**East River Column**

**Royal Asiatic Society Hong Kong Studies Series**

Royal Asiatic Society Hong Kong Studies Series is designed to make widely available important contributions on the local history, culture and society of Hong Kong and the surrounding region. Generous support from the Sir Lindsay and Lady May Ride Memorial Fund makes it possible to publish a series of high-quality works that will be of lasting appeal and value to all, both scholars and informed general readers, who share a deeper interest in and enthusiasm for the area.

---

**Recent titles in the RAS Hong Kong Studies Series:**

*Hong Kong Internment, 1942–1945: Life in the Japanese Civilian Camp at Stanley*
Geoffrey Charles Emerson

*The Six-Day War of 1899: Hong Kong in the Age of Imperialism*
Patrick H. Hase

*Cantonese Society in Hong Kong and Singapore: Gender, Religion, Medicine and Money*
Essays by Marjorie Topley; edited and introduced by Jean DeBernardi

*Early China Coast Meteorology: The Role of Hong Kong*
P. Kevin MacKeown

*Forgotten Souls: A Social History of the Hong Kong Cemetery*
Patricia Lim

*Ancestral Images: A Hong Kong Collection*
Hugh Baker

*Escape from Hong Kong: Admiral Chan Chak's Christmas Day Dash, 1941*
Tim Luard

*Governors, Politics and the Colonial Office: Public Policy in Hong Kong, 1918–58*
Gavin Ure

*Watching Over Hong Kong: Private Policing 1841–1941*
Sheilah E. Hamilton

*Scottish Mandarin: The Life and Times of Sir Reginald Johnston*
Shiona Airlie

*Custom, Land and Livelihood in Rural South China: The Traditional Land Law of Hong Kong's New Territories, 1750–1950*
Patrick H. Hase

*Portugal, China and the Macau Negotiations, 1986–1999*
Carmen Amado Mendes

# East River Column
## Hong Kong Guerrillas in
## the Second World War and After

**Chan Sui-jeung**

香港大學出版社
HONG KONG UNIVERSITY PRESS

Hong Kong University Press
The University of Hong Kong
Pokfulam Road
Hong Kong
www.hkupress.org

ISBN 978-962-209-850-3 (*Hardback*)
ISBN 978-962-209-193-1 (*Paperback*)

British Library Cataloguing-in-Publication Data
A catalogue record for this book is available from the British Library.

10   9   8   7   6   5   4   3   2

Printed and bound by Caritas Printing Training Centre in Hong Kong, China

# Contents

# Foreword

The many and varied aspects of the Second World War still hold for us a fatal
fascination even though the conflict came to an end over two generations ago.
Men and women were called upon to perform extraordinary tasks that in other
circumstances they would have thought totally beyond them. The lives of
everybody at the time were deeply affected by their individual experiences –
sometimes heroic, sometimes tragic, but in the vast majority of cases unrecorded
and often unrecognised. It is perhaps for this reason that even though so much
has been written already, there are still new angles for historians and writers to
explore.

Such is the case with this book by Chan Sui-jeung. Using his deep knowledge
of the subject and wide network of people who were personally involved, Mr.
Chan has pieced together for the first time a full account of the activities and many
achievements of the group of brave men that came to be known as the East River
Column. Whilst the existence of this guerrilla group may be known to those who
have delved into Hong Kong's wartime history, what is less known is that they
were very active for a number of years before the fighting came to Hong Kong and
for many years afterwards. It must be remembered that for the Chinese the years
of conflict were not confined to the period from Christmas 1941 to August 1945.

The Royal Asiatic Society Hong Kong Branch and Hong Kong University
Press are very proud of what they have achieved so far with the Studies Series. More
and more people, both here and abroad, are finding that Hong Kong and its unique
history and culture provides a rich and fascinating field of study. An increasing
number of schools are including the history of our city and its surroundings in
their curricula, for which we should be able to take some credit. We will continue
to bring to the public original works that will enhance this area even further.

The publications in the Studies Series have been made possible initially by the
very generous donation of seeding capital by the Trustees of the Clague Trust Fund,
representing the estate of the late Sir Douglas Clague. This donation enabled us to

establish a trust fund in the name of Sir Lindsay and Lady Ride, in memory of our first Vice President and his wife. The Society itself added to this fund, as have a number of other generous donors.

The result is that we now have funding to bring to students of Hong Kong's history, culture and society a number of books that might otherwise not have seen the light of day. Furthermore, we continue to be delighted with the agreement established with Hong Kong University Press, which sets out the basis on which the Press will partner our efforts.

Robert Nield
President
Royal Asiatic Society, Hong Kong Branch
February 2009

# Preface

Those who apply the doctrine of Dao to help the ruler will oppose all conquest by military force. War being so destructive will, as law of cause and effect, bring harm to the Maker. With the station of soldiers, thorny bushes might grow, thus affecting the livelihood of peasants. Great wars are always followed by famines. Therefore a good general will not use force to carry out invasion. After the war, he does not think it an act of glory. Despite the effect he does not boast of his merit. Despite the effect he does not take pride in it. Because he considers the force so used is only a regrettable necessity. After the war, he does not love violence. When things reach their prime, they will decay and become old. Violence by the use of force is against the nature of Dao.

— Chapter Thirty, *Daodejing*, Lao Zi. 6th Century B.C.

This book has had a long gestation. As a child who has witnessed the Japanese invasion and their atrocities inflicted upon the people in Hong Kong in 1941–42, it was a defining experience not only for me but also for members of my family. Despite the burden of having a family of eight children and holding down a full-time job in the government, my father served as an Inspector of the Special Constabulary and took up arms in defending Hong Kong. Subsequently, he took the entire family to China, where he worked for the British Information Attache's Office in Guilin and the British Army Aid Group (BAAG) in Kunming, Yunnan, China.

On V. J. Day, my father, the late Mr. Chan Kwok-wing, was a proud member of the BAAG's "S" Section. Together with his colleagues, they were flown to Hong Kong in the first week of September 1945. Their Commandant, the late Sir Lindsay Ride, landed in Hong Kong only several days ahead of them. Their task was to "identify, locate, apprehend all traitors, collaborators and enemy agents". In a way, I owe it to my father to write a book about this period of Hong Kong's history, and to him this book is dedicated.

As I resumed my primary schooling, interrupted by the war, I gradually became interested in books and articles written about the war years in Hong Kong. During my undergraduate years at the University of Hong Kong, I was influenced by Professor Ronald Hsia. He is a distinguished economist of world standing, and his knowledge of modern Chinese history is immense.

By a happy coincidence, I had the privilege of being appointed District Officer, Sai Kung, New Territories, Hong Kong in 1980. Many of the heroes and veterans of the East River Column of the Guangdong People's Anti-Japanese Guerrillas Force who lived in the district told me their stories. Another coincidence was the publication of Professor David Faure's short oral history project, "Sai Kung in the 1940s and 1950s" shortly after I took office. With limited resources at his disposal, Faure produced a useful source of background material. For the first time, the subject was published in both English and Chinese.

Shortly thereafter, Edwin Ride published the *British Army Aid Group, Hong Kong Resistance 1942–1945*. It provided an impetus for me to collect materials on the subject. However, from the Chinese side, much of the materials were still being classified as "confidential" and restricted to internal consumption only. When veterans of the East River Column celebrated their 40th anniversary in Shenzhen in December 1983, the Governor, the late Sir Edward Youde, noticed the event and suggested to me that it was a project worthy of a full-size book. The late Professor Barbara Ward of Cambridge University, who was teaching at the Chinese University of Hong Kong then, encouraged me to pursue the research in earnest, when she discovered that I was collecting materials for the subject.

With a full-time job of steering the development of a new town of some 300,000 people, it was difficult to sit down and start writing the text. In the meantime, I had the good fortune of tracking down the late K.M.A. Barnett, a distinguished member of the Administrative Officers Grade of the Hong Kong government. He personally took part in the defence of Hong Kong at the Lyemun Barracks as a soldier of the Hong Kong Volunteers Defence Force during the battle of Hong Kong. Subsequently, he was the District Commissioner, New Territories in the 1950s. In August 1945, he was one of the handful of senior government officials who marched out of the Prisoners of War Camp, Shamshuipo, Hong Kong to take control of an interim Hong Kong government. He gave me a thorough briefing on the situation of Hong Kong during its military administration in 1945–46. During that period, he met many of the soldiers of the East River Column personally before they announced their withdrawal from Hong Kong on 28 September 1945. It was him who pointed me in the right direction in looking for MacDougall's Dispatches. My meeting with him took place barely six months before he died.

I also had the good fortune of having worked under Reverend Alastair Todd, formerly Defence Secretary of the Hong Kong government who was the Private Secretary to the late Sir Mark Young, the first civilian governor after the war. He was privy to much of the Hong Kong government's dealing with General Zhang Fakui, Garrison Commander of Guangzhou in 1945–49. He and his charming wife Nancy accorded me kindness and warmth, and also gave me insights into the post-war situation.

Another person who kindly briefed me on the situation during the military administration in 1945–46 was the late Sir Jack Cater. Initially, he was a member of the military government but subsequently joined the Hong Kong civil service.

Congressman William Frenzel from Minnesota, a member of the Ways and Means Committee of the American Congress, was most generous in helping me in tracking down some detailed records of the Field Team No. 8, under General George Marshall, when the general was mediating between the Chinese Communist Party and the Kuomintang in 1946.

One other person who has been a great source of help is Ms. Elizabeth Ride, daughter of the late Brigadier Sir Lindsay Ride. Ms. Ride worked tirelessly in sorting out her father's papers in both Hong Kong and Canberra, Australia. She pointed out to me the relevant parts among her father's archives.

For over twenty years I have been an Honorary Research Fellow at the Centre of Asian Studies of the University of Hong Kong. Professor Wong Siu Lun, the director of the centre, and Professor Chan Lau Kit Ching of the History Department of the university were most supportive of my work.

On the Chinese side, I am forever indebted to the people of Sai Kung, New Territories, Hong Kong. Not only did they accord me kindness, generosity and tolerance, also they were the first ones who introduced me to some of the veterans of the East River Column, who were still living on both sides of the border. Unfortunately, many of them preferred to remain anonymous because of the sensitive nature of their experience during the difficult period when they suffered under the harsh policy of Tao Zhu in the 1950s and 1960s. Among them were the late Mr. Chung Pun, the late Mr. Lee Hokming, and the late Mr. Chan Kwaisang of the Sai Kung Rural Committee. The Chairman of the Rural Committee, the late Mr. Lau Wanhei, was most kind in facilitating much of my research. He was actually the one who introduced me to General Zeng Sheng, the Commander of the East River Column, when he visited Hong Kong in August 1984.

Among those who assisted me tirelessly in tracking down relevant materials in China is Yang Qi, who was one of the editors of the newspaper of the East River Column during the war. Since his retirement from *Ta Kung Pao* in the late 1980s, he has been living in Guangzhou. But he makes a point of coming to see me whenever he visits Hong Kong. Every time he comes, he would discover new materials for me.

In April 1999, I was appointed a member of the War Memorial Fund Pension Advisory Committee by the Hong Kong Special Administrative Region Government. Through the help of many of the staff in the Health and Welfare

Bureau, and particularly Mr. Julian Cheng, I managed to retrieve many of the records relevant to the subject from the Public Record Office in London. Another person who helped me tirelessly in this area is Anne Ozorio, a family friend. She herself is a dedicated researcher on Hong Kong history of the war years.

I am forever grateful to Elina and Daniel Lam, who are most helpful and generous of their time and computer knowledge. Without them, this book would never see the light of day. Initially, I was a computer illiterate. It was Bosco Cheng Manhang who educated me in the intricacy of IT technology.

Philip Snow, who wrote *The Fall of Hong Kong: Britain, China and the Japanese Occupation* in 2003, has been most supportive and put in a great deal of time in editing the first draft of the manuscript. Colin Day and Dennis Cheung, the publisher and the managing editor of Hong Kong University Press, have been most sympathetic and helpful.

All the photographs in the plates section are provided by courtesy of Ms. Tsui Yuet Ching, whose father was a member of the East River Column. Her generosity is much appreciated.

Last but not least is my dear and devoted wife, May. She remains a pillar of support and a relentless critic of my sometimes lackadaisical approach in pursuing the subject.

Errors and omissions in the work are entirely my own.

# Notes on Terms and Romanization

The term "dollar" in the text refers to the Hong Kong Dollar, which is approximately 0.128 of the American Dollar. One *tael*, or Chinese ounce, is equal to 37.7 grams. One *mu* corresponds to 648 square metres or 0.16 acre.

Pinyin romanization is used for nearly all Chinese names, except for well-known ones such as Chiang Kai-shek and Soong Ching-ling. Instead of adopting the Pinyin (Jiang Jieshi and Song Qingling) their Wade Giles romanization is retained.

For place names, as many of the documents were written before the Pinyin system was adopted, so it is inevitable there were references to Kwangtung, Canton, instead of Guangdong and Guangzhou. However, for place names within the territory of Hong Kong, their original names are used.

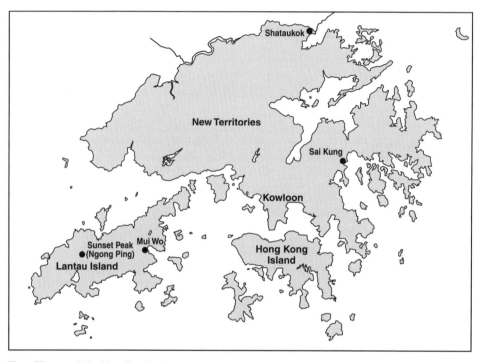

**Hong Kong and the New Territories**

- Sunset Peak, near Ngong Ping — The BAAG together with the Hong Kong/Kowloon Independent Brigade planned to install an observation post here in 1944.
- Mui Wo — This is where the Japanese and the Hong Kong/Kowloon Independent Brigade fought a fierce battle on 18 August 1945. The Japanese waged a massacre here from 18 to 26 August 1945.
- Sai Kung — Headquarters of the Hong Kong/Kowloon Independent Brigade.
- Shataukok — This is where the Hong Kong/Kowloon Independent Brigade met their worst debacle on 3 March 1943.

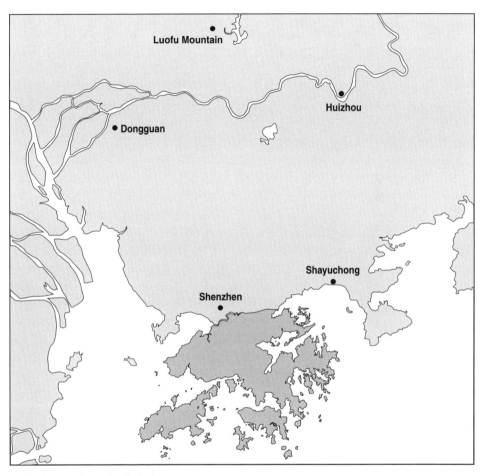

**East River region of South China**

- Luofu Mountain — Headquarters of the East River Column. An important meeting was held here on 6 July 1945. One of the meeting's resolutions was to form underground administration in Japanese occupied areas.
- Dongguan and Huizhou — Both towns were bases of the East River Column.
- Shayuchong — Embarkation point for over 2,500 East River soldiers when they were repatriated to Yantai, Shandong, on 30 June 1946.
- Shenzhen — General Zeng Sheng's hometown.

# 1 Introduction

For most people in the Western world, the Pacific War began with the Japanese attack on Pearl Harbour on 7 December 1941. The first steps towards the conflict, however, had already been taken as early as the late nineteenth century, when Japan embarked on its gradual expansion into Chinese territory. When a Japan-assisted rebellion broke out in Korea in September 1894 — Korea was a protectorate of China at this time — the Japanese not only captured Pyongyang but also crushed the entire northern Chinese fleet. The Chinese government then was forced to sign the Treaty of Shimonoseki. In addition, China was forced to abandon its rights in Korea and was made to pay Japan 200 million taels of silver in war indemnities. Other conditions of the treaty were that Taiwan, the Pescadores, and the Liaodong region of the northeast were ceded to Japan. It marked the beginning of a series of Japanese invasions.

During the Russian-Japanese War in 1905, the Japanese navy attacked the Russian fleet in Port Arthur and won from them all rights in the southern part of Manchuria. The end result was Japanese control of Port Arthur in the Liaodong Peninsula, with rights over railways and mines. Under duress, China endorsed the arrangement.

China, under the rule of the Qing emperors, was in a state of political and social instability. The two Opium Wars in 1840 and 1860 and the subsequent defeat led foreign powers to establish a foothold in the treaty ports of Guangzhou, Xiamen, Fuzhou, Ningbo and Shanghai. The cession of Hong Kong as a colony had given foreign powers further opportunity for advancement and influence in the entire eastern coastal provinces in China.

Internally, years of massive famine probably brought the most violent rebellions from its own people. The Taiping Rebellion lasted from 1850 to 1864 and raged over sixteen provinces, the Nien Rebellion lasted from 1851 to 1868, and the Muslim Rebellion in Yunnan lasted from 1855 until 1873. All three rebellions failed after cruel and violent suppression by the government, but the financial and military strain had weakened the government so much that its collapse was only a matter of time.

The First World War provided Japan with further opportunities to encroach on Chinese territory. Japan declared war on Germany and demanded the surrender of the German colony in Qingdao, thus placing China in the position of designating a specified area of its own country as a battleground between two foreign combating powers.

Japan then followed with the "21 Demands" on China in 1915, requiring China to cede to Japan all German rights in China. Other humiliating demands included supervising and supplying the Chinese army, constructing railways and mines and developing a steel industry, thus reducing China to a virtual Japanese protectorate. China was ruled by a weak and pro-Japanese president, Yuan Shikai, who had been a leader of the Beiyang warlords and had become influential towards the end of the Qing Dynasty. During this period, China was carved up into different spheres of influence by foreign powers, aided and abetted by various warlords.

At least in name, China joined other Allied nations in declaring war against Germany in 1917, but as a weak nation, it did not have the means to send any soldiers to the battlefields in Europe. The only people sent were a few thousand men who worked as unskilled labourers for the Allied forces. Japan took the opportunity to wring from the Allied nations an undertaking to support its claims to the former German rights in Shandong Province. At the Paris Peace Conference held after the war, China had to accept the Japanese stake in Shandong as a reward for its help in the European war.

In Japan, because of early diplomatic success in the international arena and the ability to manufacture cheap, light, industrial products that flooded the world market, stock prices increased at a spectacular rate. The first direct result was the emergence of some of the industrial/financial conglomerates (*Zaibatsu*). Unfortunately, the relatively short period of economic prosperity did not produce a large enough middle class, because the economic wealth did not seep into the lower stratum of society. As a result of the stock market crash in the US in 1929, followed by the Great Depression of the 1930s, Japan's economy was hurt badly.

On the political front, Japan's aggressive policy in taking over the former German interests in Shandong and north China alarmed most Western countries.

## Communism in China

In the early 1900s, China saw the appearance of Communism as a political ideology. Its origins here can be traced to the publication of Karl Marx's biography in the journal *Ming Bao*, but the influence of Marxism remained insignificant until the May Fourth Movement in 1919. Chinese intellectuals and students had been disappointed with the Western powers' unfair treatment of the Chinese government at the conclusion of the First World War. At the same time, Russia's October Revolution attracted some Chinese attention. The factor that appealed most to the Chinese was that the new government in Moscow renounced the Soviet Union's rights to Chinese territories acquired by Tsarist Russia.

Marxist and Leninist study groups appeared in Peking University. In 1918, the university librarian, Li Dazhao, openly declared that he was involved in Marxism. His move attracted young students such as Qu Qiubai, Zhang Guotao, Chen Duxiu, and Zhang's library assistant, Mao Zedong.

In July 1921, the founding meeting of the Chinese Communist Party (CCP) took place at a girls' school in the French Concession in Shanghai. Chen Duxiu founded the CCP at that fateful meeting in Shanghai, but he was in Guangzhou and was represented by Zhou Fohai.

From 1921, various Communist International (Comintern) agents such as H. Maring, Adolf Joffe and Mikhail Borodin were sent by the Soviet government to meet Dr. Sun Yat-sen, a medical practitioner who had been inspired by the Taiping Rebellion. One of the main functions of the Comintern agents was to help Dr. Sun reorganize the Nationalist Party, the Kuomintang (KMT).

The KMT was developed from the Tong Meng Hui, founded by Dr. Sun in 1905. What troubled Dr. Sun most during the period the Soviet agents were in China was the lack of unity and discipline among his party members. Under the influence of the Comintern, Sun agreed to absorb Communist Party members into the KMT, provided they join as individuals. Sun openly modified his original political ideology by adopting a policy of *lian'e ronggong* (alliance with Soviet Russia and admission of the Communists) and *fuzhu gongnong* (assist the industrial workers and peasants).

The cooperation between the two parties was actually a marriage of convenience. The KMT needed Soviet assistance in organizing the party and utilizing the Communist ties with industrial workers and peasants. Indeed, the founding of Huangpu Military Academy in Guangzhou was the idea of the Soviet agents, who thought this was the only way to build an army loyal to Sun and to create an officer corps to lead the army. The Communists thought they could use the KMT base to expand their own influence. Having built the military academy, staffed by both KMT members and Communist members such as Zhou Enlai, Sun was anxious to launch his Northern Expedition to beat the warlords in central and north China. His death in 1925, however, was a blow to the movement.

The leadership then was handed over to Wang Jingwei and Hu Hanmin, but the man who had the real power was Chiang Kai-shek, the commandant of the military academy right from its inception. A series of relatively minor battles were fought in Guangdong and Guangxi, where warlord forces were defeated in 1925. In July, Chiang led a force of about 85,000 soldiers and marched to take on the warlords in the north. In less than a year, major parts of central China were recovered from the warlords. Dazzled by his success, Chiang went on to conquer Fujian, Zhejiang, Jiangsu and parts of Anhui.

In the meantime, an impending split between the KMT and the Chinese Communist Party (CCP) was about to occur. In November 1925, some rightwing members of the KMT demanded the expulsion of CCP members from the party as well as the dismissal of Borodin as the political adviser to the party.

When Chiang marched into Shanghai in April 1927 and launched a liquidation move against CCP members, KMT troops — aided by the Green Gang, a mafia-type secret society — raided labour unions and shot hundreds of CCP members and union leaders. Similar massacres took place in Nanjing, Hangzhou, Fuzhou and Guangzhou.

Communist cadres who escaped moved to Jiangxi. The final break between the two parties came when Zhou Enlai led some of the military leaders such as He Long, Lin Biao and Ye Ting and staged an uprising in Nanchang on 1 August 1927. In September, Mao also led some peasant soldiers in staging the Autumn Harvest Uprising in Hunan. These uprisings failed after a few days, but they did provide valuable experience and a military force for the embryonic party. With some remnants of his soldiers, Mao moved to Jinggangshan, a mountainous area in Jiangxi. At this hideout, the KMT launched a series of five "bandit suppression" campaigns from 1930 to 1934.

With the help of German military advisers, KMT forces managed to encircle and blockade the CCP forces in Jinggangshan. Fighting for survival, the leaders of the CCP decided to retreat. On 16 October 1934, almost the entire Jinggangshan Soviet of about 80,000 people, cadres, soldiers, women and children left their base and went on the legendary Long March, which went through eleven provinces and covered over 6,000 miles. The main units of the march arrived in Yan'an in October 1935.

It was in Yan'an that they became relatively settled. From the caves of this desolate town, the CCP launched repeated appeals to the entire nation for the two parties and other political groups to co-operate in a "united front" in their resistance against the Japanese.

Chiang Kai-shek flew to Xi'an in December 1936. His intention was to push the commander in Xi'an, Marshal Zhang Xueliang, to attack the CCP base in nearby Yan'an. In dramatic fashion, Zhang took Chiang and his subordinates captive on 12 December.

Directed by the Comintern in Soviet Russia, Zhou Enlai emerged from Yan'an to mediate. Some of the main demands posed by Zhang were the "Reorganization of the Central Government to include all political parties as a means to resist the Japanese and to work for national salvation" and the "release of all political prisoners". Chiang was released on 25 December; he promised that the CCP could participate in the future war against the Japanese. Despite intermittent skirmishes between armed forces of the two parties, a façade of a united front was maintained from 1936 until the end of the Second World War.

## Japanese Invasion

In Japan, the conventional wisdom of the nation was that it needed to acquire new territories by military conquest, to ward off mass starvation. Political and military commentators cast their covetous eyes on countries such as Australia, Canada and the US, that had vast land masses with small populations, but these countries were separated from Japan by oceans. Yet nearby China, where Japan already had a foothold in the north, was still ruled by a weak government.

By 1930, Japan had stationed soldiers in various cities in Manchuria or the north-eastern provinces of China. What the Japanese military wanted most was an incident to provoke China into an all-out war. On 18 September 1931, the Japanese army blew up the tracks of a Japanese-owned railway in south Manchuria. The explosion failed to derail an express train, so the Japanese killed the Chinese railway guards and fabricated a story that the Chinese had sabotaged the railway. Within a matter of days, the Japanese army occupied a few cities such as Andong, Yingkou and Changchun. Shortly thereafter, the two provinces of Jilin and Heilongjiang were Japanese occupied. The end result was the creation of the puppet state of Manchukuo, and the last emperor of the Qing Dynasty, Henry Pu Yi, was installed as head of state. The central government in Nanjing appealed to the citizens "to avoid conflict with the Japanese, pending the result of the Government's appeal to the League of Nations". This weak response aroused the anger of the people throughout the country, resulting in demonstrations, a boycott of Japanese goods and the birth of mass movements of Anti-Japan and Save the Nation in all major cities like Shanghai, Qingdao, Changsha and Guangzhou, and even in the British colony of Hong Kong. Chinese communities all over the world, particularly those in Southeast Asia, reacted in a similar manner.

Anti-Japanese feelings ran so high that, in January 1932, a mob in Shanghai attacked five Japanese Buddhist monks, killing one of them. The Japanese retaliated by bombing Zhabei, one of the most heavily populated districts. The ensuing battle involved over 80,000 soldiers from both sides. For the first time, the Japanese met with stiff resistance from the Chinese that came from the 19th Route Army, commanded competently by General Cai Tingkai. Not only did the Japanese suffer heavy casualties in the battle, but the bravery of the Chinese soldiers also aroused patriotic feelings in all of China as well as in Chinese communities throughout the world. After more than a month without success and after three changes of commanders, the Japanese had to settle for peace. As a result of mediation from the League of Nations and diplomats from Britain and the US, both sides ceased firing and the 19th Route Army withdrew. At the request of the Chinese government, the League of Nations sent an investigation team to China. The team found Japan at fault in Manchuria, but Japan's reaction was to withdraw from the League in 1933.

In January 1933, the Japanese attacked Shanhaiguan and Jehol in north China, and, in just ten days, the whole province of Jehol was occupied. Throughout this period there were intermittent conflicts and ceasefires between Japan and China, with Japan nibbling away at various parts of northern China in Jehol, Hebei and Mongolia.

The point of view in north China in 1937 was that the Japanese military wanted to provoke an all-out war with China because they were confident Japan could achieve a complete and quick victory. Some Japanese generals supposedly said that they could conquer the whole of China within three months.

In the summer of 1937, the Japanese army from Tianjin was conducting an exercise near the Marco Polo Bridge (Lugouqiao) in a suburb of Beijing. A Japanese soldier failed to return to his regiment on the evening of 7 July. Using this as an excuse, the Japanese commander demanded that the city gates be opened so the Japanese could conduct a search. When the Chinese commander refused, the Japanese shelled the city wall. Intermittent firing and shelling with occasional negotiations continued for the next few days. The Japanese demanded that Chinese troops withdraw from all strategic military points in north China and the men responsible for the incident be punished, despite the fact that the Japanese soldier who had disappeared eventually did return. By then, both sides could not back down from their positions, as the question of "face", so important to Asians, was involved. Both nations sent reinforcements, and by 25 July, both sides were engaged in a full-scale war. By 7 August, all of Beijing was captured, because most Chinese soldiers were outgunned or simply surrendered.

While the battle in north China was raging in and around Beijing and Tianjin, the Japanese tried to provoke an incident in Shanghai. All major foreign powers had stationed troops in their respective concessions in Shanghai; Japan was no exception. On 9 August, a Japanese naval officer with his ratings tried to drive past the airport to the west of the city. They were stopped by a group of Chinese militiamen who objected to what appeared to be a Japanese inspection of Chinese military facilities. The Japanese refused to leave the scene and both men were shot. Realizing they were outnumbered, the Japanese initially wanted to pursue the matter through diplomatic channels. However, when the local Chinese forces fortified their defence positions in the city, the Japanese admiral, who commanded twelve warships lying just outside the Huangpu River, threatened the Chinese by having the guns on the warships stripped for action. By 11 August, Japan had landed another 1,000 marines in the city, thus making a total military strength of 4,000. Two days later, the big guns on the Japanese warships opened fire. Once again, Chinese soldiers put up a stiff fight. They outnumbered the Japanese by almost ten to one. When the Japanese attempted to land fresh troops, to their utter surprise, a hidden artillery emplacement opened fire and killed several hundred Japanese troops. The battle of Shanghai, in fact, proceeded very slowly as the Chinese defended street by street and barricade by barricade. Far from being able to conquer the whole of China within three months, the Japanese forces took several months to win control of Shanghai alone. In November, Shanghai at last fell and the Japanese moved on to Nanjing with a vengeance.

Barely 200 miles from Shanghai, Nanjing was the capital of the Chinese Nationalist government, and the capture of this city was of strategic as well as psychological importance. On 1 December, the Japanese military headquarters gave the order for its soldiers to march to Nanjing. By 5 December, the Japanese were within sight of the city walls, and by 13 December, the capture of the city was complete. The Chinese army's retreat was unplanned and disorderly. Over 100,000 officers and their men broke into uncontrolled flight, while tens of thousands of civilians also escaped. To show their displeasure over the Chinese refusal to surrender, the Japanese troops who entered Nanjing were let loose and went on an orgy of rape and massacre. By February the following year, a Japanese correspondent who went to the city concluded that there were 300,000 deaths. The Chinese estimated 600,000. The actual total has never been established with any degree of accuracy, but an educated guess must be somewhere between these two figures. After the capture of Nanjing in December 1937, the Japanese moved up the Yangtze River to capture the important industrial city of Wuhan, where the Nationalists had now transferred their government. But it took the Japanese ten months to capture Wuhan. The interim period enabled the central government to move its industrial facilities, arsenals, museums and libraries to the western provinces of Guizhou, Yunnan and Sichuan, where a longer-term government was established in due course in Chongqing. This is a city sheltered by rapid rivers, high mountains and fog. Although the city was bombed by Japanese planes throughout the war, the Nationalist government had a relatively stable situation there. Wuhan finally fell in October 1938. The Japanese then directed another strong contingent to move south to attack Guangzhou, an important commercial centre in south China that gave the Nationalist government access to the outside world. Along with Kunming in Yunnan, Guangzhou had been their sole transport link with other countries and source of external supplies since the beginning of the war. As Guangzhou was the provincial capital of Guangdong and had important industrial and commercial facilities, the Japanese concentrated their main force in the immediate area near the city and left the countryside (the Pearl River Delta area) relatively under-strength. This provided an ideal opportunity for Chinese guerrillas to operate in the countryside.

# 2 Birth of the East River Column

## The Overseas Chinese and the Anti-Japanese Resistance

For quite a few years after the Japanese imposed the infamous "21 Demands" on China in 1915, students and workers all over China and Hong Kong waged a campaign to boycott the use and purchase of Japanese goods and Japanese shops. Overseas Chinese communities, particularly those in Southeast Asia, joined in enthusiastically. Such activities outside China had a definite effect on Japan, as Southeast Asia was the dumping ground of Japanese textile and light industrial goods.

In Singapore and Malaya alone, there were over 2.3 million overseas Chinese in 1941. Because of their relatively better income than their Chinese counterparts in China and Hong Kong, these overseas Chinese became a source of strong financial support for China, in war preparation.

A significant factor in the relative ease and success in mobilizing so many overseas Chinese was the Hakka culture. The Hakka and the people from Fujian and Guangdong in general made up more than half of the overseas Chinese in Southeast Asian countries. The Hakka identified as their homeland Meixian, Guangdong and the neighbouring towns and counties such as Huizhou, Bao'an and Huiyang, and most of the other towns in the East River areas, a tributary of the Pearl River Delta. The Hakka, who made up over ninety percent of a number of the guerrilla groups, therefore enjoyed a great advantage in material and kinship support from other Hakka in Southeast Asia and, for that matter from the East River region in south Guangdong. Throughout Chinese history, Hakka have been well known for their independent spirit and hardworking culture. Another distinct characteristic of this ethnic group is they are exceptionally clannish. In countries outside China, one can always find Hakka clan associations, which carry the names of Huizhou or Huiyang Clansmen or Jiaying Clansmen Association.[1]

In October 1938, when the news of the fall of Guangzhou and other towns in the East River area spread to Southeast Asia, overseas Chinese, particularly those of Hakka origin who lived in Malaya and the Dutch East Indies, formed the Nanyang Dutch/British Territories Huizhou Compatriots Relief Association, on 30 October. They sent representatives on an inspection tour to the East River area of the Pearl River Delta. They arranged this through their contact with Lian Guan and Liao Chengzhi, the most senior Chinese Communist cadres in Hong Kong then. Liao was the son of Liao Zhongkai, a contemporary of Dr. Sun Yat-sen, and a senior member of the left-wing faction of the KMT. Liao Chengzhi had the additional advantage of being Hakka himself. Lian Guan was a Hakka born in a peasant family in a poor village of Dapu, in the mountainous area in east Guangdong. From an early age, he was a casual worker in a tobacco factory near his hometown. He did not start school until he was almost nine, and he was admitted into a teacher training school after he completed primary schooling. Subsequently, he became a primary school teacher himself in Meixian. He came under the influence of a Chinese Communist Party member when the latter was a member of Chiang Kai-shek's Northern Expedition. He joined the party in 1927. He moved to Hong Kong with the help of his clanspeople. From the 1930s, he was involved in Anti-Japan and Save the Nation activities.

Liao Chengzhi was born in Japan, where he went to primary school and secondary school. Subsequently he studied in the missionary-founded Lingnan University in Guangzhou, where he joined the KMT. When the KMT and the Communist Party split in 1927, he joined the Communist Party. Because of his command of foreign languages, he was sent by the party to foment strikes among Chinese seamen in Holland and Germany in 1928. Expelled by the Dutch authorities, he returned to China and did underground work for the party in Shanghai in 1932. He was arrested by the KMT authorities in Shanghai when he was discovered. But due to his parents' previous standing in the KMT and Soong Ching-ling's intervention, he was released and went to Hong Kong where his mother had relatives and connections.

After the tour, the association met up with other Hakka residents in Hong Kong. Through the encouragement of Liao and Lian, the association joined up with the Hong Kong Huiyang Youth Association, the Hailufeng Residents Association and the Yu Sian Le Association to form "service teams" to visit various towns and counties in the East River area of the Pearl River Delta. Young people from Hong Kong and overseas Chinese from Singapore, Vietnam, Malaya, the Philippines, Thailand, and Macao, particularly those of Hakka origin, were recruited. Even in a small place like Macao, eleven groups of such young people were mobilized to join in the work of the service teams. The work of such service teams was mainly propaganda, indoctrination and relief. Within six months, separate teams had been organized to serve Huiyang, Hailufeng, Boluo, Zijin, Heyuan, Longchuan and Houping. In addition, there was a mobile and roving song and dance troupe that went from county to county in the unoccupied areas in the Pearl River Delta in south Guangdong, to spread the Anti-Japan and Save the Nation propaganda message.

In the meantime, the Hong Kong Huiyang Clansmen Association, together with a few other similar groups, began to mobilize their clanspeople from Southeast Asia to form the East River Overseas Chinese (*huaqiao*) Service Team. In Southeast Asia alone, excluding Vietnam and Thailand, there were the Singapore Overseas Chinese Wartime Service Group, the Overseas Chinese Hui Xiang Service Team, the Dutch East Indies Overseas Chinese Ambulance Team, the Malaya East River Overseas Hui Xiang Service Team and the Northwest Overseas Service Team.

In addition, various small-time traders like stevedores, trishaw coolies and shopkeepers formed their own small fundraising committees. One person who, not a Hakka himself, instigated all such activities was Tan Kah Kee. He was born in Fujian Province in China but immigrated to Singapore at the age of seventeen in 1890. Initially he worked as a shopkeeper at his father's small grocery store. Then he branched out to operate his own provision store by selling imported canned food. By maintaining a thrifty and hardworking lifestyle, he accumulated sufficient wealth to go into business in rubber plantations and other business all over Southeast Asia. He was a millionaire by 1911 and a multi-millionaire at the end of the First World War. During Dr. Sun Yat-sen's fundraising campaigns in Southeast Asia, he helped Sun and joined him as a member of the Xing Zhong Hui, the precursor of the KMT.

As a leading member of the Singapore Chinese Chamber of Commerce, he was the person who organized all such activities. In addition to fundraising activities, he recruited about 3,200 lorry drivers and motor mechanics throughout Southeast Asia to work on the road connecting Kunming in Yunnan with Lashio in Burma. After the fall of Shanghai and Guangzhou, China's only transport link with the outside world was by this road.

Initially, Tan and other members of the Singapore Chinese Relief Fund Committee and the Southseas China Relief Fund donated the funds and the materials raised mainly to the KMT government in Chongqing. In December 1939, Tan organized a "comfort mission" to China. The objective of the mission was to console the combat soldiers, to inspect and scrutinize the actual war conditions in China. Some of the fifty members of the mission who came from Singapore, Malaya, the Philippines, Hong Kong, Burma and Indochina went by way of Saigon and Hanoi to Kunming. Other members gathered in Singapore and sailed to Rangoon. On arriving in the wartime capital of Chongqing, Tan was appalled by the substantial budget prepared by the KMT government for entertaining the mission. What he discovered was summed up by a saying circulated among the people that described the situation, *qianfang chi jin, houfang jin chi*, translated roughly as "while the frontline was fighting a tense and bitter battle, the officials in the wartime capital were engaging in intensive and indulgent pleasure seeking". Despite Tan's dismay and disappointment, he did not openly criticize the KMT government, except for the fact that he lamented to General Bai Chongxi, the deputy chief of staff, that he was saddened by the "rift between the two parties.... And that it would be tantamount to suicide should there be a civil war". Subsequently, when he had the opportunity of meeting with Ye Jianying and Dong Biwu, he expressed the wish to visit Yan'an. Later on he received a formal invitation from Mao.

Next to Mao Zedong, both Ye and Dong were highly respected senior members of the party. Ye was Hakka, born in Meixian, where his father ran a small grocery store. He went to a primary school run by missionaries where he excelled in school work. During his younger days, he went to work as a primary school teacher in Ipoh, Malaya. He joined the Yunnan Military Academy in 1917, and graduated in late 1919 with distinction. When the Huangpu Military Academy was opened in Guangzhou in May 1924, he was appointed one of the instructors in weaponry when he was barely twenty-seven. He joined the Communist Party around the same time, in 1927, and staged the Guangzhou Uprising in December. Despite its ultimate failure, Ye made his name because the revolutionary soldiers that he commanded formed the Guangzhou Commune that existed for a few weeks. He then joined Mao and Zhu De in Jinggangshan, Jiangxi, via Shanghai.

Dong Biwu was one of the few party members to be veteran of both the 1911 Revolution and the civil war between the KMT and the CCP. Born in Hubei, he was one of the founders of the CCP. As a communist, he had a most unusual background, as he was a Chinese classical scholar. He was the son of a classical scholar who was a teacher of rich families in Wuhan. During the split between the KMT and Communist Party in 1927, he had to escape to Japan and then to Russia in September 1928. He studied for a few years at Lenin University and returned to China in 1932. He joined the Jiangxi Soviet by going through Shanghai and Shantou. He joined the Long March and was appointed the head of the party school in Yan'an.

Mao Zedong was born into a moderately well-off landowning family in a village in Hunan in 1893, when China was crumbling in degradation and despair, having lost a series of battles with foreign powers. As a student, Mao did quite well in school, particularly in the Chinese classics. But what affected him more was the May Fourth Movement which was undoubtedly a national awakening of China, particularly among young people of that generation.

After graduating from Teachers College in Changsha, Mao and some Hunan students went to Beijing, initially with the intention of going to France to join the work-study programme. But he got a job as an assistant librarian at Peking University, where he came under the influence of Professor Li Dazhao. A brilliant intellectual, he was the first to introduce the ideology of Marxism-Leninism to China. After staying in Shanghai for four months, Mao returned to Hunan and obtained a job as a primary school teacher. By then he was already a party member who was busy recruiting new members for the party.

In 1926, he was asked by the KMT government based in Guangzhou to run training classes for peasants at the Peasant Institute. He used this as a base, not only to train cadres from among peasants who came from other provinces and from Guangdong, but also to recruit members for the Communist Party despite the fact that he was occupying a post in the Propaganda Department of the KMT government.

In July 1927, Mao and a few of his close comrades planned an uprising in his own province, Hunan, to be co-ordinated with similar uprisings in Guangdong and Hubei. The uprising began on 8 September and ended in October. In military terms, it was not a success. But it left a myth that Mao was a capable organizer and a leader. He then led a group of some 800 soldiers comprising peasants, students and miners and marched to Jinggangshan.

From the time of his arrival until 1934, a "soviet government" was established in Ruijin, Jiangxi, a relatively large market town near Jinggangshan, where Chiang Kai-shek launched a series of extermination campaigns. In October 1934, the entire Jiangxi "soviet" went on the legendary 25,000-*li* Long March. When about 30,000 of the original group of 80,000 who set out from Ruijin arrived in Zunyi, Guizhou, the entire politburo of the party rested and held a large meeting. It was at this meeting that Mao established his leadership position when he proved the strategy of the Russian-trained intellectuals was wrong and had caused immense loss. When Tan met him in Yan'an, it was a few years after Mao and the remnants of his soldiers had arrived and settled.

During his stay there, Tan was impressed by what he saw. At his first meeting with Mao, they were interrupted by students who came to visit Mao, and then by members of the Communist Party who were junior to Mao in rank and years. Such visitors came without any prior appointment. When they entered the chairman's house, they did not bow to or salute him.

To Tan, Mao was an approachable and honest man. The Communist leadership, Tan found, was hardworking, frugal, honest and led simple lives. Before he left China for home, Tan had a further meeting with Chiang in Chongqing. What Tan did and his favourable comments about the Chinese Communists did not please the KMT regime and Chiang in particular. When Tan and his party returned home via Burma in early December 1940, he lost no opportunity to tell overseas Chinese communities that China would win the war with Japan and that KMT and Communist conflicts would flare up. Despite the fact that Tan was a member of the Tong Meng Hui, after the visit he was completely disenchanted with the corrupt regime in Chongqing. From that point onward, the funds and materials that he and his organizations managed to raise were sent mainly to the New Fourth Army and the Eighth Route Army. Both armies were created after the KMT and the Communists came to an agreement to cease their civil war in December 1936 and Communist armed forces were given KMT military designations in the overall KMT government military establishment. In rank and uniform, they were indistinguishable from regular KMT soldiers. But Chiang Kai-shek seldom allocated them adequate resources during the Anti-Japanese War.

Within a year, from 1938 to 1939, the Singapore Chinese Relief Fund Committee and the Southseas China Relief Fund, both under the direction of Tan, managed to raise nearly HK$5 million worth of goods, which included 300,000 suits of warm clothing and pharmaceutical items, such as vitamin and quinine tablets for the central government in China and the Communist-led guerrillas. In order to coordinate and consolidate the various organizations that were engaged in similar kinds of activity, a Southeast Asia Federation of China Relief Funds was formed on 10 October 1938. The representatives were Tjung Siengan from Jakarta, Lee Chengchuan from the Philippines and Tan Kah Kee from Malaya and Singapore.

## The Response in Hong Kong

The Shenyang Incident occurred on 18 September 1931, when a bomb exploded on the Southern Manchurian Railway outside Shenyang. It was only a minor incident, and normal railway service was not disrupted. But the Japanese, who engineered the incident, used the excuse that Chinese soldiers fired on them after the explosion, so they fought back in self-defence. The Japanese crack Kwantung Army quickly moved in and occupied most of the three north-east provinces. For a long time, Chiang was so preoccupied with his "pacification campaign" in fighting the Communist forces in Jiangxi that he directed the commander in the north-east not to engage the Japanese.

But the Japanese aggression, and even more Chiang's policy of "non-resistance" against the Japanese, angered the entire population. There were massive demonstrations by students in all major cities, particularly in Beijing and Shanghai. Their main demands were that the central government should stop its campaign against the Communist regime in Ruijin and unite all the resources to resist the Japanese. The movement came to a head on 9 December 1935, when students from all the schools, including primary schools, in Beijing boycotted their classes and demonstrated all over the city. The central government reacted by sending anti-riot police to beat up the demonstrators. Over a hundred students were injured and over thirty were arrested. But the anti-Japanese movement soon spread to every major city.

During this period, quite a few of the Chinese Communists and their sympathizers in the literary circle moved to Hong Kong, e.g. Qiao Guanhua and Zou Taofen.

Qiao Guanhua was born into a family of landowners in Suzhou, in 1913. Exceptionally bright as a student, he was successfully admitted to Qinghua University when he was barely sixteen. Graduated at twenty, he enrolled in the Imperial University in Tokyo. But he was involved in anti-Japanese imperialism activities organized by the Japan Communist Party and soon deported. He then went to Germany in 1935 where he successfully obtained a Ph.D.

Zou Taofen was born into a family of scholars in Fujian, in 1895. His father was a patriot who hoped that his son would one day qualify as an engineer or a scientist as a means to serve the country. The family was not financially well off. Zou Taofen managed to study in good schools in Shanghai by winning scholarships every year. Eventually, he was admitted to the prestigious St. John University, where he graduated in 1919.

After graduation, he worked for a few years as an English teacher at the YMCA in Shanghai. Because of his good command of both English and Chinese, he was offered the job of editor-in-chief of the weekly journal *Life* in 1926. Deeply disappointed with the KMT government's corruption and incompetence, he was highly critical of the central government in his editorials.

Later on he also openly attacked the Japanese government's aggression against China. He was personally involved in many student demonstrations and boycott movements of Japanese goods. Eventually, his journal was banned by the government. Knowing that the government was after him personally, he went to Hong Kong in March 1936.

Since the Shenyang Incident, when Japan launched an undeclared war on China, every year on the anniversary, Hong Kong Chinese have waged different kinds of protests and meetings to commemorate what they call National Humiliation Day. On 18 September 1936, some secondary school students joined hands and formed an organization called the "Hong Kong Resist Japan and Save the Nation Society" in secret, after having observed a National Humiliation Day commemoration ceremony at the Lap Tak School. The object was to rouse Hong Kong Chinese to join the society's anti-Japanese activities with their propaganda. As the society was not properly registered in accordance with the colony's *Societies Ordinance*, it was clearly illegal. Eighty of the society's members were arrested by the police. While some officials in the Hong Kong government were sympathetic towards the Chinese anti-Japanese activities, they did not wish to antagonize Japan openly. Therefore, the eighty who were arrested were treated leniently and released. The office bearers of the society quietly disbanded it.

Some undergraduates of the University of Hong Kong teamed up with the Chinese Pharmaceutical and Relief Association and appealed to about 300 schools, primary and secondary, to form an umbrella group called the Hong Kong Students Relief Association in September 1937. An undergraduate, Lee Chingyiu, from the university, was elected chairman. From the 300-odd schools, students from some of the most élite schools like King's College, Queen's College and St. Paul Secondary School (founded by the Anglican church) joined in. Parents of such students helped their children in raising funds and organizing patriotic anti-Japan activities throughout the colony. Within three days in the first week of October, 1937, the association managed to raise forty individual teams to visit practically every school in Hong Kong to spread the message. Concerts were organized to raise funds by the Diocesan Boys' School. Most other students raised funds by forgoing their lunches. Some of the funds raised were donated to the New Fourth Army, the Eighth Route Army and other guerrilla groups, through Soong Ching-ling's contact and channels in China.

Soong was one of the three daughters of Soong Yaoru, known to his foreign friends as Charles Soong, who went to Vanderbilt University in 1882. He became quite affluent by importing American tobacco to China.

He sent all six of his children, three sons and three daughters, to American universities. Ai-ling eventually married Kong Xiangxi, the finance minister of the KMT government. Ching-ling, the middle one, married Sun Yat-sen. The youngest one, Mei-ling, married Chiang Kai-shek. The Soong sisters went to Wesleyan College in Macon, Georgia. Ching-ling graduated and sailed home in 1913. She had met Sun when she was a little girl, as he had visited her parents in Shanghai. When Sun relinquished his presidency for Yuan Shikai, she re-established contact with him in 1913, when her father took her to see him in Japan. Sun was actually on the run from the warlords. He stayed in Japan to launch a new form of the KMT Party called the Zhonghua Gemingdang or Chinese Revolutionary Party. While her father was helping with Sun's finances, Ching-ling became Sun's English language secretary. Despite the difference in age, and that Sun was a married man with children, the two fell in love in Japan and decided to marry after Sun obtained a divorce from his wife, who was then in Macao.

In 1925, Duan Qirui, the premier of the regime, and other warlords in Beijing took the initiative of inviting Sun to Beijing to "discuss the affairs of the State". Sun could not possibly refuse. So Sun and Soong set sail for Beijing, via Shanghai in November. Shortly after their arrival in January 1925, Sun passed away. Soong was a widow when she was barely thirty-two.

With Sun out of the way, Chiang Kai-shek, who as the commandant of the Huangpu Military Academy, had the advantage of having armed forces under his command, made plans to consolidate his control over the country. In the meantime, a left-wing group of KMT members in Wuhan elected Soong to the central executive committee of the party in 1926. When Chiang led his army on the Northern Expedition, the split between the two wings of the party was inevitable.

When Chiang's army arrived in Shanghai in 1927, he enlisted the support and help of the Green Gang, the secret society of underworld thugs, and unleashed a massacre of Communist party members, students and workers in Shanghai, Nanjing and Guangzhou.

Firmly on the side of the left wing of the party, Soong condemned Chiang for having betrayed Sun's ideal and principles in April 1927. Among those who signed a circular written by her, addressed to the whole nation were left-wing members of the KMT, and Mao and Dong Biwu of the Communist Party.

In July 1927, Soong Ching-ling decided to visit Moscow. In her own words, this was not a "flight" but she came to "express appreciation for what the people of the Soviet Union have done for revolutionary China...". She returned home in May 1929. For the next few years, until 1937, she led the China League for the Protection of Civil Rights in Shanghai. Because of her prestige and help from many foreign friends, she was deeply involved in the protection and rescue of political prisoners who were not on Chiang's side.

Against this background of strong patriotism and popular demand, Soong Ching-ling played an active part as a leader in the political scene because of her prestige and courage in standing up to Chiang Kai-shek and the right-wing warlords. Concurrently, she assisted and encouraged the student movement and other similar groups in arousing anti-Japanese sentiments, first in Shanghai and then in Hong Kong, in 1937. During the Japanese occupation in Shanghai, Soong's house was in the technically neutral French concession. But she was being watched by spies not only from the Japanese but also by the KMT. With the help of her New Zealand friend, Rewi Alley, she escaped, and landed in Hong Kong on Christmas Day 1937.

In January 1938, Zhou Enlai negotiated with the British ambassador in Chongqing, Sir Archibald Clark-Kerr, and obtained his agreement to set up a liaison office of the New Fourth Army and the Eighth Route Army under the CCP, in Hong Kong. The office was staffed by Liao Chengzhi, who operated behind the façade of a tea trading and import-export firm called the Yue Hua Company, right in the heart of the city at Queen's Road, Central. Because of his Cantonese background and his mother's extensive network of friends and relatives in Hong Kong, he was particularly active and successful in raising funds for the Eighth Route Army, the New Fourth Army and the embryonic guerrilla force.

Zhou Enlai, unlike Mao, came from a well-educated mandarin family in Zhejiang. He went to élite schools in Tianjin and Shenyang when he was young. After graduating with flying colours in 1917, like many of his contemporaries, he felt that acquiring a foreign education was necessary for the salvation of the nation. Therefore, he went to Japan. Initially he studied the language with a view to entering a teacher training college. He returned to China in 1919. It was the time of the May Fourth Movement, when most Chinese students were involved in anti-government activities.

Li Dazhao, a professor and librarian of Peking University and one of the founders of the CCP, saw the need to recruit new members for the party. A work-study programme was launched to send young men to France. In November 1920, Zhou was one of a group of 196 students who sailed for France. By then there was already a small cell of the CCP. It was not long before Zhou became a member of the party.

In 1924, his political career took an unusual turn. Sun set up a rival regime in Guangzhou as an opponent to the warlords based in north China. Counselled by his Russian advisers, Sun allowed Communist Party members to join the KMT in their personal capacities. Zhou was summoned to China and took the post of head of the Political Department of the Huangpu Military Academy in Guangzhou. This was the period of the First United Front.

In Hong Kong, Soong and her many friends, both foreign and Chinese, founded the China Defence League in March 1938. Prominent among the leaders were Hilda Selwyn-Clarke, Liao Chengzhi, Norman France, Liao Mengxing, Deng Wenzhao, Israel Epstein and the New Zealand journalist and writer, James Bertram.[2] Because of his command of foreign languages and engaging personality, Liao was elected secretary general and Deng was treasurer. John Leaning, a young Englishman who was the editor of a monthly magazine called *Democracy* with Edgar Snow in Beijing before he came to Hong Kong, was in charge of publicity. Later on, this role was taken up by Epstein.

Epstein was born in Warsaw in April 1915. He came with his parents to China when he was only two. His parents settled in Tianjin after having fled Poland when the German army was approaching the city. He began his career as a journalist when he was fifteen, when he worked for an English-language paper, the *Beijing and Tianjin Times*. He covered China's war with Japan for the United Press. Subsequently Epstein was appointed assistant editor of the *Hong Kong Daily Press*. Soong arranged for Epstein to visit the Shanxi-Suiyuan Anti-Japanese Base areas where he interviewed Mao Zedong, Zhou Enlai and other senior Chinese Communist Party leaders. In 1938, Soong invited him to join the league. Having a good command of English and other foreign languages, Epstein was the ideal choice for the post of editor of the league's newsletter.

Despite their political differences, Soong Ching-ling invited her brother, T. V. Soong, the finance minister of the central government in Chongqing, to fill the nominal post of president of the league. He accepted the role but resigned in 1941, when Soong Ching-ling openly attacked Chiang Kai-shek after he unleashed his soldiers on the Communist New Fourth Army. It was through Bertram's introduction that Soong met and got Hilda Selwyn-Clarke to join the league. Hilda was the wife of Dr. Selwyn-Clarke, director of Medical and Health Services in Hong Kong. In the days of pre-war colonial Hong Kong, both of them had prestige and influence. But despite her high-society connections, she had Fabian Society background and a burning concern for the poor and the underprivileged. Hence by her British friends in the colony she was quickly nicknamed "Red Hilda". She was appointed joint-secretary or English secretary with Epstein. Of all the non-Chinese office-bearers of the league, she probably did more useful work than the sum total of all the other members. Even by the Chinese it was acknowledged that "she actually ran the entire operation of the league".

Another foreigner who was involved was Norman France. He worked as co-treasurer with Deng Wenzhao. France was a professor of history at the University of Hong Kong. He was born in China and in general sympathetic with China's war effort.

Liao Chengzhi, by relying on his parents' prestige and contact with senior and influential members of KMT, actually raised money from all sorts of benefactors. It was reported that, by his persistence, even T. V. Soong donated 100,000 yuan to the league. But one major source of local donations from the Chinese people in Hong Kong undoubtedly came from the "One Bowl of Rice" movement organized by both Soong Ching-ling and He Xiangning. The idea was that donors were asked to give up eating one bowl of rice or donate the equivalent amount in money, which was twenty cents in Hong Kong currency. Some of the funds were spent on materials such as clothing fabric. These were supplied to female students to make warm clothing for the soldiers. Within a matter of only three weeks or so, they managed to raise HK$6,000. Famous Cantonese opera performers were mobilized to stage free performances to raise funds.[3]

To provide prestige and appeal to a wider section of the community, Soong even managed to attract the then colonial governor, Sir Geoffry Northcote, to serve as the patron of the function, and M. K. Lo and Hilda Selwyn-Clarke as chair and vice-chair.

Northcote's term in Hong Kong coincided with the period when the KMT army was in a series of defeats and retreats. Japanese soldiers arrived and camped in Shenzhen, just over the border from Hong Kong, as early as 1938. When most of the coastal areas were occupied by the Japanese, Hong Kong became an important supply depot of war and other materials to China. Despite that, the War Cabinet in the UK issued an urgent order on 28 June 1940, for the evacuation of all British women and children from the colony to Australia. Business was good and the mood of the high society was one of complacency. But Northcote was certain that war with Japan was imminent. Probably this was why he lent his support to Soong Ching-ling's activities. But plagued by indifferent health, he left Hong Kong in August 1941.

M. K. Lo was the prosperous lawyer son-in-law of Sir Robert Ho Tung, the most prominent and probably the wealthiest Eurasian businessman in Hong Kong at that time.

Ho Tung was the son of a Dutch-British father and a Chinese mother. Sent by his mother to an Anglo-Chinese school where he learned English, he made his fortune by working through the ranks in the biggest British firm Jardine Matheson, where he became the comprador when he was still quite young. Despite his Eurasian features, he always considered himself Chinese and identified with the Chinese community.

Through He Xiangning's contacts and connections, Lo donated generously. And through his influence, other Chinese entrepreneurs followed suit. He Xiangning was the daughter of a rich landowning family in Hong Kong. She became a keen supporter of Dr. Sun and Soong Ching-ling because of her husband's connection. She and Soong Ching-ling were close friends, both personally and politically, for the rest of her life.

The appeal attracted such wide support from the grassroots elements of the community that Soong Ching-ling managed to raise HK$25,000 within eighteen months. One could gauge that the sum was a substantial amount, as the price of one ounce of gold was only HK$90 then. The league also managed to attract donations in kind, such as blankets, mosquito netting and pharmaceutical items.

## The East River Guerrillas and Their Leaders

It was the more than 3,000 young people of diverse background and training who were initially members of such service teams and who eventually took up arms and formed the bulk of the East River Column. By the mid-1930s, it was estimated there were about 650 Communist Party members under the direct control of the Hong Kong Municipal Committee of the Communist Party, and an additional 50 among the members of the Communist-led Hong Kong Seamen's Union and another 50 in Macao.

With specific approval from Yan'an, Liao Chengzhi decided to send 250 party members from this total of 750 to the various service teams made up of young people from Chinese communities in different countries and regions, to provide the organizing structure and leadership. But by early 1939, many of these young people in the East River area were arrested by the local KMT authorities and many teams were disbanded.[4] The decision to disband the teams came directly from the Communist Party in Yan'an, through Liao Chengzhi. Liao then gave the direction to Zeng Sheng.

Zeng Sheng, like most soldiers of the East River Column, was a Hakka, born in 1910 in Pingshan, a village about twenty miles north of Shenzhen. His father was an overseas Chinese in Australia. Since his youth, he had worked as an apprentice chef on an ocean-going liner that sailed between Hong Kong, the Pacific region and Australia. He jumped ship when he travelled to Sydney and started a small grocery store. After accumulating some money, he managed to move his wife and son to Hong Kong. Zeng Sheng started his primary education in Hong Kong and in 1923 went to join his father in Sydney. Initially his father sent him to the Fort Street Secondary School in Sydney, for some intensive training in English.

During his stay, he felt humiliated by the racial taunts of his white classmates. So when his father decided to return home to Pingshan for retirement in 1928 and took along Zeng Sheng, he gladly went. By then he was ready for his university entrance examination.

It was during this period that he came under the influence of his teacher Pan Zishan, who was anti-KMT. Eventually he managed to be admitted to the Faculty of Education at Sun Yat-sen University in July 1933.

Left-leaning intellectuals like Lu Xun, Yu Dafu and Guo Moruo were faculty members of the university at the time. By then there were cells of Communist Party members among the students of up to 300. It was through the influence of some of these students that Zeng became a party member in the winter of 1934. He then joined, and in some instances actually organized, many student rallies in opposing the university authority and the central government. The target of many demonstrations held inside the campus was Zou Lu, president of the university. Zou was concurrently a government official who tried to suppress all student activities. The main thrust of the students' activities was to demand the KMT regime cease the intermittent conflict between the KMT and the Communist Party and to defend the country against Japanese aggression.

It was his participation and leadership during the mass demonstration held on 9 December 1935 that caught the attention of the KMT government. On that day he led a mass rally of 20,000 students and industrial workers who marched through the streets of Guangzhou. Subsequently, an order for his arrest was issued. It was through the help of other students, who provided him with protection and cover, that he managed to escape to Hong Kong in mid-January 1936.

His status as a student was suspended. When he arrived in Hong Kong, he found a job as a waiter on an ocean-going liner, S.S. *Empress of Japan*. He worked for a few months until September 1936. Then he returned to Guangzhou as the warlord Chen Jitang, who issued the order for his arrest, had been toppled by Chiang Kai-shek's central government in Nanjing. He continued his final year of study and completed a bachelor's degree in Chinese. That made him one of the very few Chinese Communists with a university degree during that era. In October 1936, he formally joined the Communist Party in Hong Kong.

After his graduation in July 1937, he moved to Hong Kong. When the incumbent secretary general of the Hong Kong Seamen's Union was called to Yan'an, Zeng took over as the head of the organization section of the union, and performed the duties of the secretary general. The union made use of a recreation body for seamen, the Yu Xian Le She, as the façade to recruit young people to join the Anti-Japan and Save the Nation movement.

The influence and the organizational ability of the Seamen's Union were impressive. As one of the first trade unions founded in Hong Kong, the union organized one of the most successful strikes by Chinese workers in the twentieth century in January 1922. The cause of the strike initially was entirely industrial, as Chinese seamen were dissatisfied with the wide disparity in wages paid to white seamen and to Chinese seamen. Later on some of the Communist labour organizers like Su Zhaozheng, Deng Zhongxia and Deng Fa stepped in to provide leadership. Undoubtedly the union was one of the best organized and most radical trade unions in Hong Kong. With Zeng Sheng's leadership and the union's involvement, it was quite a success in attracting able-bodied young men to the Anti-Japan and Save the Nation movement.

After China and Japan went into a full-fledged war following the Marco Polo Bridge Incident on 7 July 1937, Zeng returned to Pingshan to launch the Huiyang Bao'an People's Anti-Japanese Guerrillas in November 1938.[5] The bulk of the soldiers were Hong Kong-based seamen, junior staff from foreign firms, students, junior civil servants and peasants.

A less well-known man who was a co-founder of the Huiyang Bao'an People's Anti-Japanese Guerrillas was Zhou Boming. Zhou and Zeng had similar backgrounds, as both of them started out as students. Zhou attracted the warlord Chen Jitang's attention in Guangdong because of his participation in the anti-Japanese demonstration in December 1935. As he was about to be arrested, he escaped to Beijing and joined the Communist Party there in 1936.

As he was a relatively well-educated student, the party sent him to Xi'an to join Marshal Zhang Xueliang's Northeast Army. He quickly rose through the ranks and was appointed a lieutenant to command a company of soldiers, a little over a year after he joined. After the 12 December Xi'an Incident, when Chiang Kai-shek was held captive by Zhang and Yang Hucheng's soldiers, Zhou was directed by the party to go for military training in Yan'an. When war broke out between Japan and China on 7 July 1937, the party ordered him to make his way to his hometown in Huizhou. He was then sent by Liao Chengzhi to Hong Kong and appointed to head the propaganda section of the municipal committee of the Communist Party in Hong Kong.

In October 1938, Liao directed Zeng, Zhou and another member, Xie Heming, to lead a nucleus unit of about sixty people, that included cadres and seamen from Hong Kong, to move to the Huizhou, Huiyang and Pingshan areas to launch the Huiyang Bao'an People's Anti-Japanese Guerrillas. It was during the period of the United Front between the KMT and the Communist Party that Zeng's unit was given a formal designation and recognition under the central government authority. Zhou and Zeng formed the Chinese Communist Party Huiyang and Bao'an District Works Committee. Zeng was the commander of the guerrillas unit and Zhou was the political commissar.

At the same time, Wang Zuorao formed a team in nearby Dongguan. Initially, Wang's team had a nucleus of no more than thirty soldiers or so. But it quickly attracted young peasants and seamen, and within a year or so it had grown to a team of 600 strong.

Wang was the son of a minor county official under a KMT warlord. He was born in March 1913 in Dongguan. When he was due to begin his primary schooling, his father was unemployed. He entered a village primary school when he turned seven. But due to ill health, his schooling was a series of fits and starts, so that he could not finish his primary education until he reached 13. In 1926, his father took him to Guangzhou, with the hope of finding better job opportunities in the provincial capital. It was in Guangzhou that Wang Zuorao's father came under the influence of such Communist Party members as Zhou Enlai, who joined the KMT in their personal capacities. Finally, Wang senior managed to find a job as an apprentice draftsman. But after a year or so, he became unemployed, as the firm where he worked went bankrupt.

In 1931, when the warlord Chen Jitang was ruling Guangdong, Wang Zuorao joined a junior secondary school in Yan Tang, a suburb of Guangzhou. He graduated in 1934 and was appointed a sergeant in a KMT army under another warlord, Li Yangjing.

As a sergeant, his workload was not particularly onerous, so he could go home every weekend and meet people outside his barracks. Later on he met some Communist Party members, among them his own sister. Gradually he became disenchanted with his life as a KMT soldier. As a result of the warlord Chen Jitang's suppression of the student Anti-Japanese movement, he decided to leave the army. But before he could do so, his superiors noticed his pro-Communist sympathy. When he was absent from his barracks in February 1936, they thoroughly searched his room. He knew that his arrest by the KMT government was imminent and escaped in disguise to Guangzhou. In September 1936, he joined the Communist Party. In January 1938, the local party cell sent him to his hometown in Dongguan. The directive given to him by the party was to organize the local people into anti-Japanese guerrilla units. On 14 October, the Dongguan Model Able-bodied Young Men Guerrilla Team was formed.[6]

Right at the outset, leaders of both teams realized the importance of mobilizing the peasants, who made up the bulk of the population in the area. Most of the peasants were illiterate. But they were keen to support the guerrillas' anti-Japanese activities. With Zeng Sheng, Wang Zuorao and a nucleus of some of the relatively better educated cadres provided the leadership and the organizing abilities in mobilizing the peasants. One important aspect of the peasants' support was that they hid the foodstuffs and medical supplies obtained from Hong Kong and elsewhere, with the tacit understanding that they would be held in storage for the guerrillas for their use in the future when the need arose. In early 1939, the two teams, the Huiyang Bao'an People's Anti-Japanese Guerrillas and the Dongguan Model Able-bodied Young Men Guerrilla Team, were amalgamated. But it was not until 3 December 1943 that this team was formally named the Guangdong People's Anti-Japanese Team, East River Column. Zeng Sheng was appointed commanding general and Wang Zuorao was appointed chief of staff.

One senior leader of the column who was responsible for political activities more than combat and command duties throughout the war was Fang Fang. He was born into a family of a failed entrepreneur in Puning, Guangdong, in May 1904. As a young man, he was attracted to the May Fourth anti-feudalism and anti-imperialism activities in 1919. In 1924, he left school and joined the Peasant Training School in Guangzhou, founded by the KMT but where Mao Zedong taught for a while. In 1926, he joined the Communist Party and launched peasant liberation activities in his hometown in the Chaozhou district. By 1929, he was appointed to the important post of party secretary in the district, when he was barely 25 years old. Subsequently, he was given the task of working in the border areas of Guangdong, Fujian and Jiangxi. In the early 1930s, he mobilized the peasants in the East River area of Guangdong to join Wang Zuorao's embryonic guerrilla unit. By early 1940, he was appointed to the important post of secretary of the Southern Work Committee, answerable directly to Zhou Enlai in the Central Committee of the party. In the hierarchy of the party, he was senior to Zeng Sheng, despite the fact that Zeng held the rank of general.

It was ironic that these 600 soldiers were initially armed, given military rank and some financial aid by local KMT warlords like Xiang Hanping and Luo Fengxiang, as at least some of the KMT generals superficially observed the policy of the United Front. One single factor which helped the guerrillas in mobilizing so much support from the local populace and in acquiring arms and ammunitions at the early stage of their formation was the failure and desertion of the KMT soldiers. When the Japanese tried to attack Huizhou by landing in Daya Bay on 12 October 1938, over 2,000 KMT soldiers who defended the area deserted the city and surrounding area, without firing a single shot. Some of them actually deserted well before the enemy arrived. The end result was that the entire Huiyang district west of the Kowloon-Canton Railway was left completely undefended. So, without any effort, the Japanese marched on and occupied the provincial capital, Guangzhou, within seven days. Many people who eventually joined the guerrillas were apolitical able-bodied young peasants who just felt the need to take up arms to defend their own hometowns. One example was the young people in Humen, who just picked up the arms and ammunitions abandoned by the KMT army. They dumped into the East River the heavy artillery and the cannons that they could not carry.

Soon thereafter, however, the guerrillas alienated some of the local populace by imposing harsh land reform measures waged on the landlords in the Dongguan and Huizhou areas. What made their position worse was that they were involved in intermittent small-scale armed conflicts with the local KMT forces, because the guerrillas were expanding too fast for the comfort of the local authorities. Therefore, they were fighting a multilateral war with the KMT forces, the Japanese, local bandits and some local quisling soldiers who were under the command of the Wang Jingwei regime in Nanjing. In fact in many instances, it was difficult to differentiate between the bandits and the KMT soldiers, as many bandits were given military rank and recognition by local KMT generals. This combined group of KMT soldiers and bandits was given the disparaging nickname of *he he ji* ( 呵呵鷄 ), i.e. chickens afflicted with parasites, by the people and the Communist-led guerrillas. Initially, in late 1939, General Xiang Hanping had meant to control the guerrillas by appointing a few KMT officers into the guerrilla unit commanded by Zhou Boming and Wang Zuorao, under the pretext of assisting Wang in his "political" work.

The KMT forces gradually tried to exercise control over the guerrillas. In early 1940, General Xiang Hanping actually directed these guerrillas to move to Huizhou to be "integrated" formally into the KMT army establishment. By March 1940, as Wang was playing for time by using delaying tactics, Xiang unleashed over one division of his soldiers, who surrounded and attacked the guerrillas in the Pingshan area. Poorly armed and inexperienced in warfare, the guerrillas were soundly beaten. The pervasive mood among the soldiers was defeatism, so much so that they decided to "move east", i.e. to retreat to the Chaozhou and Hailufeng areas without the approval of the provincial military command. The excuse was that this was the area where the Communist Party forces, led by Zhou Enlai and He Long, moved after their uprising in Nanchang on 1 August 1927. This is where they believed they still had "a strong base of support from the masses".[7] The nearly 1,000 soldiers and civilians led by inexperienced commanders were once again routed, and some deserted, leaving only 108 soldiers who were relatively fit and willing to carry on. The talk among the survivors, with a touch of dry humour, was that they were like the 108 heroes in *Water Margin*.[8]

After over a month on the run, they finally arrived in Shishan, where they took some rest. With a nucleus of about 100 soldiers, they regrouped into three small separate contingents of one rifle team (*dui*), one pistol team of about 70 initally and one team of about 30 who were tasked to handle "political" and propaganda work. The first team was led by Wang Zuorao with Zhou Boming as the political commissar. The latter team was led by Zeng Sheng and underpinned by the legendary Cai Guoliang, who subsequently featured very prominently in the Hong Kong and Kowloon Independent Brigade.

Cai, one of the few non-Hakka leaders of the East River Column, was born in Xiamen in 1912. In 1928, he joined the Amoy Canning Factory in Xiamen, and there he became active in labour union activities. In 1932, his employer transferred him to the Hong Kong and Kowloon Amoy Canning Factory in Hong Kong. It was the time when Chinese all over the world were involved in the Anti-Japan and Save the Nation activities. Cai quickly became active in some of such bodies such as the *Qiao Tou* (Bridgehead) Society and the Women's Education Service Team. In May 1938, he joined the CCP.

When China and Japan formally came to war in July 1937, Cai led seventeen of his co-workers in the factory and walked all the way to Huizhou to join the Huizhou and Bao'an People's Anti-Japanese Guerrillas. By March 1940, he had risen to the rank of deputy political commissar.

For non-Chinese or English-speaking people who came into contact with the column, Huang Zuomei (Raymond Wong to some of his friends) was probably the best-known member of the column, next to Cai Guoliang. Huang's ancestors were from Fujian. But his grandfather moved to Guangdong and then to Hong Kong, where he worked as a teacher at a government primary school.

Huang Zuomei was born in 1916 into a family of nine siblings. After attending a private primary school, he successfully enrolled in 1932 in Queen's College, which was one of the two élite secondary schools in Hong Kong. Later he could have enrolled at the University of Hong Kong, but as his father was struggling to raise a big family, he gave up the opportunity for a university education and sat for the Hong Kong government civil service recruitment examination. Passing successfully, he began to work as a clerk in the Government Stores Department and later in the Royal Navy Dockyard.

In the 1930s, Huang was swept into the various forms of Anti-Japan and Save the Nation activities in Hong Kong. Initially, he joined a choral group which sang patriotic songs to mobilize students and workers to join the various service teams. Chen Daming, a communist cadre in Hong Kong, noticed Huang's activities and recruited him into the party in 1941.

Fluent in spoken and written English, he worked in the International Liaison Unit of the Hong Kong and Kowloon Independent Brigade. Nearly every prisoner of war and non-Chinese civilian who escaped from Hong Kong through the New Territories met Huang and was received by his unit.

Next to Huang Zuomei, the person who met and looked after most English-speaking prisoners and escapees was Lin Zhan. She also was a fluent speaker of English. Lin was born in Hong Kong in 1920 and went to Belilios Public School, the only government-run Anglo-Chinese girls' school. After completing secondary school, she worked as a physical education teacher at the Catholic Sacred Heart School. In spring 1939, she came under the influence of a friend who worked in one of the many service teams in Huiyang. She then became involved in some of the Anti-Japan and Save the Nation activities organized by students in Hong Kong, one of which was the Rainbow Choral Group. Through such activities, she became a member of the Communist Party in July 1941. Because of her membership in the choral group, she was assigned by the party to liaise and recruit young people into various *minyun* bodies.

After the Japanese started their occupation in December 1941, the party directed her to go underground and attempt to infiltrate any Japanese military unit. She successfully found a job as a laundry worker/domestic maid in a Japanese military quarter in urban Kowloon. On one occasion, a Japanese officer tried to sexually harass her. She put up stiff resistance. Out of revenge, the officer falsely charged her with theft and put her through two days of physical torture. Eventually she was released, as the Japanese could not prove her guilt. During her eight months of recuperation, she learned to speak Japanese, which was useful for her work in the column. Chen Daming, the political commissar, met her and assigned her to work alongside Huang Zuomei in the International Liaison Unit of the column.

It was Lin Zhan who met Dr. Selwyn Selwyn-Clarke through one of his junior colleagues, Dr. Lai Baozhu. The task given by Lin's superiors was to mobilize Dr. Selwyn-Clarke to escape from Hong Kong. However, he felt it more useful to stay and look after the civilians and prisoners of war. He turned down Lin's offer of help.

## Directive from Yan'an

A directive dated 8 May 1940 from the Central Committee of the Communist Party in Yan'an was relayed to Zeng via Liao Chengzhi in Hong Kong. Zeng's "move east policy" was severely criticized. During that difficult period, the directive was probably sent by human courier, as it did not reach Zeng Sheng until early June. The message came from Zhou Enlai himself who said:

> The present overall situation throughout the country is a situation of stalling and stalemate on the part of the KMT Government. They still maintain the façade of engaging in anti-Japanese activities. But concurrently, they are more active in pursuing anti-communist activities. The possibility of KMT units surrendering to Japanese units in isolated locations cannot be ruled out. We must maintain our anti-Japanese guerrilla campaign bravely and should not be afraid of armed conflict. Only through such a move can we survive and develop further. Units commanded by Zeng Sheng and Wang Zuorao should return to the Dongguan, Bao'an and Huizhou areas. With such favourable political conditions and the support from the local populace, you should find a way to operate in the areas between the Japanese occupied territory and that controlled by the KMT. But do not stay in an area for too long. If you resort to total avoidance of armed conflict with the enemies and hide in the hinterland, it is not only a wrong political move, but it is also doomed to fail militarily. In such an event, the KMT forces will eliminate you under the pretext that you are but local bandits. If you move to the Chaozhou and Meixian areas, you are leaving your base of support.

The second part of the directive was that they should discard the rank and the designations given to them by the KMT forces. From then on, they renamed themselves "the Guangdong People's Anti-Japanese Guerrillas East River Column". Part three of the directive stated:

> When you move back to the East River area, you should go through some appropriate rectification among your soldiers. Strengthen unity and mobilize anti-Japanese sentiments politically. On your way to your destination, reduce loss as much as possible so that you can have an intact unit when you arrive in the Huizhou, Dongguang and Bao'an areas. When you arrive, strengthen your United Front work.

The directive was of course very much in keeping with Mao's teaching that "the guerrilla soldiers are like fish and the people are the water". Returning to the East River area, they could travel and obtain supplies from Hong Kong with less difficulty. So Zeng Sheng temporarily handed over the command to Wang Zuorao and Zhou Boming and made his way to Hong Kong in July 1940. During his short stay in Hong Kong, he managed to raise funds and supplies for his soldiers.

With some seventy soldiers, the embryonic guerrilla unit re-established a base just a few miles south of Dongguan and west of the Kowloon-Canton Railway. Before long, he managed to recruit up to 500 soldiers and started rebuilding his guerrilla army. Then he launched two local newspapers to promote anti-Japanese propaganda and mobilize the people.

The person who virtually launched and operated the two newspapers was Yang Qi. He was born in Zhongshan County in 1923. His father used to own a small fabric shop in Guangzhou. The Great Depression of the 1930s wiped out all his capital and savings. Equipped only with primary education, he had to fend for himself. Virtually penniless, he made his way to Hong Kong and found a job as an apprentice in an herbalist shop in 1938. Through hard work and self-education, he was admitted as a part-time student in the Institute of Journalism, where Qiao Guanhua, the German- and Japanese-educated journalist, taught. In the meantime, Yang switched jobs and became a proofreader of a left-wing magazine, *Literary Youth*. Before long, he was promoted to editor of the magazine and was involved in the editorial work of *Hua Shang Bao* (Chinese Merchants' Daily).

By then his brother, Yang Zijiang, had joined the East River Column. Yang Qi came under the influence of his brother and joined the party in early 1941. When the magazine's anti-Japanese slant caught the government's attention, it was raided by the Special Branch of the police. Finally the magazine ceased operation. Other party members alerted him that he might be arrested by the government. He was then directed to report to the East River Column's headquarters in Bao'an. His talent as a journalist was noticed, so he was given the job of publishing *Qianjin Bao* (Forward Newspaper) throughout the war.

# The Hong Kong Government and the Guerrillas

It was somewhat strange that the British government's overall policy in Southeast Asia in dealing with Liao Chengzhi and his comrades was not consistent. Liao was eyed with a great deal of suspicion by the colonial authority in Malaya, as his recruitment of young overseas Chinese attracted the local Special Branch's attention. He was criticized for "using Hong Kong as a base to organize communist disturbances against the Government of Malaya". The Hong Kong government, however, held a different view from that of the Malaya government. It stated that the latter government's policy was a "misconception of the overseas Chinese organizations' patriotic activities" and that "suppression of these patriotic movements as being inimical to the Imperialist policy of Malaya encouraged their growth and gave rise to so much internal trouble".[10]

In the meantime, Liao Chengzhi's activities in Hong Kong went through a rather hot and cold period of treatment from the Hong Kong authorities. As the UK government still maintained diplomatic relations with Japan, an overly active recruitment centre for anti-Japanese guerrillas was definitely not a welcome move. As a result, the Yue Hwa Company was raided on 11 March 1939. Five of the staff, including Lian Guan, who was probably the most senior communist cadre in Hong Kong then, next to Liao, were arrested by the Special Branch of the Hong Kong Police. The firm was forcibly closed until Zhou Enlai protested to the UK ambassador in Chongqing.[11] Then all the staff were released and all documents seized were returned. However, under strong pressure from the Japanese, the Hong Kong government forcibly closed the Yue Hwa Company later in 1939. Liao and his colleagues continued with their fund-raising and recruitment activities even without the façade of the shop. But their real activities were an open secret to their Chinese compatriots and to the Hong Kong Police.

However, the relations between Liao and Hong Kong government took an unexpected turn in mid-1941. As the Pacific War loomed on the horizon, the British intelligence knew that the Japanese army was conducting military exercises in Hainan Island, then under Japanese occupation. Indications were that the Japanese army was attempting to acclimatize their soldiers, before their attack on Malaya and Singapore. On 24 October 1941, the head of the Special Branch of the Hong Kong Police approached Liao with a rather unexpected request: to enlist the East River Column and the Qiongya Guerrillas (commanded by Feng Baiju on Hainan Island since 1927) to sabotage the military airport and other military facilities built by the Japanese. The British side made it quite clear that what they wanted was co-operation in the military area only. Any such negotiations did not imply any overtone of politics or recognition of Liao's political status. For quite some time since the late 1930s, Premier Tojo of Japan had been planning and directing a detailed study of what would be required for the capture and occupation of Malaya

and Singapore. Therefore, the Taiwan Army Research Centre was founded in
Taiwan. It was run and directed by Colonel Masanobu Tsuji. Initially, Tsuji was
given a year for the planning of the invasion of Malaya and Singapore. By the
beginning of 1941, because of the American embargo on all petroleum products,
he was told that his period of planning was reduced to six months. The main
emphasis of his planning and study was to collate "all conceivable data connected
with tropical warfare" for Malaya, the Philippines, Indonesia and Burma. Coming
from a temperate climate, the Japanese army had never fought in the tropics. So
with the beaches in Malaya in mind, amphibious exercises were staged initially
in Kyushu, the most southerly island in Japan. Subsequently, such exercises were
held on Hainan Island, which was as tropical as they could get.[12] Occasionally,
Japanese aircraft also flew over Malaya from French-occupied Saigon and from
Hainan Island.[13]

The secret negotiations went on back and forth for a few weeks. Initially
Liao cabled Mao in Yan'an for instructions. Mao gave his agreement for Liao
to proceed with detailed negotiations, in a cable on 26 October. Representing
the British side was the head of the Special Branch of the Hong Kong Police,
Superintendent F. W. Shaftain. While the British were anxious to enlist the
help from the East River Column, they were highly concerned that if the
news of the secret negotiations was leaked out, that would no doubt cause a
serious diplomatic disaster. Not only would it offend the Japanese but also the
sensibilities of the British authorities in Malaya and the Dutch, who maintained
a strong anti-communist policy in the Dutch East Indies. So the negotiations
went back and forth right up to a few days before the outbreak of the Pacific War.
As late as 14 November, Mao cabled Zhou Boming and Liao to tell them not to
be "too greedy in their demands". Finally an agreement on the following four
points was arrived at:

(1)  The Communists agreed to sabotage the military airfield built by the Japanese
     on Hainan Island. But they hoped that the agreement would not be a one-off
     operation. They hoped that there would be a long-term co-operation between
     the two sides. The British, while remaining non-committal, agreed to assist
     the Qiongya Guerrillas as much as possible.

(2)  The Communists agreed to undertake the operation provided that the British
     would supply all the necessary arms, ammunition, technology and training to
     Feng's soldiers in undertaking the sabotage work. The dynamite required was
     to be shipped to Zhanjiang, then known as Guangzhouwan, in Guangxi, at that
     time a French Colony. It would be picked up by Feng's soldiers. The British
     agreed to supply 1,000 pistols and 250 sub-machine guns to Feng.

(3)  The Communists requested that Feng be allowed to set up a liaison office and
     a radio station in Hong Kong, somewhat like the Yue Hwa Company operated
     by Liao. The British rejected this request but agreed that Feng be allowed to

operate a "commercial firm" in Hong Kong, named "Guang Nam Company" under the management of the Comintern representative in Hong Kong. The Communists considered the possibility that the "company" be formed by a left-leaning New Zealand journalist, James Bertram. There was evidence that Bertram was the intermediary who brought both sides together.[14] The British agreed not to interfere with the firm's activities but expressed the hope that the "company" would not organize a "mass movement" among the people in Hong Kong. The request to set up a radio station was turned down.

(4)  The Communists requested the British to supply the East River Column and the New Fourth Army with arms and medical supplies. The British agreed to supply them with 500 pistols and 50 sub-machine guns initially. The Chinese side would provide the transport to send the weapons to the areas of operation.

Throughout the negotiations, Liao kept Yan'an informed by telegram, the last one sent to Yan'an on 7 December 1941, one day before Pearl Harbour and the invasion of Hong Kong. It was obvious that the Communists were anxious to obtain the weapons and ammunitions, because they sent Zhou Boming, a deputy of Zeng Sheng, to Hong Kong to take delivery of the weapons. But the British were somewhat hesitant and tardy for fear of offending the KMT government and that of the Japanese. Ultimately, the deal was never implemented because of the outbreak of the war on 8 December. Many guerrilla leaders involved were still bitter at the British side's failure in fulfilling their conditions of the deal, when they recalled the negotiations many years afterwards.[15]

# 3 Hong Kong and the War Years

Hong Kong Island was the product of the first Opium War, and the British took full possession in 1842. Eighteen years later, they acquired the tip of the Kowloon Peninsula, opposite Hong Kong Island across from Victoria Harbour. The island covers an area of thirty-two square miles, with a chain of steep hilly ridges throughout its length of eleven miles. The distance from the northern coastal strip to the farthest point to the south of the island is only five miles. Up to this point, the role of the Hong Kong government, except for a few Indian and Chinese police at the rank-and-file level, staffed by British expatriate civil servants, was to foster a peaceful environment for the British firms to use the area as a trading post. In 1898, to forestall against Russia's and France's increased influence in China, a treaty was negotiated with the Qing government to lease the land mass north of the Kowloon Peninsula and over 250 mostly uninhabited islands to the British government for ninety-nine years. The subject of the treaty was a piece of land and the islands, which measured some three-fifths of the county of Xin'an or Bao'an. The Hong Kong government called this piece of leased territory the New Territories. The main land mass of the territories consisted of sparsely populated villages hidden in the valleys of steep hills. Most of them were accessible only through unpaved footpaths. The fertile cultivable land was mainly occupied by Cantonese-speaking people. But since the Ming Dynasty, through hard work and thrift, many Hakka who arrived and settled later had successfully moved from their first settlement on the hillside terrace down to the fertile valleys. By the 1800s, Hakka-speaking people became the majority in the New Territories.

In 1899, when the Hong Kong government took control of the New Territories, there were about 100,000 people in various villages that had been settled since the Song Dynasty. Their main economic pursuits were a subsistence form of farming of rice and sugar. The other main interest was fishery. Except for a few major market towns like Yuen Long, Tai Po, Fanling, Tsuen Wan and to a lesser extent, Sai Kung, the Hong Kong government did not invest any significant resources in the territory. The New Territories was really the backwater of a highly developed city. Except for some single-lane rudimentary roads, as late as the 1930s, round most of the market towns and isolated police stations, the really only significant sign of government administration were the British district officers. They were administrators and concurrently police magistrates, land officers and the dispensers of government funds in the districts. Up to the mid-1940s, there were only two such district officers in the entire New Territories and the outlying islands. They were respectively the district officer north and district officer south. The Kowloon-Canton Railway, the only major transport link with Guangzhou (the closest major city), was built only because the then governor was a trained army engineer.[1]

In short, the people in the New Territories were living in a way not significantly different from that of their compatriots north of the Sino-British border at the Shenzhen River and in a way little changed for the past several hundred years. In fact, the New Territories for long remained a kind of traditional Chinese hinterland to urban Hong Kong. Administration was not, by British standards, intensive; changes were not rapid; and before the Second World War there could have been, but for the guarantee of peace, little difference in conditions and atmosphere between the New Territories and China across the border. In topography, except for a piece of flat land measuring about ten square miles in Yuen Long and Ping Shan, most of the land mass is hilly and heavily wooded.

## Japanese Invasion of Hong Kong and Entrenchment of Guerrillas in the New Territories

When war broke out in Hong Kong early in the morning on 8 December 1941, the immediate move of the Japanese forces was to bomb the minuscule British Air Force stationed at Kai Tak Airport. At 8:00 a.m., thirty-six Japanese fighters appeared over the airport and deliberately flew to as low as sixty feet. The entire British Air Force of three obsolete torpedo bombers and two amphibians were totally destroyed within minutes, before they had any chance of taking off. The Pan America Clipper flying boat that was due to fly to Manila that very morning was also destroyed. General Maltby, the general officer commanding British forces, commented, "the aircraft were no match for enemy fighters and I gave orders that they were not to be employed unless the opportunity occurred... In any case, all were put out of action in the first raid by the enemy....". Immediately afterwards, the Japanese Air Force bombed several military installations in Kowloon and those in the New Territories.

Concurrently, two battalions of Japanese soldiers moved across the Shenzhen River. One moved along the Kowloon-Canton Railway into the various market towns of Sheung Shui, Fanling, Tai Po Market and Shatin. Another battalion landed by small boat in the south-east coast of Tai Po.

Defending the Gin Drinkers' Line's key point, the Shing Mun Redoubt were the Royal Scots and a few Indian ranks. This was the key defence line on the New Territories mainland, as it was ten-odd miles from the Shenzhen border. On the other side were the battle seasoned Japanese soldiers. Overall, the Japanese commander, Lieutenant General Sakai Takashi, had 15,000 men at his disposal. Despite an initial minor success in warding off the enemy, the order from the high command was to delay the Japanese advance and to offer protection to the army engineers whose priority was to destroy all the bridges as a means to delay the enemy's rapid advance. Before long, the Japanese occupied Golden Hill and the Shing Mun Redoubt. Both these points were key positions in the overall Gin Drinkers' Line. On 11 December, General Maltby decided to withdraw all his troops from the New Territories mainland and the Kowloon Peninsula, to concentrate his defence on Hong Kong Island.

Before they retreated, they thoroughly destroyed the Green Island Cement Works, the China Light and Power stations and all the shipyards. Therefore, Hong Kong Island was left wide open to defend itself. As Hong Kong was without any air power for protection, Japanese planes bombed some of the vital installations such as the Shell Oil depot in North Point and some of the water supply systems. But before the British troops' retreat from the Kowloon Peninsula, the Japanese had captured Hong Kong's main reservoirs at Shing Mun that provided most of the territory's potable water supply. This was no doubt one of the most difficult problems faced by the defending soldiers and the general public for the next few days.

Starting on 13 December, the Japanese artillery fired at all the important targets on the island with pinpoint accuracy. The guns at Mount Davis and those at Belcher's Fort were knocked out by direct hits.

On the evening of 15 December, the Japanese assembled a large number of small boats in Kowloon Bay. Despite the fact that early and initial attempts to land on the island were repulsed, they successfully landed in Lyemun Fort on 18 December. Outnumbered and outgunned, many defenders were butchered after they surrendered to the Japanese. Despite gallant efforts put up by various units at places like the Hong Kong Electric Power Station at North Point, Wong Nai Chung Gap, the Repulse Bay Hotel and Stanley, they were fighting a hopeless war. By 24 December, there was no more co-ordinated defence on the island. What was left for the Japanese to do was a series of mopping up operations, the main thrust moving into Stanley. By 3:00 p.m. on Christmas Day, General Maltby went to Government House to advise the governor that no useful resistance was possible. At 3:15 p.m. he gave a general order to all commanding officers to stop fighting and surrender to the nearest Japanese commanders. The same evening, Sir Mark Young crossed the harbour and formally surrendered to General Sakai at the Peninsula Hotel in Kowloon.

In the hiatus between the day of the Hong Kong government's surrender and the Japanese military's formal entry into the city on 27 December, the colony was in a state of anarchy. Poor Chinese went on widespread looting and robbery. Then the commander-in-chief of the Japanese, Lieutenant General Sakai Takashi, issued a proclamation placing the entire territory under martial law. The proclamation detailed Sakai's absolute power and made any action or opposition against the Japanese army, any act of espionage or "any action which endangers the safety of the members of the Imperial Army or causes any obstruction to military movement" crimes against martial law and punishable under it. The sentences included death, imprisonment, banishment, fines and confiscation of property.

Sakai tried to put on a façade of civility and friendliness by hosting a luncheon at the prestigious Peninsula Hotel on 10 January, for 133 former Chinese Justices of the Peace and community leaders. At the luncheon, he spoke of "the currency problem and the tasks of restoring order, the cleansing of the city and the reopening of business". He said he would make every effort for the reconstruction of Hong Kong and Kowloon, and he hoped that the Chinese leaders would do their best to co-operate.

Sakai then outlined in some detail what he intended to do. Among other items, he said that the task of restoring "order" was the responsibility of the military authorities. But to avoid "inconvenience" to the people from the deployment of too many soldiers, the Chinese police were being re-employed. In fact many of the so-called "Chinese police" were not police but collaborators, fifth columnists and triad society members who had little or no proper training in police duties. Despite being designated "police", the Japanese used them mainly as interpreters, and they were given few law-and-order duties. One of the main emphases of his speech was that "the Chinese and the Japanese are the same people and have the same culture and belong to the same 'Great East Asian race'." He would spare no effort to make Hong Kong and Kowloon a place "where people may reside in peace". He then appealed to his guests to form local assistance committees to help him.[2]

It was under such an atmosphere of coercion and pressure that the Chinese community leaders quickly took action as a sign of their "co-operation". Shortly thereafter, the Executive Committee of the Chinese Chamber of Commerce called a meeting of nineteen members of the chamber to "discuss ways and means of re-starting business in Hong Kong". After the meeting, those present elected a committee of nine. The nine then formed themselves into a "Rehabilitation Committee". Then on 14 January, they were received by the Japanese authorities at the Peninsula Hotel, where they "submitted their proposals for the immediate settlement of several important problems, such as rice supply, opening of communications and re-opening of business". As a follow-up, all those who attended Sakai's luncheon earlier on were asked to register with the government their business and profession with the Rehabilitation Committee.

On 21 January, the government announced that the whole urban area of Hong Kong and Kowloon was demarcated into eighteen "administrative districts", twelve on Hong Kong Island and six in Kowloon. Each was to be placed under a "District Bureau" headed by a Japanese official in charge, and some Chinese staff. The bureaux were supposed to handle "general welfare of the residents in their particular district, matters such as public health, business and repatriation". But the main functions and the more important ones were, in fact, the taking of census, the management of rice rationing, removal and travel permits, and issuing of birth and death certificates.[3] It was evident that the Japanese military authority was not adequately covered in the vast suburbs as far as administration was concerned. Except for some of the secret agents who worked and lived in Hong Kong before the war, the Japanese soldiers' command of the local language was not perfect, particularly in the countryside. They had to rely on their Chinese staff and collaborators, who were mainly Chinese of Taiwan descent. Therefore, in the New Territories, some of the district bureaux were infiltrated by members of the East River Column.

Then in April 1942, the Japanese government created three "Area Bureaux" on top of the District Bureaux. There was one for the whole of Hong Kong Island and neighbouring islands as far as Cheung Chau, a second one for Kowloon and Tsuen Wan, and a third for the rest of the New Territories. Despite the fact that the Japanese military had fairly good intelligence on the urban areas, their demarcation of the New Territories in such a manner showed that they either did not understand the situation on the ground or they relied too much on the word of the collaborators. Another factor was that the New Territories was under-administered before the war by the Hong Kong government, because of its peculiar status as a "leased" territory as against the status of Hong Kong Island and the Kowloon Peninsula as a Crown Colony. A good example was that telephone lines were not installed in many market towns until years after the Second World War. Population in the New Territories was no doubt sparse. But it was evident that the Japanese were not in complete control of most of the countryside during the early months of the occupation.

## Movement of the East River Column

During the initial stage of the eighteen-day war in Hong Kong, the British and Indian soldiers retreated from the New Territories and Kowloon. It was not an orderly retreat. Except for some of the heavy equipment that they destroyed, they left behind a sizeable quantity of guns, ammunitions and hand grenades. The guerrillas managed to pick up some of the materiel and weapons left by the British and Indian soldiers. They were poised to move into the New Territories, behind the Japanese line. Lin Ping, who held the position of party secretary of the Third and the Fifth Detachments and the chairman of the Guangdong Frontline Military Committee, gave the order to three teams of guerrilla soldiers to move in when the British retreated from the countryside to urban Kowloon and Hong Kong Island.

Lin was born into a poor peasant family in Jiangxi in 1908. After attending primary school in his hometown, he joined a peasant society organized by the local party cell. He joined the Communist Party in 1931 and was a guerrilla soldier in Jiangxi since then. Rising through the ranks, he was appointed secretary of the Guangdong Provincial Military Committee in 1938.

One group came in from Shataukok, through Luk Keng, Wu Kau Tang, Sheung Shui, Fanling and camped in the wooded hills of the Pat Sin Range. In topography and environment, Sai Kung and the Pat Sin Range areas were ideal for guerrilla warfare, as both areas were heavily wooded and linked to the nearest market town by unpaved village paths. Another point to their advantage was the people in nearly all the towns and villages in the New Territories spoke the local Hakka or Wai Tau dialect, unintelligible even to their compatriots in the city, let alone the Japanese. In Sai Kung, the overwhelming majority of the population spoke Hakka exclusively. Although the fishermen who landed their catch and used the town as anchorage spoke a different dialect, they made an effort to learn Hakka. The majority of the guerrillas of the East River Column were Hakka. The minority who were not native Hakka made an effort to learn to speak the dialect, particularly those who worked in the propaganda and courier divisions of the column.

One of the strongest detachments in weapons, human resources and able leadership was that led by Cai Guoliang, Huang Guanfang and Liu Jinjin.[4] This detachment moved in via Mirs Bay (also known as Dapeng Bay), through Kat O Island, and then to Sai Kung where most of them hid in the hills in Cheung Sheung in Pak Tam Chung, Sai Kung. This location was accessible only after a steep climb. Hence this group used the place as their headquarters and kept their radio transmitter throughout the war years. Some moved into the urban areas near Ngau Chi Wan, in urban Kowloon. The guerrillas had made an excellent choice, as Sai Kung was the most inaccessible from urban Kowloon because there was no road for vehicles linking it with the rest of Kowloon. The third detachment moved into Yuen Long, Shap Pat Heung and Tsuen Wan.

The East River Column operated under the name Guangdong Anti-Japanese Guerrilla Column from 1942. It openly declared that it "came under the leadership of the Chinese Communist Party" only as late as 2 December 1943. The news was first announced in a Xinhua News article published in *Jiefang Ribao* in Yan'an on 23 August 1943. General Zeng Sheng was the commander, Lin Ping was the political commissar and Wang Zuorao was the deputy commander. Because of the unique position of the group led by Cai Guoliang and its relative military success, it was given the designation "the Hong Kong and Kowloon Independent Brigade" on 3 February 1942, when the order was relayed by Lin Ping to Cai Guoliang in

Sai Kung. The ceremony of the establishment was held in a Catholic chapel, in the isolated village of Wong Mo Ying, Sai Kung, when Cai Guoliang was appointed commander and Chen Daming was appointed political commissar.

The guerrillas were quite well organized. Shortly after they moved into various areas in the New Territories in early 1942, they went about doing propaganda work and recruitment from among the general populace. In Sai Kung alone, they managed to recruit 300 young men and women within the first six months of 1942. Some of the villagers recruited were given proper training in political indoctrination in the column's training school near Huizhou, and some were trained to work in the paramilitary section.

In addition, the guerrillas were successful in launching their *minyun*, i.e. propaganda, logistics, and hearts and minds work combined. In Sai Kung, for example, they staged plays with songs and dances. The contents of such performances did not stress Communist ideology but patriotism. The local people were also taught to organize themselves to defend against the bandits. Better cultivation methods were also taught. All in all, they won the support of the local people not by coercion but through soft "heart and mind" indoctrination.[5]

Right from the outset, they followed Mao's teaching that "in order for a guerrilla unit to survive, it must have a reasonably secure base" and "the unit must develop an anti-Japanese military unit before it can mobilize the people". During the hiatus between the retreat of the British forces and the regular Hong Kong Police and the Japanese takeover, the whole of the New Territories, and for that matter the urban areas, was a free-for-all during which bandits and triads operated at will. Once the guerrillas moved into Sai Kung, they realized that the first priority was to eliminate the bandits from the district before they could win the trust of the local people. The people could then be mobilized to offer co-operation and protection before the guerrillas could build a secure base. Within months of their arrival, Huang Guanfang and Jiang Shui caught seven of the most notorious bandits. After a public trial was held in Ho Chung, near Sai Kung, the bandits were executed on the spot.

Huang was born in Shenzhen in a peasant family in 1911. He was an industrial worker in Hong Kong just before the war and was recruited into the Communist Party in 1938. As he had a few years of primary schooling before he started to work, he was appointed to the post of captain of a pistol detachment when the Hong Kong and Kowloon Independent Brigade was formed.

Jiang Shui was born in Sai Kung in 1927. When the war started, initially, he was given the rank of "Little Devil" which required him to be courier of messages and handle odds and ends duties in the brigade. But because of his detailed knowledge of the Sai Kung area, he was allowed to carry weapons, despite his young age.

Among the bandits and pirates, there were a few who were so powerful and had such well-entrenched influence that the column, and for that matter, the

Chongqing government, had to co-opt rather than defeat them. A notorious one known to the British Army Aid Group (BAAG) agents was Liu Pei. He was a well-known pirate leader who could command a large number of young men in the Mirs Bay and Bias Bay areas. In February 1944, the column announced that he had joined them. It was well known that he managed to acquire a fairly large quantity of arms and ammunitions by attacking central government units. But his so-called allegiance certainly did not deter him from operating more like a pirate than anything else.

Liu Pei, originally called Liu Tian, was born in Hong Kong in 1922. His father was a second-hand garment trader. But because the family had five children, Liu's father found it difficult just to feed them. So Liu's mother had to work as a vegetable farmer to supplement the family income. Liu Pei had just a few years of primary schooling when he and his brother, Liu Zhenpeng, were caught up in the Anti-Japan and Save the Nation activities in Hong Kong when they were barely teenagers.

After the Japanese landed in Daya Bay in October 1938, Liu and his brother joined one of the "Return to Hometown Service Teams" in the East River area. He led a group of barely fifty young peasants to provide protection to his hometown in the Huizhou area. In order to garner whatever financial and other resources he could, Liu accepted an offer from the local KMT commander to incorporate his team of young men into the KMT's formal army establishment.

Another man was Liang Yongyuan, who was so powerful in 1941–42 that he practically controlled the entire Dapeng Peninsula. In 1941, he was actually recognized by the central government as an official guerrilla leader under the KMT military establishment. He had his first brush with the East River Column in October 1942 and suffered a crushing defeat. He wisely switched his allegiance, but his allegiance was only valid when it was convenient.

In addition to being brave in battle, Huang Guanfang and Jiang Shui were the hardest working and most enterprising in the recovery and collection of weapons left behind by the British soldiers. Before the Japanese could fully occupy and administer some of the periphery of urban Kowloon and Hong Kong Island, Huang, Jiang, and a platoon of guerrilla soldiers went as far as Aberdeen in the south of Hong Kong Island and the Kowloon City area to retrieve some of the Bren guns left behind by the retreating British soldiers. It was in the period right after the British surrendered while the whole city was still in a state of chaos and confusion. In the areas along the waterfront near Kai Tak Airport, there were fishermen who made it a daily routine to find shellfish. Huang and his soldiers posed as fishermen and mingled with them to try to find some of the weapons. As some of the fishermen had already collected some of the weapons before Huang's arrival at the scene, he had to resort to other means and in some instances he had to acquire them with hard cash. But with the help of the fishermen, Huang managed to retrieve some of the mines left by the British Navy, during ebb tide. They then extracted the TNT inside the mines for their own use.

Despite its relatively small size compared with guerrilla units in other parts of China, the East River Column, and for that matter the Hong Kong and Kowloon Independent Brigade, followed closely Mao's strategy that he spelled out in detail in his lectures in Yan'an from May to June 1938. The strategy was eventually published under the title "On Protracted War". In his thesis, the guerrillas are three types: the élite hard core, who are well trained, disciplined, experienced; the party's future top leaders; and the part-time guerrillas who are concurrently part-time peasants, who are recruited to fight and defend their own village area. They would form the bulk of the rank and file of the combatants. The third type belongs to the auxiliaries, who are not well armed and are used mainly as support troops, couriers, runners and labour units. In as early as February 1942, the Hong Kong and Kowloon Independent Brigade already had a well-defined organizational structure remarkably consistent with Mao's teaching. In addition to the main combatant forces under the command of better educated cadres and seasoned soldiers, there were departments responsible for logistics, intelligence, medical and field hospitals, political indoctrination, propaganda or *minyun*, and United Front work. Details of their initial organization in January 1942 are as follows:

1. Main Detachment
   Captain: Cai Guoliang. Political Commissar: Chen Daming.
   Deputy to Cai: Lu Feng. Training: Zhai Xin, Chen Jiatian.
2. Logistics: Yuan Dachang, A.D.C.: Luo Oufeng (based in Shataukok). Couriers and Intelligence: Cai Zhongmin. Translation and Interpretation: Tan Tiandu.
3. Medical and Field hospital: Mai Yazhen, Li Kun.
4. Political Indoctrination: Huang Gaoyang.
5. Organization: He Jie. Guard Duty: Huang Yunpeng.
6. Minyun: Wang Yue'e. Propaganda: Chen Guanshi.
7. United Front: Fang Juehun. Printing: Liang Buke.
8. Sai Kung Detachment
   Pistol Unit: Huang Guanfang, Lee Tang and Liu Jinjin. Minyun: Liu Zhiming.
   Fishermen Work: Xiao Chun.
9. Shataukok Detachment
   Rifle Unit: Zhuo Juemin. Political Commissar: Zhang Liqing.
   Pistol Unit: Lu Jinxi. Minyun: Huang Siming.
10. Sheung Shui Detachment
    Pistol Unit: Lin Chong. Deputy: Mo Haobo. Minyun: Yang Fan.
11. Yuen Long Detachment
    Captain: Su Guang. Deputy: Gao Pingsheng. Minyun: Chen Hai.
12. Lantau Island Detachment
    Captain: Liu Chunxiang. Deputy: Su Guang.

13. Iron and Steel Detachment. This detachment was somewhat like the special force of a regular military establishment that is given more vigorous training and tasked to handle difficult operations.
    Captain: Xiao Guangsheng. Deputy: Yang Jiang.

14. Marine Detachment
    Captain: Chen Zhixian. Deputy: Wang Jin.[6]

By April 1942, when the Japanese were relatively settled in the urban areas, they began to move into Sai Kung. Preceded by six plainclothes collaborators, the Japanese police (*Kempeitai*) moved in a team about ninety strong and set up a road block in Tun Cheung, a village some 1.5 miles outside Sai Kung. The *Kempeitai* were the military police, who nominally belonged to the overall establishment of the army, but actually operated independently. Throughout the war, they were feared, as they were notorious for being brutal and cruel in their handling of anyone whom they considered an enemy or suspected of being involved in subversion.

By using rough treatment in their interrogation of the local villagers, the Japanese tried to extract intelligence to track down the guerrillas. By then, Cai Guoliang and his soldiers had already been tipped off by the local villagers. They then retreated and hid themselves and their radio transmitters in the mountain hideout in Cheung Sheung. This location is about fifteen miles outside Sai Kung, up a steep climb on Sharp Peak. The Japanese never managed to come anywhere near the main body of the guerrillas.[7]

Zhang Xing, a villager from Tai Long Village, Sai Kung, remembered that the guerrillas came into the district in April 1942. Under the command of Cai Guoliang, only a handful of them came into Sai Kung while the rest of the detachment hid in the hills nearby. Initially they either attacked the local bandits who had been robbing and kidnapping some of the people, or they threatened them so much that the bandits retreated across the border at Shenzhen River, to China. In fact, before the guerrillas came into the district, Zhang Xing, being a member of the Hong Kong Seamen's Union, had come under the influence of the underground cell of the Communist Party. He recalled with delight when I interviewed him that, well before he joined the column, he personally witnessed the biggest haul of weapons and ammunition, recovered by the guerrillas from the retreating British soldiers in Yuen Long.

When the guerrillas came, they publicized their aims and organized the local people against the bandits. In every village they went to, they left a couple of their cadres from their *minyun* department. In addition to their duties of indoctrination, they were responsible for recruitment. Zhang recalled that, within six months of their arrival, they successfully managed to recruit over 300 able-bodied young men in some parts of the New Territories. Zhang Xing was one of those recruited, not only as a soldier but subsequently to Communism. When I interviewed him some forty years after the war, he was still a card-carrying member of the party.[8]

As the leader of the brigade, Cai was always on the move to be one step ahead of the Japanese. Another part of his important duties was to contact the various detachments. On one occasion, before Cai left Sai Kung, Zhang Xing was appointed to lead one of the subunits of the Sai Kung Detachment, after having attended about six months' training in politics and weaponry. Fang Fa, an able-bodied young man from the neighbouring village of Chek Keng, was appointed his second in command. It was Luo Rucheng who was the instructor in tactics while Lin Wu took the task of political indoctrination. As many of the peasants recruited were barely literate, they had to be taught the basics of political ideology, such as communism and capitalism, from scratch before they were taught the famous *San da jilü, ba xiang zhuyi* ("The Three Rules of Discipline and Eight Points for Attention"). These were the rules and standards of behaviour that Mao first introduced to his soldiers when they were in Jinggangshan in the spring of 1928. But first and foremost, the emphasis of their training and indoctrination was on patriotism. The new recruits were then taught the basics of guerrilla tactics. Some of the better educated were then sent to the column's headquarters north of Shenzhen for further training. Subsequently many of these were appointed cadres.

Liu Jinwen from Shek Kip Mei Village, Sai Kung, was one of those who had partially finished secondary school when the war began and had worked in a newspaper office as a typesetter. He was so attracted by the message of patriotism featured in the plays staged by the guerrillas that he and a friend walked for hours just to find and join a fighting force, regardless of political ideology. Initially they thought they could just walk all the way to Qujiang, some 300 miles away in north Guangdong where the KMT had an army base. But no sooner had they reached Long Ke, some fifteen miles away, than they met one of the captains of the Hong Kong and Kowloon Independent Brigade, Jiang Shui. Liu and his friend were persuaded to join the guerrillas. As Liu was relatively better educated, he was appointed a cadre instead of a regular combatant. He was then sent back to his village to recruit more young men. Later on, when the Japanese moved into Sai Kung and established the Sai Kung District Bureau, he found a job in the bureau and managed to gather intelligence for the brigade.[9] Because of the recruitment effort, by the summer of 1943, the Sai Kung Detachment had grown to a size of 500 strong.[10]

In Yuen Long, it was Zeng Hongwen who led a company of soldiers that moved in quickly after the British retreated. They found over ten pistols, eight machine guns and a large quantity of ammunition. The haul was so substantial that they had to mobilize more than one company of soldiers to transport it by boat. It took them three days to complete the job of transporting everything to one of their bases in Shataukok. Zeng and Huang Guanfang collected about 30 machine guns, 100 rifles, 50 Bren guns, over 100 pistols and 100 hand grenades between them.[11]

Throughout most of the war years, the Independent Brigade maintained their communication centre in Cheung Sheung, Sai Kung. But in early 1942, the brigade had deployed a considerable number of soldiers in the area around Wu Kau Tang, near Tai Po Market. This was a logical and wise strategic move, as the road leading from Tai Po Market to Wu Kau Tang was no more than an unpaved village path. The entire area was also heavily wooded. Before the Japanese tried to tackle their problems in Sai Kung, they tried to deal with the guerrilla base in Wu Kau Tang. On 25 September 1942, two companies of Japanese soldiers moved into Wu Kau Tang. The date was of some significance, as it was Mid-Autumn Festival, an important occasion for family reunions. The Japanese thought that they would certainly net some important cadres of the brigade. First, all villagers were forced to leave their houses and move into the open ground in front of the village. The Japanese then went from house to house searching for guerrillas. Finding no one, they turned their anger on the village elder Li Saifan. He was subjected to water torture followed by the cruel treatment of having a horse trample over him until he was unconscious. The Japanese then took another village leader, Li Yuenpui. They subjected him to the same water torture until he was unconscious. Li Yuenpui also told them nothing. Then they withdrew under the protection of darkness. The result of the ill-treatment witnessed by the villagers was to arouse their anger and persuade them of the need to defend their own hometown. After the Japanese departure, over 200 able-bodied young men in the area joined the brigade voluntarily.

## Rescue of Leftist Cadres and Intellectuals

When Sir Mark Young, the Hong Kong governor, surrendered to the Japanese after eighteen days of resistance, quite a few senior Communist Party officials at the provincial level were stranded in Hong Kong, as members of the Chinese Communist Party South China Work Committee were meeting in Hong Kong in secret when the war broke out. In addition, there were about 800 political figures, writers, journalists who were either sympathetic to the Communist cause or were anti-KMT in their outlook. Therefore, the Central Committee of the Communist Party in Yan'an issued a directive, stating that the immediate and most urgent task for the guerrillas was to rescue these people and escort them to safety. Two cadres, Lian Guan and Liu Xiaowen, who were familiar with the local scene, were given the duty by the Communist Party Central Committee and the South China Bureau of rescuing these people.

Mainly for this purpose, the guerrillas had managed to establish two separate routes of escape and communication in January 1942. The western route was from urban Kowloon to Tsuen Wan, Tai Mo Shan, Kam Tin, Yuen Long to Lok Ma Chau, then across the border. Secret reception points were set up in all the major towns like Tsuen Wan, Yuen Long, Kam Tin and Lok Ma Chau, with guides and couriers.

The eastern route was from the Ngau Chi Wan area (in urban Kowloon), to Sai Kung, Ki Ling Ha, and then by boat to the northern shore of Mirs Bay. In fact, an overwhelming majority of the cadres and literary figures used this route, as Sai Kung was the strong base of the guerrillas. As well, the guerrillas had some usable, dependable boats and fishermen who were also guerrillas. Hence sailing to the shore of Mirs Bay was inevitably the route of nearly all escapees. Among those who were rescued and taken on the western route were Mao Dun, Zou Taofen, Ge Baoquan and Feng Zi.

Mao Dun, whose real name was Shen Yanbing, was not a Communist. But he came under the influence of Russian literary figures like Maxim Gorky and Alexander Pushkin, so he was always sympathetic to the anti-Japanese policy of the Chinese Communist Party and had chosen to live in Hong Kong since 1936, where he could write and publish freely.

Ge Baoquan was a famous translator of many literary works of the Western world. He taught in many top universities in north China. Feng Zi was a famous stage actress in Shanghai. She was an underground Communist Party member for a few years before she came to Hong Kong in 1937.

One group who took a different route were He Xiangning and Liao Mengxing, mother and sister of Liao Chengzhi, and the famous poet Liu Yazi. They were escorted from urban Hong Kong to the outlying island of Cheung Chau, where they hid for a few months before they sailed under cover to Haifeng.

The regular ferry service that served the passenger traffic between the two sides of the harbour, Hong Kong Island and Kowloon, before the war was not operating after the Japanese took over in December 1941. So even taking the escapees on the island to the Kowloon mainland before going on to the border was already a major challenge. In addition to the problem of physical distance, Japanese military motorboats patrolled the water virtually non-stop.

The Japanese military government just could not cope with the management of a fairly sizeable city of 1.5 million people. After the eighteen-day battle, the Japanese found that much of the infrastructure such as the water supply system, the power plants on both sides of the harbour and public transport was either damaged during the fighting or sabotaged by the retreating British soldiers. The most urgent and serious problem was the serious food shortage. By early spring 1942, many people had died after weeks of starvation. The whole population had to rely on a system of food rationing at the rate of 7.5 ounces of rice for each person daily. All other items of food such as fruit and vegetables were either in short supply or just not available.

In January 1942, the interim Japanese military government issued a public notice warning that people who had "no employment or place of residence", or "who had to beg for their food" should be repatriated to the towns and villages in China from where they had come. Then the Japanese government set up a "Repatriation

Bureau" under its civil affairs department to handle the evacuation of people from Hong Kong. For this purpose, the Japanese military administration enlisted the help of various Chinese district and provincial associations. Representatives from these associations were invited to sit on the "committee". Initially the procedure in respect of such departures was quite simple. Those who wanted to leave had to apply for a repatriation certificate at various District Bureaux or their sub-stations. Such documents were subject to vetting by the Japanese sentries at the border. In June 1942, the military government imposed compulsory registration of all the residents. After this date, it was necessary to apply to the *Kempeitai* for permission to leave. No transport tickets were obtainable without the production of a *Kempeitai* permit. People who departed under such a scheme had to go through a lengthy process to obtain the necessary papers, as the Japanese were keen to vet their background and more importantly their political outlook. There were Hong Kong Chinese residents who took part in the defence of Hong Kong during the eighteen-day battle, such as soldiers in the Hong Kong Defence Force, the auxiliary police and the air raid wardens. They discarded their uniforms and melted into the civilian population when the governor announced the surrender on 25 December 1941. Such obstacles provided a golden opportunity for some of the Chinese collaborators who worked in the Japanese-controlled police force to extort money from the poor victims. Once anyone was accused of being a "Chongqing element" he or she could be subject to all sorts of torture or even execution by the Japanese. Anyone who showed any signs of sympathy with the KMT government in Chongqing, or even anyone who dared to tune in on the radio broadcasts from Chongqing, was considered a Chongqing element. Those who had obtained the necessary papers had to leave on the specified route from Yuen Long to Shenzhen. Various "welcome" and "interrogation" stations were established by the quisling elements of the Wang Jingwei government and Japanese sentries at the border. However, except for those unfortunate enough to be found by the Japanese and forced to leave, most people who chose to leave did not bother to apply for the necessary papers and just left on foot through the New Territories. It is estimated that within a year from January 1942, up to half a million people left Hong Kong in this manner. But the food shortage was so serious that there were cases of the Japanese soldiers just cordoning off a block in the urban area and forcing the residents to leave, by putting them on boats which were towed out to the outlying islands. There were also cases of people being forcefully shipped to Hainan Island to be mine workers for the Japanese.

People rescued by the guerrillas had to avoid the route specified by the Japanese. As subsequently described by Mao Dun in great detail, the selection of the date and the time of the escape from the island was of great importance. As the people who were most knowledgeable about the safe escape routes and various means of evading the Japanese were the triads or bandits, who collected "protection" money from everyone who relied on them for assistance, even the guerrillas had to co-operate and work closely with them. Out of respect and probably in awe of the East River Column's superior weaponry and organization, the triads did not levy any such "protection money" on the people rescued by the guerrillas.

The guerrillas who helped Mao Dun and others in their escape from the island picked one night when the moon waned in early January 1942. In order not to arouse suspicion by any Japanese sentry who would stop and search them, Mao Dun and his party not only dressed like ordinary workers but discarded all books, diaries and any papers that would incriminate them. Mao carried a well-thumbed copy of the Bible with him as a disguise as a religious minister. Initially they had to walk for quite a distance and then hid themselves with about fifty others in a big fishing boat for the night. Then they were transferred to small fishing boats that could accommodate four to five passengers. These small boats then sailed out just before daybreak when the harbour was fog-bound. It was in the big fishing boat that Mao Dun came across Zou Taofen. Zou was surprised to find that Mao actually took his entire family on such a hazardous journey, because Zou left his wife and children to the guerrillas' care. For a short harbour crossing that usually took less than twenty minutes under normal circumstances, their crossing took over an hour to reach Kowloon. The entire party was then taken to a disused warehouse in urban Kowloon. After hiding there for two days, a group of about fifty was escorted to travel over the hilly paths between Kowloon and Tsuen Wan. Tsuen Wan was quite a desolate town — virtually a no-man's-land during the daytime — and the East River guerrillas hid in the highest mountain, Tai Mo Shan. But the guerrillas moved into the town at night and had actual control. Hence the escaped party was well looked after with good accommodation and adequate food. After resting for two days, the entire party was taken to climb Tai Mo Shan. This was controlled by a team of guerrillas led by Captain Jiang Shui.

When they reached Tsuen Wan, Jiang not only made sure that Mao's group was adequately fed and provided with good potable water for the rest of the journey, but he also organized able-bodied porters to carry their luggage. By the time they reached the outskirts of Yuen Long, the biggest town just south of the border, it was night-time. Some "not overly friendly" bandits occupied the area. The guerrillas and the bandits operated under a symbiotic situation. Both groups were armed but with different aims and objectives, so they tolerated one another as long as each did not interfere with the other's activities. Mao's group of over 100 stragglers and some early arrivals were escorted by the guerrillas. Feeding such a large group at such short notice posed a serious problem. But after some persuasion, and probably owing to Jiang's prestige, the bandits actually provided a reasonably adequate meal for the group. Accommodation was provided in a large house abandoned by a local landlord; some were housed in the local ancestral hall.

As the guerrillas and the triads had virtual de facto control of the area around the border, Captain Jiang Shui had actually obtained exit passes — with the help of officials of the local District Bureau — which were a requirement laid down by the local Japanese commander.

Japanese entries checked Mao and his group. It was evident that the number of refugees leaving Hong Kong was so large that the Japanese sometimes just could not cope with a long process of checking and verifying the refugees' identities. The group was then taken on two wooden boats that sailed across Shenzhen River and landed on the north shore of Bias Bay in a village near Shayuchong.

The whole group then walked for another twenty-odd miles before they reached a township that had been attacked and burned down by the Japanese the previous week. They rested for the night. Then General Zeng Sheng, the commander of the East River Column, came out to welcome them. Mao Dun described Zeng as "ponderous, soft spoken, medium built. He looks like a scholar more than a soldier. We were told that he used to be a schoolteacher in Guangzhou before the war. He certainly fits the description". When Zeng met me in Hong Kong some forty years after the war, he impressed me with his mild and humble manners. Of medium stature, gentle, soft-spoken and self-effacing, he was quite different from some of the firebrand and eloquent senior Communist cadres I had met in the past.

Zeng extended the group a warm welcome, as he had been expecting them to arrive the previous day. Then dinner was served. Zeng apologized for the simple dinner, because it certainly was not a "proper welcome dinner" except for a vegetarian dish and some dog meat. The next morning, both Zeng and Lin Ping, the political commissar, extended a formal welcome to the group. Lin then gave a speech outlining the history of the East River Column. After resting in the small township for three days, the group set out again on their journey. For the next three days, they took a route close to the Kowloon-Canton Railway. The area was occupied by the Wang Jingwei elements. But militarily, the East River Column was stronger and so dominating that the quisling soldiers did not dare question Mao Dun's group. The guerrillas in fact were so daring that they posted all over the electric lamp posts and trees along the route slogans that mobilized the local people to "resist the Japanese". It took something like four days before they reached the suburb of a previously prosperous market town, Shi Long. While the group rested there, the guerrillas received intelligence that the Japanese were deploying their main force nearby to attack Shi Long, with the object of plundering the food supply. Immediately the group marched out of Shi Long and moved to Huiyang. As this town was the main concentration point of the Hakka, the group most of the guerrillas belonged to, they felt safe and secure there. Mao and his group rested and spent Lunar New Year there. In the meantime, the KMT army and the Japanese were going through a see-saw battle nearby, so the group had to evacuate by taking a rickety boat and sailed for fourteen days on the East River. Finally, they reached the sizeable town of Lao Long. Their journey took more than a month, which in normal circumstances would take only a day or so. The group were by no means home and dry, but at least they were in an area controlled by the KMT government.

The whole rescue mission took a little over three months, until the end of May 1942, by which time the entire contingent of 800 cadres and intellectuals had been rescued successfully.

As pointed out by Dr. Douglas Scriven and Colonel Lindsay Ride, two of the non-Chinese people who were rescued by the guerrillas, it was a magnificent feat by any standard, as these people were rescued right under the noses of the Japanese. As described by some of those from among the 800-odd Chinese who were rescued, the success was due to great organizational skills and co-operation from the local people and some of the local bandits that roamed the countryside before the war. In addition to the provision of safe passage through rugged terrain, board and lodging, in some instances, porter service was provided for some of this group who were mostly elderly writers, poets and politicians and were physically unfit to walk with their own luggage over such rugged terrain and difficult circumstances. The whole operation of rescuing Chinese under this category started on 25 December 1941 and continued until 22 May 1942, when the overwhelming majority of these people were successfully rescued.

Not one escapee from a prisoner of war camp or a Chinese refugee who departed from home for China, of his or her own volition, could have survived the journey without the guerrillas' assistance.

## Rescue of Allied POWs and Civilians

Besides the 800-odd Chinese political figures who were rescued and assisted by the guerrillas in their escape to China, non-Chinese soldiers and civilians were rescued. According to a rough estimate provided by the East River Column, about 100 British and American Air Force personnel, Indian soldiers, and other non-Chinese prisoners, civilians and military personnel were rescued between January 1942 and early 1945 from Hong Kong and repatriated to Free China. The guerrillas failed to rescue only two of the American Air Force personnel who parachuted into Hong Kong during that period, as both were seriously injured and then captured by the Japanese before the guerrillas arrived on the scene. The total number of American Air Force personnel rescued by the Hong Kong and Kowloon Independent Brigade came to thirty-eight.

One of the earliest successful escape parties was undoubtedly that of four soldiers, led by Colonel Lindsay Ride. He was interned with the other British soldiers in the Shamshuipo Prisoner of War Camp at the end of December 1941, after the surrender. As there was a serious shortage of medical supplies even of the most basic type and the Japanese captors refused to help, Ride considered the chances of dying due to illness and malnutrition in the camp greater than the risk of being caught while trying to escape. It was during the early stage of the Japanese occupation when the camp was inadequately guarded. Ride discovered that there was a slipway and a jetty at the western side of the camp that was not guarded, and prisoners were allowed to sit on the jetty at night. So he sent Francis Lee Yiupiu, his Cantonese-speaking lance corporal, to bribe a fisherman who paddled a sampan to come near the jetty at night. The party was made up of Ride, Lee, Lieutenant D. W. Morley and Sub Lieutenant D. F. Davies. On the night of 9 January, they were taken across the bay in Lai Chi Kok, landing at a beach near Castle Peak Road. Within a few hours they were out of the camp and in the foothills of Kowloon. Under the protection of darkness, they walked from Tai Po Road. Before daybreak on 11 January, they were in Siu Lek Yuen Village, outside the small rural town of Shatin. They climbed the mountain ridge that separates Shatin and Sai Kung, where they rested. Throughout these two days, they had to overcome the difficulties of the lack of reliable maps and unkind weather, as most of the hill areas that separated Shatin and Sai Kung were fog-bound most of the day. It was a sign that the guerrillas had already established a reliable system of communication and intelligence. By relying on the Little Devils, who roamed the hills, the guerrillas were aware of this party's escape. The Little Devils were children, sometimes as young as seven or eight, who were recruited by the guerrillas to work as couriers and sentinels. As they were knowledgeable about the areas of their hometown and generally more mobile in their activities, they were a useful source of human resources for intelligence and in general doing errands for the soldiers.

It was the guerrillas' determination to find and rescue the group before the Japanese and the Wang Jingwei elements found them. It was due more to a stroke of good luck than by design that they managed to wander into the outskirts of Sai Kung. By 12 January, the third day of their escape, they had met up with one of the leaders of the East River Column, Cai Guoliang, in the village of Pak Kong Au. Ride briefed Cai in great detail about the situation in the camp as well as the ammunition and weapons left behind by the retreating British soldiers in various pillboxes in the hills nearby. In Sai Kung, they rested and were well fed for two days.

Even then, so soon after the East River Column had first moved into the New Territories, they had established an intelligence station in Sai Kung. It was a café that operated virtually round the clock. The station was staffed by Zhang Wanhua, a female guerrilla. This café had the distinction of looking after so many escapees, Chinese and foreign, that it was dubbed the "Night and Day Café" by many people who patronized it during their escape. Ride's party rested and were supplied with food and drinking water before Zhang gave them the all-clear sign that it was safe to sail across the sea. Then they were taken in a junk that sailed through Tolo Harbour to the island of East Peng Chau, which is about a mile from the north coast of Mirs Bay.

Ride and other escapees who met Cai were impressed by the morale, the bravery and the discipline of the East River Column guerrillas in general and with Cai's personality in particular. As a result of this brief encounter, as early as mid-1942, shortly after the British Army Aid Group (BAAG) was established in Guilin, Guangxi, Ride and his colleagues made up their minds to work closely with Cai and his soldiers. It was a rather fruitful relationship for both units. In fact, in one of his reports, Ride wondered why not many other prisoners of war made the attempt to escape, as he said that "safety lay almost at the gates of the camps". That was not an exaggerated claim; most of the camps in Kowloon were within a few miles from the foothills of Lion Rock, where guerrillas of the Hong Kong and Kowloon Independent Brigade were operating, particularly after dark. Small units of them actually came right into the city.

Ride was born in Newstead, Victoria, Australia, in 1898, and was appointed professor of physiology at the University of Hong Kong in 1928. He saw active service as a private in France during the First World War and was twice wounded. A keen sportsman, he was convinced that sporting ability was one of the factors that determined the Australian forces' success during the First World War. He also believed that the best way for other prisoners of war was to tell the outside world of their plight in the hands of the Japanese. Another objective of his was to send medical and other supplies to civilians and prisoners in Hong Kong. Right from the outset, BAAG belonged to a unit under the British MI9, which was an organization to help prisoners of war and to engineer their escape from prisoner-of-war camps. As the commandant of BAAG, he soon exceeded his remit by intercepting refugees who escaped from Hong Kong, as a means of obtaining intelligence. Secret agents were also sent from Free China back to Hong Kong to gather intelligence.

Forty days after Ride and his party escaped from the camp, he and Francis Lee Yiupiu reached China's wartime capital in Chongqing. He then obtained approval from General Sir Archibald Wavell, commander-in-chief in India, to set up BAAG. The British ambassador in China then took him to see Chiang Kai-shek, when he explained to Chiang that BAAG had to deal with the East River Column in Chinese territory. Due to the sensitive political situation in China, he needed Chiang's endorsement. In addition, the ambassador gave Chiang assurance that Ride would not engage in any political activities. In the presence of his wife, Chiang gave his endorsement.

Obviously encouraged by the success of Ride's party in escaping from the camp, another party of three planned their escape from the same camp less than a month later. The three were Captain Anthony Hewitt of the Middlesex Regiment, Dr. Douglas Scriven, the Regimental Medical Officer, and New Zealand Pilot

Officer Edmund Crossley. Following practically the same way out of the camp, the three escaped by a sampan hired outside the camp and ferried across Lai Chi Kok Bay on 2 February 1942. Like most escapees, they stealthily climbed up the steep hill along Tai Po Road at night. After reaching Shatin, they did not follow the usual route by turning right, to climb the hill of Ma On Shan to find shelter and food in Sai Kung, where the East River guerrillas had a strong presence. Instead, they went by the mountain route through the foothills of Tai Mo Shan. It was an unfortunate choice for the party, as they encountered not only a number of unhelpful villagers but bands of local bandits. Over the hill near Lam Tsuen, north of Tai Po Market, eventually they arrived somewhere near the Shenzhen–Lo Wu border and were again surrounded by a gang of local bandits. Fortunately out of the blue, a Jamaican Chinese called Percy Davis Chang, who lived nearby, appeared at the site to rescue them. Percy Davis Chang had some influence over the local bandits, who were persuaded to leave Hewitt and his group alone. They were then taken to meet a leader of the East River guerrillas, Fang Fang. They were protected by Fang's soldiers, who took the group to cross the border through Wu Tung Shan. They were then taken to meet one of the political commissars of the guerrillas.

There they were looked after by two English-speaking Straits-born Malayan Chinese, Lim Koonteck and Chan Pengleong, who had answered the recruitment drives by other Hakka before 1941. Like many rank and file members of the column, initially they joined as members of the service teams to do propaganda work.

At the camp just north of the border where Hewitt and his group stayed for a few days, they were well looked after by the guerrillas and struck up friendly relations with them to the extent that the guerrillas invited the three of them to inspect their own soldiers and help train them. Scriven, a professional medical practitioner, gave the young soldiers training in hygiene and sanitation in the camp. In whatever spare moments he got, he treated the sick and the wounded soldiers with the precious store of medicine that he carried all the way from the prisoner of war camp. They stayed in this camp for a few days waiting for the commander, Huang Guanfang, to return to meet them in person. Huang finally appeared on 10 February. The three escapees not only were given a good meal but also a good briefing from Huang, who told them the status of the East River Column vis-à-vis the KMT central government. During their brief sojourn in what Hewitt called "the Communist camp", he noticed that soldiers worshipped the Buddhist goddess, Guanyin, the Goddess of Mercy, and Tin Hau, the legendary Goddess of Heaven, the traditional patron saint of fishermen and peasants who live near the sea. Before their departure from the camp on 13 February 1942, Lunar New Year, the party was given a warm farewell by Huang, who even supplied them with some Chinese currency.

The guerrillas managed to find some flour to make some dumplings and a goose to give the three a New Year's feast. They were deeply touched and impressed, as all the people in the area were experiencing a food shortage. The goose was the only one left in the whole village. After another day of marching, they said a fond farewell to the guerrillas, who accompanied them as they were near the market town of Danshui, which was in the hands of the KMT army.

Another party of British soldiers who escaped early from the Shamshuipo camp were Douglas Clague, Lynton White, John Pearce and David Bosanquet. Faced with a starvation diet and the side-effects of malnutrition, they felt that they would have a bleak future if they decided to stay in the camp, so they planned to escape. With precise planning, they escaped from the camp in mid-April, by going through the utility hole covers into the storm water drain, and then into Lai Chi Kok Bay.

Armed with only a sketch map provided by John Barrow, a pre-war district officer north in the New Territories, and some canned food, they followed the route taken by other escapees. Once they swam across Lai Chi Kok Bay, they climbed the foothills in north Kowloon and tried to find their way to Shatin. Their aim was to cross Tolo Channel and Mirs Bay with the help of local fishermen. But their rudimentary map was no help in providing any direction and bearing. Instead of anywhere near Tolo Channel, they ended up in the village of Ho Chung, which was some three miles outside Sai Kung. Fortunately for them, they were ferried in a boat across Hebe Haven. Not one of the four could conduct any meaningful conversation in Chinese. Despite their being helped by some friendly villagers, they were actually groping in the dark. Fortunately, a local school teacher who spoke "near perfect English" was roused from his sleep and came to their aid. Then, they were taken to meet the local leader of the East River Column, who identified himself as Zhang Ming.

They were housed in the village of Tai Wan, a mile or so from Sai Kung, where they were met by one of the oldest of the cadres, Tan Tiandu, who identified himself as Henry Tam. They were then told that a police superintendent from Hong Kong also escaped successfully. He was W. P. Thompson, who escaped from the Stanley Internment Camp together with probably the only non-Chinese woman who successfully escaped, Gwen Priestwood. After a brief meeting with Thompson, the party were taken by junk and sailed to Plover Cove. After landing in Plover Cove, they were met by an escort party of armed guerrilla soldiers, who led them to the village of Chung Mei.

The intention of the guerrillas was to use this village as the starting point to sail across to the northern shore of Mirs Bay. After they had been settled in the cockloft of a village hut, Cai Guoliang of the Hong Kong and Kowloon Independent Brigade came to see them. He briefed them on the history of the East River Column. Most people who met the East River Column guerrillas for the first time had very little idea about the origin of the column. In fact, the column and for that matter, the Hong Kong and Kowloon Independent Brigade, was not particularly keen to show that they were led by cadres of the Chinese Communist Party. Therefore, Cai was at pains to explain that they were not a "Communist" guerrilla group, despite the fact that they were so "labelled by the central government". "They were no more than men and women committed to do all within their power to lift the Japanese yoke from China."[14] The following day, Cai met up with them again and briefed them in greater detail about the Independent Brigade. He told them that one of the serious problems was the shortage of "money", as they were relying largely on "remittances sent by overseas Chinese through banks in Hong Kong in the past". Now that Hong Kong was occupied by the Japanese, this source had dried up. The only source of income were "fees" extracted from people in Hong Kong who wanted protection while they travelled through the New Territories into Free China. This was a difficult period that the brigade went through early in its formation. The situation was improved only in late 1943–44, when they were so well organized that they could levy import and export duties on goods and commodities that passed through their area of control.

After a few days of good rest, they were taken to the shore, from where they sailed in a little flotilla of three sampans. Their aim was to reach the village of Shayuchong on the northern coast of Mirs Bay. Unfortunately, the village had been raided by Japanese soldiers two days before. So the party landed in Kwai Chung instead, from where they were taken by the guerrillas to Danshui, a sizeable market town. They continued on their journey by using an unconventional form of transport, riding pillion on the back of bicycles, after leaving the guerrillas. David Bosanquet, one of the four in the party, was so grateful to the guerrillas that he vowed to let the British and US forces "hear about their case". The last stretch of about thirty miles brought the escapees to Huizhou. Dr. Douglas Scriven, who had escaped and who was operating as the medical officer at the Red Cross centre, welcomed them. Like all the escapees, they made their way to Guilin and then to Chongqing.

The last prisoner of war who escaped successfully was Lieutenant R. B. Goodwin, a New Zealand member of the Royal Navy Volunteers Reserve, who got out in 1944. He had arrived in Hong Kong via Singapore in late September 1941. When Governor Sir Mark Young surrendered to the Japanese invaders on Christmas Day 1941, Goodwin was recuperating in a military hospital with a light leg wound. Like most other soldiers, he was sent to the North Point Camp, and then the Argyle Street Camp and subsequently to the Shamshuipo Camp. Of all the camps in the Kowloon Peninsula, the Shamshuipo Camp provided the most tempting opportunity for anyone incarcerated there to escape, as it was on the seafront. Anyone who could manage to ford the shallow patch of water during ebb tide needed to go only a few miles to the foothills of Lion Rock. This was consequently the favourite route taken by previous successful escapees. After being transferred to the camp, Goodwin made up his mind to escape but was surprised to find so few other prisoners who attempted to do the same. Most feared reprisals. Goodwin was the last prisoner of war to make the successful attempt in getting away, a little over a year before VJ Day in 1945.

On a warm and rainy night on 16 July 1944, he escaped from the camp by just going under the barbed wire fence. He swam through the shallow Lai Chi Kok Bay before he touched ground. Following the well-trodden route taken by some of the previously successful escapees, he made his way from the Kowloon foothills to Shatin. Probably because he was alone, he did not come across any of the East River guerrillas until he reached a village close to the border town of Shataukok, ten days after he left the camp. Like many of his predecessors, he was given a square meal and a clean change of clothes, and then he rested before he was taken to the nearby coastal village of Xiaomeisha, about twenty miles east of Shataukok. After a brief stay in the village, he was taken to another village five miles away, where he met the English-speaking cadre, Raymond Wong, or Huang Zuomei. Huang briefed him on the strength of the Hong Kong and Kowloon Independent Brigade and the overall situation. According to Huang, the brigade had over 1,000 soldiers who carried arms, not including others such as those involved in logistics, propaganda and intelligence. Apparently, the brigade was operating in the Japanese-occupied territory of Hong Kong from north and east of Shataukok right down to Kowloon City, within the heart of urban Kowloon. Other units of the column were operating along the Kowloon-Canton Railway. The guerrillas sabotaged the railway repeatedly and interrupted the traffic that the Japanese depended on. According to Huang, it was such a serious problem that the Japanese had mounted at least one major offensive against the saboteurs. Unfortunately for the Japanese, the guerrillas just melted into the local populace and hid in the neighbouring hills. The guerrillas did not suffer one single casualty. In fact, two nights after Goodwin passed through the border village of Shataukok, the guerrillas attacked the Japanese police station, killed the guards and made off with all the weapons and cash.

During his more than two-week stay with the guerrillas, Goodwin was deeply impressed with their kindness and generosity. Despite the fact that most of the people he stayed with were living on a starvation diet, he was given a more than adequate food supply of fresh fruit, meat, eggs and rice. What was most important for his morale was that Huang Zuomei kept him informed of the latest news in the war theatre in Europe and in China. He was told that the Russians were within twenty miles of Warsaw, Hitler was wounded, and Premier Tojo had resigned in Tokyo.

Following the standard practice of the guerrillas in handling the Allied prisoners of war who had escaped and fallen into their hands, Goodwin rested, was well fed and debriefed. The story of his escape and the assistance given by the guerrillas was featured in their newspaper, *Qianjin Bao*. After making sure that it was safe to travel to the nearest town in Free China, Goodwin was escorted by a team of fourteen soldiers and a couple of bearers who actually carried Goodwin on a sedan chair. Eventually, the party arrived in Pingshan, a small town near the major market town of Huizhou. Goodwin was then handed over to the staff of BAAG. It was in Huizhou that BAAG had an advance headquarters, virtually throughout the war.

In the meantime the Communist Party Southern Work Committee convened a meeting in Yantai Mountain, Bao'an County, in January 1942. One of the decisions of the meeting was the reorganization of the Guangdong People's Anti-Japanese Guerrillas into five detachments. The Third and the Fifth Detachments were grouped under the Hong Kong and Kowloon Independent Brigade with Cai Guoliang as the leader, Chen Daming the political commissar and Huang Gaoyang as Chen's assistant.[15]

## Guerrilla Relations with the British (Early Part of the War)

By mid-1942, the guerrillas who obtained most of their arms and ammunition left behind by the British and Indian soldiers who retreated from the New Territories after only a few days of resistance, had established a considerable area of control and operation in Guangdong. According to Colonel Lindsay Ride, the commandant of BAAG, "Eastern Guangdong was divided into belts or spheres of influence: (i) the Japanese occupied belt — Hong Kong and the New Territories, Canton (Guangzhou), and the Kowloon-Canton Railway, (ii) the East River guerrillas belt occupied by the so-called Communists, (iii) the pro-KMT guerrillas belt occupied by the official guerrillas and (iv) the Central Government belt occupied by central government troops". In Ride's opinion, "the Reds formed the buffer between the Japanese and the Central Government forces ... They were the most active, reliable, efficient and anti-Japanese of all the Chinese organizations, and their control extended right through the Japanese-occupied areas, even through the New Territories and into Kowloon".[16]

In Ride's words,

> It should be stressed that almost all this activity was assisted by the Chinese Communist guerrilla forces, who controlled the buffer zone between the enemy-occupied territory and that part of Free China still in the hands of the KMT forces, and who virtually dominated the hills and outlying districts of the New Territories. There was no overland route into or out of Hong Kong other than through Communist territory, and no one either Chinese or foreigner, could pass in or out, without their agreement or assistance...

Strategically and numerically, the East River guerrillas often suffered, as they were quite inadequately armed. On quite a few occasions, they were attacked by both the KMT and Japanese forces concurrently. But they made up this deficiency by their knowledge of the local terrain and the support they received from the local people.

In August 1942, not long after the formal establishment of BAAG in Guilin, Ride sent probably his best trained officer in espionage work, Captain Ronald Holmes, to go from the advance headquarters in Huizhou back to Hong Kong for a reconnaissance tour. Huizhou, situated at the heart of Hakka culture, was a large market town south of the East River some sixty miles north of Hong Kong. It was the headquarters of the KMT's Seventh Military Region. There was a well-equipped American Seventh Day Adventist hospital called Wai Oi Hospital, that had been offering relief and accommodation to refugees who arrived from Hong Kong for quite a while before Ride set up the advance headquarters there.

Holmes, a well-known Sinophile and fluent speaker of Cantonese, was a member of the Special Operations Executive (SOE) at the outbreak of the war. On 4 August, he left Huizhou and eventually went through areas controlled by "official guerrillas" recognized by the KMT government and those controlled by the East River Column. According to Holmes, the "official guerrillas" made a bad impression on him, as "not one of them seemed either satisfied with his lot or very efficient at his work. They were an unruly lot who preyed on commercial and refugee traffic passing through the area assigned to them".[17]

Holmes stayed with the guerrillas of the Hong Kong and Kowloon Independent Brigade from 4 August to 7 September. He had detailed discussions with Cai Guoliang, whom he referred to as captain of "Kong Kau", the British term used for the Independent Brigade. He said he had "a considerable respect for this man's ability" and guessed that "he is the most powerful man working for the Allied cause in the New Territories".

Prior to his arrival, Holmes had been briefed by an escapee about the prisoner of war camps in Kowloon. Therefore, he had an ambitious plan — if he could obtain the East River Column's assistance — of entering the Argyle Street Prisoner of War Camp through the underground storm drain system in Waterloo Road.

Although Holmes's knowledge and understanding of the organization structure and other aspects of the column was imperfect, the observations from a trained staff member of SOE enabled outsiders to have quite a good picture of the situation and the difficulties that the column was facing. To begin with, Holmes quite correctly guessed that the Independent Brigade was an offshoot of the East River Column, which he termed "Tsang Wong", from the names of the two commanders of the two separate teams in Cantonese, Zeng Sheng and Wang Zuorao. Holmes discovered that, by 1942, the Independent Brigade already had 1,000 men under arms and they completely controlled the eastern part of Sai Kung to Kei Ling Ha and that "the Japanese even by day only enter this area in fairly large numbers". Cai also briefed Holmes about the presence of the Independent Brigade's soldiers in Tsuen Wan, Yuen Long and Shataukok. In addition, the Independent Brigade had a special unit which operated in the urban area. Holmes also discovered that the brigade's non-commissioned officers fell into two types: those who were "reticent about their recent history and do not know Hong Kong" and those who know Hong Kong and were "thrown out of work by the Japanese attack on Hong Kong". Those who belonged to the first category were obviously the peasants who joined Wang's group from areas around Huizhou and Dongguan. Students, shop assistants, peasants, junior government servants and unskilled labourers were members of the second group.

Holmes's mission was the first one launched by BAAG after its establishment in Guilin that dealt with the East River Column, and Holmes was specifically tasked to handle a difficult and ambitious mission. He was rather hesitant in dealing with Cai, so he played his cards quite close to his chest. Initially, he did not tell Cai his real intentions. What he told Cai was that he wanted to conduct "reconnaissance from the Kowloon Range". His intention was to reveal his plan by stages. Eventually, when Holmes had time to meet and talk with Cai in greater detail, he revealed his rather ambitious plan of going through the underground storm drain system in urban Kowloon into the Argyle Street Prisoner of War Camp. His aim was to establish contact, and if possible, engineer a mass escape among the prisoners of war. When he revealed the plan in detail and asked Cai to lend his assistance, initially Cai agreed to help but on two conditions: that he was to be the sole judge of wherein lay the best interests of the Allied cause within his area, and Holmes would do nothing without consulting him beforehand. In the end, the plan was not implemented because of the great risks involved and, as we shall see, the withdrawal of the brigade's assistance and co-operation. Despite the failure to carry out the plan to enter the storm drain system, two guerrilla soldiers were provided to protect Holmes. To conduct a reconnaissance, the three once went as far as Beacon Hill, which was about two miles from the target storm drain. It was at this point that the guerrillas withdrew protection of Holmes and co-operation with Holmes's daring plan, because they were aware that the Japanese were suspicious of something unusual taking place. Later on Holmes admitted that his decision to reveal his plan by stages was a mistake. He said that he should have entered the New Territories armed with a letter from the highest available British military authority asking Cai to do all in his power to help him enter the Kowloon drainage system. After all, despite the less than orthodox and irregular status of the brigade, Cai was the commander of 1,000 armed soldiers and had been operating and seen active service in the area since 1938. In his eyes, Holmes was no more than a junior army officer of the British.

Holmes's long discussion with Cai provided a fascinating and rather detailed record of the situation faced by the Independent Brigade. Cai told him that, in 1942, his work was no more than "preparation" and that he hoped to bring his unit to a much higher degree of organization before he started aggressive warfare on a large scale. He said that the potentialities of the brigade could not be realized until the question of his unit's status was settled. In passing, he told Holmes that the difficulties faced by his soldiers were first of all food. According to him, in agriculture, the New Territories was not self-sufficient. To make matters worse, the Japanese had collected forty percent of the first rice crop in the summer of 1942. Therefore, it was anticipated that a famine of up to three months would occur in the spring of 1943. Further, the area east of Sai Kung, where the Independent Brigade was most secure, was the poorest area in the New Territories, the most inaccessible and hilly. Therefore, it could not provide cultivable land to provide even subsistence farming, except for a few crops of sweet potatoes. In addition, it was liable to be blockaded by Japanese and KMT forces. So, even if they had the money, there might come a time when they could not buy food.

The second problem was the military supplies. Most of their supplies were the weapons retrieved from the retreating British soldiers. Some were obtained from the open market after the fall of Hong Kong. Cai admitted that they had about six months' supply of ammunition, but little could be bought now and whatever was expended could not be replaced. Limited arms and ammunition therefore made the expansion of the brigade impossible beyond a certain point. The third difficulty was the unsatisfactory strategic position because of the lack of liaison with the KMT authorities, despite the fact that, at least in name, they were allies.

Holmes questioned Cai at some length about these "difficulties", particularly the brigade's finances. Cai stated that the initial capital was provided partly by subscriptions from Hong Kong merchants and partly by trade protection fees. It was in fact confirmed by some of the people who operated as small-time two-way traders between the Japanese-occupied Hong Kong and Free China that the Independent Brigade did charge "protection fees". Indeed, by 1943, when the East River Column was much better established, a comprehensive set of import and export duties was promulgated and levied on the two-way trade.

According to Holmes, Cai made some rather strange claims, such as that he had no connection with the Communists and that most of the members of his units were British subjects. He asked Holmes to help clarify this "misunderstanding with the British authorities" about his Communist links, despite the fact that Holmes was a relatively junior army officer. Technically these claims were accurate, in that some of his soldiers were born in Hong Kong or in other British colonies like Singapore and Malaya. The Communists provided the leadership in the positions of commanders and political commissars only. In addition, he requested Holmes to transmit to the "proper authorities that his unit be brought into some properly defined relationship with the British Government". Holmes had the impression that the guerrilla soldiers were keen to have a share in the Allies' counter-attack on Hong Kong, when the time came. Holmes thought that these soldiers were "well armed, well led, but inadequately trained. But they could be made into a useful guerrilla force".

Being conversant in Chinese, Holmes read the newspaper published by the column's headquarters, *Qianjin Bao*, and sat in on their daily lecture or indoctrination. To his surprise, he found very little evidence of Communist propaganda. The troops were given a lecture every afternoon, always by a practised speaker, who was obviously the political commissar. But the contents of the talks were mostly lessons on guerrilla tactics, sometimes of an exhortation in general terms. He had never heard anything in the nature of political propaganda. Nor did he find anything of this nature in *Qianjin Bao*. What he found in the newspaper were veiled attacks against the KMT commanders in the East River region. In addition, Holmes found that there was a mobile library where all the textbooks on Communist ideology were available to whoever was interested. Eventually, Holmes and his party were escorted back to Cheung Sheung, which was probably the most secretive and inaccessible part of Sai Kung. Hence it was where most of the senior command and the radio station of the brigade were based.

In addition to Cai and his political commissar, Chen Daming, Holmes met Huang Zuomei for the first time. They had a thorough discussion about the situation of all the prisoner of war camps in Hong Kong. Apparently Huang was in regular contact with Dr. Selwyn-Clarke, so Holmes passed 1,000 vitamin B tablets to Huang, who promised to deliver them to the prisoners of war in the Shamshuipo Camp.

Before Holmes and his party departed the occupied area around Hong Kong and the nearby areas, Holmes lent a few detailed maps of the New Territories used by the British military personnel to Cai, with the proviso that the maps should never be taken out of the New Territories and should be made available to any British officer working in the New Territories "in the future".

Holmes then gave HK$1,000 to Captain Jiang Shui, "in recognition of his services to escaping British personnel" and parted with Cai on the most cordial of terms. Although Ronald Holmes's daring plan of going through the storm drain system was not implemented, the visit was considered a success, as it laid the foundation of co-operation between BAAG and the East River Column.[18] E. Maxwell-Holroyd, a trained medical practitioner and a Petty Officer in the Royal Navy travelled with Holmes.

During their six-week sojourn in the field, Holroyd offered his expertise in treating guerrilla soldiers and civilians in every area they passed through. In the words of Holmes, he "never failed to win the confidence of his patients". It was undoubtedly a beneficial side-effect of their trip that won the respect of the column's soldiers.

Shortly after Holmes's abortive mission to Hong Kong, Douglas Clague, major in charge of BAAG Advance Headquarters in Huizhou, decided to send Sergeant Francis Lee Yiupiu, and another soldier, Vincent Yeung, to carry a personal letter to Cai in November 1942. Other instructions given to Lee were ambitious and specific. The senior command of BAAG realized that the guerrillas had a strong presence and influence in the area south of Huizhou that extended all the way into urban Hong Kong. BAAG, which operated as an MI9 unit tasked to assist prisoners of war and other escapees, had to rely heavily on the co-operation and help of the guerrillas. The instructions given to Lee were:

1.  To find out the guerrillas' exact situation in the New Territories East of Shataukok, as it affected the BAAG;
2.  To reconnoitre the Sai Kung area and see if it was possible to set up a forward BAAG post. The function of the post would be to collect reports from its own agents in Hong Kong and to liaise with the guerrillas.

The letter carried by Lee to be delivered to Cai was interesting and daring. BAAG had been warned and obstructed at every turn by the KMT authorities whenever they tried to deal with the guerrillas, whom the officials described as "Reds" or "Kong Kau". The letter appealed directly to Cai to "establish closer liaison". Furthermore, the letter expressed the hope of sending Captain Ronald Holmes to the guerrillas' area of control in the future. It asked whether Cai would be prepared to supply armed men to accompany Holmes in a military operation.

During their week-long stay in Chek Keng Village in Sai Kung, Lee and Yeung were given accommodation. They were dealt with initially by Fang Fang, who was in charge of United Front duties. While Lee was waiting for Cai, the captain in charge, Yeung was accompanied by a guide provided by the guerrillas and went to urban Kowloon to contact other BAAG agents. In Lee's detailed report submitted to Clague, it was evident that the guerrillas had a strong presence in Sai Kung, to the extent that the Japanese would not dare patrol the area, unless they moved with at least a group of 150 fully armed soldiers, and they could only do so during daytime. The guerrillas could also move with ease and confidence in the rest of the New Territories. During Lee's discussion with Cai and his political commissar, Chen Daming, Cai welcomed the proposed plan for a forward post, as he had previously met Clague. But he was sceptical of the real motive behind BAAG's request. He openly asked Lee whether the post was to be set up for the benefit of the KMT forces and for the purpose of "spying on the guerrillas". Obviously, Cai and his colleagues were aware that BAAG had more formal and regular relations with the KMT military establishment.

Finally, Cai proposed the following plan to be relayed to Clague in Huizhou for his consideration:

> Shayuchong: One agent from BAAG would be stationed in this coastal village for the collection of intelligence from Sai Kung and its despatch to Huizhou. He should be responsible for maintaining liaison with the East River guerrillas. In addition, he should handle the money necessary for the agents coming from BAAG's Advance Headquarters in Huizhou.

> Sai Kung: One agent from BAAG would be attached to the East River guerrillas. But he was tasked to visit the other agents in urban Kowloon. In addition to the intelligence reports coming from BAAG's own source, the man in Sai Kung should collate whatever intelligence reports were passed to him by the East River guerrillas.

> Kowloon: One man from the East River Column would work alongside a BAAG agent to collect intelligence reports from a group of five agents. The BAAG man should pass the intelligence reports to Huizhou through Sai Kung.

The proposals show that virtually everything was to be routed through Sai Kung, where the East River Column had a strong presence. It was obvious that, despite the objection from the KMT authorities, this British underground unit had to rely on the Communist guerrillas for guide duties and protection.

As for BAAG sending Ronald Holmes to the guerrillas' control area in Sai Kung, Cai's response was that "Holmes and any other British would be welcome". But in view of the difficult situation prevailing then, he suggested waiting "until the Advance Intelligence post is properly organized and the communication system running smoothly". Then he would give the signal to start the implementation of the proposed plan. However, Cai said that he was not prepared to receive any Chinese staff from BAAG to do the same work. This was again a consistent policy on the part of the East River Column, as it was keen to be recognized as a fighting unit on the side of the Allied forces. Chinese people were always suspected of working for the KMT government or, even worse, for the Wang Jingwei collaborators. Before Lee's departure, Cai gave him a rather detailed briefing on the overall strength and deployment of the Japanese. Probably one of the most useful pieces of intelligence given to Lee was that the Japanese were seriously planning to build a road from urban Kowloon to the village of Tseng Lan Shue initially and then extend it to Ho Chung, a village some two miles from Sai Kung itself. It was evident that the Japanese felt threatened by the presence of the East River Column guerrillas in Sai Kung. Later on, two guerrilla soldiers who acted as escorts and guides took Lee to a site quite close to Kai Tak Airport. The two had done a thorough reconnaissance the previous evening. Then, on the next day, Huang Guanfang and Liu Jinjin personally escorted the BAAG agent to the foothills of Lion Rock, which was as close and as safe as one could get to, to take some pictures of the extension work on the runway being carried out daily. Both prisoners of war and civilians were forced to work as labourers on the project.

Cai told Lee that the guerrillas had helped three Indian prisoners of war escape from the camp in North Point, Hong Kong Island recently. They were hiding in Shaukiwan. He asked Lee to delay his departure by a day or two, in case the three Indian prisoners of war could join him on their way to Free China. In addition, he requested Lee to ask the British to supply him with a binocular case, medical supplies of unspecified quantities, Mauser ammunition and a complete set of maps of the New Territories. As a goodwill gesture, Cai offered to give to the British the engine of a wrecked Japanese aircraft that the guerrilla soldiers had salvaged with the help of local fishermen, for what it was worth.[19]

According to a report filed by Holmes in late 1943, the East River Column had managed to consolidate their sphere of influence and controlled the entire Sai Kung Peninsula, in addition to the entire Kowloon-Canton Railway area south of the important market of Shi Long. Also, their soldiers moved freely in the desolate mountainous area of Wu Tong Shan in late 1943. They also controlled the important coastal fishing village of Shayuchong, the most important landing point on the northern coast of Bias Bay. The nearest KMT regular troops were in Danshui.[23]

While the Independent Brigade was anxious to eliminate traitors and collaborators with the Japanese, such as the Japanese interpreters, there was evidently a policy of dealing leniently and humanely with lesser traitors. One report filed by a BAAG member who personally witnessed the capture of six bandits and collaborators in Tai Po, in the New Territories in June 1942, described how he was surprised by the lenient treatment. He fully anticipated that they would be summarily executed. Instead, this group of six was given a stern lecture on their "unpatriotic conduct". The six were genuinely reduced to tears. They were given some money for travelling expenses and released. They were told to return to their original home, be it north of Shenzhen in China or Japanese-occupied Hong Kong. It seemed that the policy was that, as long as such bandits or collaborators had not killed any Chinese, they were treated more leniently. The treatment meted out to Japanese prisoners of war was equally humane. Once they were captured, they were repatriated to the safe sanctuary of the column, somewhere in Luofu Mountain in Dongguan. Again, they were lectured on the "evils and crimes of the Japanese Imperial Government" and told that "the Japanese and Chinese peoples should never be at war".[20]

As the tide of war was beginning to turn against the Japanese in the Pacific in 1944, the Allies' bombing raids over Hong Kong became more frequent. The brigade's co-operation with BAAG agents became more effective to the extent that the guerrillas became more daring. There were a number of occasions when the guerrillas fired flares and tracer bullets, which were supplied by BAAG agents, into the night sky, even in urban Kowloon, to direct the Allied planes to drop their bombs on the right targets, such as the Whampoa shipyard in Hung Hom. Despite the extensive search launched by the *Kempeitai*, those who fired the flares could not be located. The Japanese had to mobilize their soldiers on the reserve list to operate an observation post on the roof of the tallest building in urban Kowloon, the Peninsula Hotel. To the Japanese, the problem was so serious and frustrating that a directive came directly from the Japanese governor calling for an immediate settlement. The task fell on the *Kempeitai* warrant officer, Omura Kiyoshi, to devise a plan whereby false air raid alarms were sounded to trick and smoke out the guerrillas (see note 11 in Chapter 4). But the plan had little effect on the guerrillas' operation.

Earlier on during one of their operations in Sai Kung and Shatin, the Japanese found some useful documents that provided important information, showing that the brigade's main body of soldiers and their base were in Sai Kung, so the Japanese conducted repeated raids in the area (see note 12 in Chapter 4). The brigade's headquarters then made a conscious decision to distract the enemy's attention by sabotaging some of the infrastructure in urban Kowloon. On 22 April 1944, Captain Fang Lan led a company of soldiers who carried nearly thirty kilograms of dynamite from their supply depot in Pak Tam Chung in Sai Kung into urban Kowloon. As Japanese sentries guarded most of the road junctions, the guerrillas relied on an eleven-year-old Little Devil, Ya Yingzai, who posed as a cowherd. The dynamite was hidden in the cattle's bamboo harness and successfully transported to Kowloon on time. Then the guerrillas conducted quite a few hours of reconnaissance of the Japanese army's movements before they planted the bomb under the railway bridge at the Argyle Street junction. The noise of the explosion was heard by the prisoners of war inside the Argyle Street Camp. No doubt it was a boost to their morale. The railway track was rendered inoperable and stayed that way for a few weeks. At the time of the sabotage, hundreds of civilians were being forced by the Japanese to work as labourers to level a hill at the foot of Argyle Street to provide the aggregates and soil for the extension of the Kai Tak Airport. For five days after the explosion, the levelling work at the hill had to be suspended, as all traffic was brought to a complete standstill throughout nearly all of urban Kowloon. In desperation and frustration, lorry loads of Japanese soldiers raced around urban Kowloon at high speed. The Japanese vented their anger and frustration by inflicting brutality on the civilians. Many were arrested on the streets and taken to the nearby police station where they were interrogated and severely beaten (see note 13 in Chapter 4). After the explosion, the shock and psychological impact were so great that the Japanese imposed a curfew in Kowloon for the following few weeks.

## The Guerrilla Economy

After the Hong Kong government's surrender on Christmas Day 1941, Zeng Sheng's first priority as commander of the East River Column was to maintain a safe sea route for the supply of materials to his soldiers. So, despite the fact that he and Liu Pei were in two separate political camps, they had a symbiotic relationship. Zeng had to depend on Liu to provide protection for the transport of material and personnel, as well as the escort duties of escaped prisoners of war, almost all of whom went through the Hong Kong border through the waters of Dapeng and Daya Bays. At the same time, Zeng tolerated Liu's pirate activities in collecting protection money from itinerant entrepreneurs. By 1942, despite the fact that Liu had joined the East River Column as a leader of the Marine Detachment and held the rank of lieutenant, he co-operated actively with a notorious bandit, Huang Zhuqing. Liu's excuse was that he was under the column's headquarters' order to promote "united front" activities. Despite his constant harassment of the Japanese marine traffic in the area, he kept on with his pirate activities.

In late 1943, Ronald Holmes led a group of Chinese BAAG agents together with the help of the American OSS staff to set up an observation post near the coast in Dapeng Peninsula. Among the Chinese agents was Francis Lee Yiupiu, who escaped with Colonel Ride in early 1942. Initially, Holmes had obtained permission from the local KMT commander. Everything was in order when the wireless set, arms and equipment were left with Lee in October 1943. However, a party of armed men led by Liu Pei appeared on the evening of 15 October. Lee and his party were captured together with his equipment. BAAG had to negotiate under duress when Liu demanded 5 million yuan of Chinese currency.[21]

Holmes counter-offered 100,000 yuan. After a few weeks of bargaining and pressure from the column's leaders, Zeng Sheng and Cai Guoliang, Holmes's offer was accepted. Despite the fact that the column recognized Liu and his soldiers as a member of the column, he was generally viewed as "more of a bandit than a Communist guerrilla". In late 1943, during one of his skirmishes with other bandit groups in the Dapeng Bay area, Liu was seriously injured. He was hospitalized during much of the period until late 1944.

According to an MI9 report filed in July 1944, another way where the East River guerrillas had the upper hand was that they controlled over ninety percent of the trade between Hong Kong and the Pearl River Delta. Since the Japanese occupation in Hong Kong in December 1941, regular interregional trade as conducted by business firms before the war had virtually ceased. What took its place was a number of itinerant small-time traders known to the local Chinese as *shuike*, who carried strategic goods like pharmaceuticals and rubber footwear to south China from Hong Kong in exchange for foodstuffs such as rice and sweet potatoes. As nearly all of them had to pass through the East River Column's area of control on foot, they needed the guerrillas' protection against the bandits. For that, the East River Column instituted a system of charging of import and export duties. By 1943, the guerrillas were so well organized and confident that they disseminated notices to all itinerant traders their rate of import and export duties to be levied. For example, a notice issued on 1 October 1943 to all the itinerant traders who passed through "The East River Liberated Area" specified that animal produce, food produce (e.g. eggs and dried meat), charcoal and bamboo products exported from the East River area to Hong Kong were taxed between twelve and fifteen percent. Corn, flour, rice and wheat products were taxed at only five percent. Goods such as cosmetics and tobacco imported from the opposite direction were taxed between ten and twelve percent. Rubber tires, machinery, cement, metal goods and second-hand garments were taxed at only five percent. The notice also spelt out that the object of such regulations was to facilitate the two-way trade between Hong Kong and the "Liberated Area". Hence, traders who paid such duties, according to the notice, were exempted from paying any transport costs, as in some instances, transport was provided by the guerrillas. For any consignment of goods valued under HK$2,000, the levying of such duty was waived. For goods valued from HK$2,000 to $10,000, a thirty percent discount on the standard rate of duty was offered. For goods valued between HK$10,000 and HK$20,000, a twenty percent discount was offered, and for goods valued at $100,000 no discount was offered. It was evident that, even in the levying of import-export duties, the guerrillas were aiming to win the hearts and minds of the small-time traders. And it was not an idle boast that they were trying their best to "help and feed the people under the Japanese yoke of oppression".[22]

# 4 Guerrilla Organization and Activity

By mid-1943, the Hong Kong and Kowloon Independent Brigade had nearly 5,000 full-time soldiers who were divided into six *duis*, or detachments, with from 100-odd to over 600 full-time soldiers. They were the Lantau *zhongdui*, Shataukok *zhongdui*, Sai Kung *zhongdui*, Marine *zhongdui*, Urban *zhongdui* and the Yuen Long *zhongdui*. As the name used by the Hong Kong and Kowloon Independent Brigade was *dadui*, i.e. a brigade, all detachments that came under the brigade were called *zhongdui*, medium-sized *dui*, irrespective of their size.

At the formation of the brigade, the strongest and best organized team was the Marine Detachment. Fishermen were the most exploited and discriminated stratum in the community, as most were illiterate, so the guerrillas did a great deal of propaganda work in various fishing villages at a very early stage. Consequently, a significant proportion of the soldiers of the Marine Detachment were ordinary fishermen before the war. Even as early as February 1942, Cai Guoliang, who initially headed the Hong Kong and Kowloon Independent Brigade, decided to have two separate marine detachments, each handling different duties. One team was active in the eastern part that covered the route from Daya Bay to Shanwei and was led by Liu Pei. This team was responsible for providing protection and convoys to escapees from Hong Kong, nearly all of whom were taken to the northern shore of Mirs Bay on ordinary fishing boats. The second team was active in the High Island and Hang Hau areas of Sai Kung. Initially, the team was led by Cai himself, but the command was handed over to Chen Zhixian and Wang Jin. The main duty of this team was to harass and attack the sea traffic of the Japanese military.

In order to win over the fishermen, the guerrillas decided early on as a priority to assist them in eliminating the traditional intermediary system, called the "fish *laans*", who were known to be the most exploitative. As the overwhelming majority of fishermen were illiterate, they had to rely on the fish *laans* for keeping the books and other matters related to their commercial transactions. When the guerrillas stepped in to replace these intermediaries, the fishermen were easily won over. Another important activity undertaken by the Marine Detachment was the barter trade they conducted with the Pearl River Delta towns. By offering their catch, which was a rich source of protein, they obtained rice and other foodstuffs to help the civilian population in the New Territories. Other *minyun* activities were literacy classes organized for fishermen and the children and women.

In July 1943, Cai, Chen and a few senior comrades convened a meeting in Pak Tam Chung, Sai Kung. It was then decided that, in addition to the two main duties of providing convoys to escapees and harassing the Japanese military units on the sea, they would collect taxes. Wang Jin was charged with setting up an import-export duties collection station on Town Island, a strategically located site that controlled the sea route going to the northern shores of Mirs Bay. The duties collection was so successful and efficient that this station on Town Island managed to collect between HK\$40,000 and HK\$100,000 each month throughout the war.

The Marine Detachment, launched with only a handful of weather beaten fishermen and political cadres in early 1942, eventually grew to nearly 300 strong by June 1943, most of whom were full-time combatants. By December 1944 it had grown to nearly 500. The commander then made the decision to reorganize the original two teams. One was called the Great China Detachment and the other the Sea Eagle.

Besides the convoy and import-export duties collection activities, the marine *dui* conducted skirmishes and sabotage against the Japanese. One relatively major engagement was launched in August 1944, when it was discovered that the Japanese had set up a mobile marine squad operating from the border village of Shataukok. The squad was led by a Japanese captain with nearly a whole company of soldiers who sailed out of the village in two motorized boats and four non-motorized fishing boats. The main objective of this mobile team was to protect the Japanese marine traffic in the area and to harass fishermen who were sympathetic to the East River Column. Wang Jin, who was then the captain of Marine Detachment, decided to mount a counter-attack the week before Mid-Autumn Festival.

Under normal circumstances, there is a full moon during the festival. Fortunately for the guerrillas, that night brought unusually heavy rain. Wang Jin sent two fast motorized fishing junks that set up an ambush in a village barely three kilometres from the Japanese base in Shataukok. Under the cover of heavy rain, the two boats moved close to the two Japanese boats. Unable to match the Japanese in guns, the guerrillas made up the difference with courage. They moved close to the Japanese and hurled dozens of rudimentary explosive devices at the Japanese boats. One of the boats caught fire and began to sink rapidly, but the other one that was still seaworthy tried desperately to get away. Using their skill in boat-handling, the guerrillas jumped onto the surviving boat and killed twenty-five Japanese and puppet soldiers and captured the boat with its entire crew of thirteen. The guerrillas also retrieved a haul of six machine guns, twenty rifles and four pistols. In the darkness, the Japanese captain jumped into the sea and got away.

Encouraged by the success of this battle, the guerrillas became bolder and more daring. In late November 1944, they discovered a large Japanese motorized junk berthed in the fishing village of Nan Ao, on the northern coast of Dapeng Bay. Luo Oufeng, the captain in overall command of both marine detachments, together with Wang Jin mobilized non-motorized fishing boats and nearly 100 soldiers. Protected by sea fog and darkness, the three boats moved to within twenty metres of the junk without being discovered. The guerrillas opened fire first and then followed with a rain of explosive devices. As the Japanese were caught by surprise, they could put up only token resistance before surrendering to the guerrillas. As a means to protect themselves, the Japanese jettisoned every weapon into the sea and then claimed that they were only civilians. What was found on the Japanese boat was a consignment of expensive tobacco. The seven Japanese soldiers captured were turned over to the East River Column Headquarters. About twenty puppet soldiers were given a heavy dose of indoctrination before they were set free.

## Lantau Island Detachment

In addition to the various detachments operating on land, an important one which contributed significantly to the overall war effort was the Lantau Island Independent Detachment. Situated at the western end of Hong Kong's territorial waters, Lantau Island is of strategic importance as it controls the marine traffic between Hong Kong and the Pearl River estuary. Su Guang and Chen Man, the two political commissars, led a handful of soldiers who sailed from Tuen Mun to Chimawan in April 1942.

Other soldiers included Qiu Qiu, Zeng Kesong and Chen Hanping. The main objective of setting up this detachment was to sabotage the Japanese marine traffic between the Pearl River Delta and Hong Kong and the South China Sea. Another purpose was to eliminate the bandits on the island. But an even more important purpose was to open up another safe sanctuary for the main body of the Independent Brigade, in the event that they had to retreat from the New Territories. This platoon of soldiers went on their mission, initially armed only with one sub-machine gun, four rifles and one pistol. Each soldier was given only HK$5. One evening in April, they set out from the waterfront in Tsing Lung Tau, a fishing village on the fringe of Tsuen Wan. Chen Liangming, a young political commissar who preceded the rest of the platoon in arriving in Lantau, provided a small wooden boat for the entire platoon to sail to Tai Long Village, the most isolated and deserted part of the island. Shortly after their arrival, they ran into a group of local bandits in Shek Pik Village. It was the annual Tuen Ng, or Dragon Boat Festival, and the bandits tried to rob the local villagers when the latter were celebrating the festival. Caught by surprise, the bandits could not put up much of a fight and had to leave in a hurry. But the news of the platoon's arrival and the gunfight soon spread like wildfire. So, rural leaders from the neighbouring villages of Tong Fook and Shui Hau approached the guerrillas and asked for their protection. There were such a small number of soldiers and they were so under-armed, the guerrillas could only teach the villagers to set up a district watch system organized jointly among several villages.

Chen Liangming was born in Dongguan in May 1920. After having completed his junior years in secondary school in his hometown, he worked for a while as a salesman in the market town of Huizhou. Attracted by the call by Wang Zuorao to resist the Japanese and save the nation in the 1930s, he joined Wang's Dongguan Anti-Japanese Able-bodied Model Guerrillas Team in 1938. Because of his relatively better education, he was promoted to the rank of political commissar in 1942.

Before long, the gang of bandits who were beaten off earlier returned. Led by their ringleader, Lin Rong, they managed to mobilize a group of about 400 who marched from Tung Chung to Tong Fook. The guerrillas were led by Chen Man and a few able-bodied young men but were no match for the bandits. Fighting to the last few bullets, the guerrillas had to beat a hasty retreat to Tai Long Village. Faced with such a serious situation, one of the leaders, Su Guang, returned to the column's headquarters to appeal for help. So another platoon, led by the experienced Liu Chunxiang, was sent in September 1942. Better armed and better commanded, the guerrillas took the initiative by attacking the bandits' hideout in Tung Chung. Caught by surprise, most of the ringleaders were killed. The rest dispersed or escaped by boat.

After the battle, Chen Liangming went to the several villages around Tung Chung to investigate the real reasons why banditry was so rampant on Lantau Island. In typical Chinese Communist guerrilla fashion, a mass meeting was called when the local villagers were urged to "spit bitter water", i.e. to utter their grievances to everyone at the meeting in public. It then became evident that some of the rural leaders were hand in glove with the bandits in their activities. Some of them were actually collaborators with the Japanese. It was Fan Mao and Xie Mao, the headmen of Tung Chung and San Tau Village respectively, who supplied intelligence to the bandits in exchange for a share of the spoils every time the bandits robbed the surrounding villages. So after a public trial, the two were executed in the village square in front of all the victims.

No doubt it was this victory that caused the detachment to be more ambitious. Soon after their victory, they tried to extend their area of operation to Laufaushan Village, near Yuen Long, on Deep Bay. They intended to occupy some of the small islands near Lung Ku Tan and even tried to move as far as Lin Tin Island. Their plan was to establish a secure base on these islands, so they could link up with the Pearl River Guerrillas Column.

The Pearl River Guerrillas Column, different from the East River Column, was formed much later. It was established by some young industrial workers in the suburbs of Guangzhou as late as August 1942. Led by a Communist Party member, Peng Ru, and underpinned by political commissar Lu Weiliang, it was relatively weak in weaponry and human resources. Its strength seldom exceeded 1,000 strong throughout the war.

On a moonless night in May 1943, Liu Chunxiang sailed with a platoon of eleven of his more experienced soldiers to Lung Ku Tan. When they were near the two small islands of Lung Ku and Sha Chau that were normally uninhabited, they were caught by surprise, as they were ambushed by two well-armed Japanese gunboats. All twelve soldiers were killed and their boat was sunk. The only survivor was the woman coxswain, who swam ashore. It was undoubtedly the Independent Brigade's worst defeat during the entire war. Liu Chunxiang was killed in the battle — a great loss to the column of an experienced combatant.

He Guoliang, a captain of the detachment, was then ordered by the column's headquarters to investigate the cause of the defeat and if possible retrieve the soldiers' bodies. Posing as a local fisherman, he was detained by the Japanese *Kempeitai* for a few days but was then released and deported to Bao'an. This market town northwest of Shenzhen was desolate, despite the fact that it was the seat of the magistrate who used to rule over the entire Pearl River Delta, including the New Territories of Hong Kong, before the British occupation in 1898. It was one week before He Guoliang could return to report his findings to his headquarters.

Shortly after this crushing defeat, the detachment again ran into difficulties. Su Guang, who commanded a platoon of soldiers, was trying to hide in an old temple behind the hills in Tung Chung. Su reckoned that it was a safe sanctuary, as the Buddhist monks in the temple were sympathetic to the guerrillas. A few days after the platoon arrived, a company of Japanese marines landed at dawn in Tung Chung. Obviously they were tipped off, as the Japanese trained their machine guns at the temple. Outnumbered and outgunned, Su and his platoon had to beat a hasty retreat along a mountain stream. The Japanese were close on their heels. A young soldier, Chen Xiang, who could not follow the rest, was captured. He was executed on the spot. It was discovered later that one of the Little Devils, Huang Wei, who was responsible for carrying messages earlier, had been caught. He had become a turncoat and led the way for the Japanese marines to the secret hideout.

By early May 1943, the Lantau Island Detachment encountered difficulties of a different kind. As the preceding summer had just experienced an uncommonly long period of drought, most of the villagers had to consume the grain stock that was saved as seeds for the coming planting season. So, the guerrillas had extreme difficulty in obtaining their food supply. Most of the soldiers had to subsist on barely three ounces of rice, supplemented with sweet potatoes, daily. Furthermore, they had to go on long marches most of the time over hilly, rough terrain, to evade the Japanese. But some of the soldiers did not even have shoes. The memory of the tragic loss of their experienced leader Liu Chunxiang and other soldiers affected their morale badly. So in late May, the entire detachment assembled in Tung Chung to conduct a memorial service for Liu and the other soldiers who died in service. The leaders took the opportunity to conduct a brainstorming session with the cadres. One of the results of the session was that the leaders of the detachment were criticized for being overly ambitious. The terminology used in the criticism was that the leaders had committed "the errors of adventurism".

In June and July, the deputy political commissar, Lu Feng, and a senior leader from the column's headquarters, Huang Gaoyang, organized some intensive training sessions. Talks on "qualities" of party members and the theory of "guerrilla tactics" were given. Huang repeatedly told the gathering and particularly the new recruits about the strategic importance of Lantau as it was the key military base in the entire war against the Fascists. Military drills were beefed up to the extent that the soldiers were put on such drills daily. A direct result of the training session and the criticism levelled against the leaders was that the leader, Chen Man, was transferred back to the headquarters for further training.

Huang fully realized that the near starvation diet was one of the key factors that affected their morale. Su Yanliu, the quartermaster, and Qiu Qiu were ordered to return to the headquarters area in the Pearl River Delta to obtain food supplies. Food was then transported by boats to Lantau Island, not only to nourish the soldiers but the starving civilians as well. Intensive training in agriculture techniques was taught to the local peasants to help them improve their yield. The situation continued until almost the end of the war in August 1945, and the detachment managed to harass the Japanese every now and then, particularly in the Mui Wo area.[2]

## Urban Detachment

Another important detachment, the Urban Detachment, was formed in June 1944, initially with only 150 soldiers. It grew steadily and doubled in size after about six months. It was then commanded by a woman, Captain Fang Lan. The special feature of this team was that most of the soldiers were usually unarmed. Their main function was intelligence gathering. Some of the important intelligence on Japanese army deployment, locations of their ordnance depots, details of the movement of the work gangs that were working on the repair and building of the airport and Japanese navy shipping movement, were passed to Allied forces via some BAAG agents with whom they worked closely. This detachment never engaged the Japanese in actual combat. But the intelligence gathering and the propaganda work it handled, particularly towards the end of the war, was a significant contribution to the overall activities of the column.[3]

# Sai Kung Detachment

The column realized right from the outset that Sai Kung was so desolate and inaccessible that the Sai Kung Detachment was formed in early February 1942. Initially it was led by Huang Guanfang, with Liu Jinjin (better known as "Darkie Liu" or Liu Heizai) as the second in command. As Huang was heavily engaged in the important task of collecting import-export duties on cargoes passing through some of the Sai Kung checkpoints, Liu was the de facto commander throughout the war.

As Sai Kung was the most inaccessible, the Hong Kong and Kowloon Independent Brigade used it as the most important stronghold. Not only did the brigade have a strong presence there, but it also kept its radio transmitter in the steepest village in Cheung Sheung throughout the war.

According to Chen Daming, to succeed in winning the support from the local populace, particularly those in the New Territories, the first priority of the brigade was to eliminate the local bandits. After the Hong Kong government's surrender, it took a while before the Japanese could establish themselves in the New Territories. During the hiatus, many bandits who used to operate in the areas around Shenzhen moved south to the New Territories. It was estimated that there were over twenty gangs of bandits in the New Territories, each numbering 200 strong and armed with rifles and sub-machine guns. Some of them not only robbed the local people of their valuables but also demanded regular monetary contributions as a form of protection money. Some villagers were even kidnapped for ransom.[4]

To win the support from the local people, bandits were dealt with seriously. In February 1942, a gang of local bandits raided the village of Ho Chung, about three miles outside Sai Kung. The villagers alerted the guerrillas, who immediately sent a company of soldiers led by Huang Guanfang and Liu Jinjin into the village. Seven of the most notorious bandits were captured. As a warning to the other bandit gangs, a public trial was held at which the local villagers took part, at the pier in Sai Kung Town itself. The choice of the site of the trial was significant, as it was the point where all the Sai Kung fishermen landed with their daily catch. The bandits were then executed on the spot. The local people were so grateful to the guerrillas for their protection that they gave them food from their meagre stock. Another gang of bandits that was eliminated was led by Li Guanjie, who also raided the village in Ho Chung in March 1942. Again, his entire gang was captured by Liu Jinjin and his soldiers. Li and most of his assistants were executed after a public trial held in the village square in Sai Kung.

In addition to the execution of bandits and collaborators, the Sai Kung Detachment displayed courage and a strong message of their control in February 1942. The Japanese established various area bureaux all over Hong Kong early in 1942 as a means of control, the gathering of intelligence and the important function of the distribution of rice rations. To the local people, particularly those who were sympathetic to the guerrillas, the Chinese who worked in the bureau were the "eyes and ears" of the Japanese. As a show of defiance, the guerrillas set fire to the Sai Kung Area Bureau in broad daylight the day the bureau was inaugurated. The building was burned to the ground. By setting it on fire, the guerrillas sent a strong message to the local community about who was in control.

Of all the junior leaders in the column, Liu was probably the most colourful and most fondly remembered by his comrades. Born into an extremely poor peasant family in Da Peng in 1920, he often suffered from severe hunger as a child. The only way that he could manage to obtain an adequate meal was for him and his brother to do odd jobs as lion dance performers or kung fu fighters. His courage and sense of justice were noticed by the Communist party secretary, Lai Zhongyuan, in his hometown when he was a teenager. He was then recruited into the party in early 1939. When the war came to Hong Kong in December 1941, he was sent by Lai to Huizhou and then to Hong Kong as a soldier in the column. His courage and toughness in character were noticed by the leaders of the column, and he was promoted to the post in the Sai Kung Detachment.

In addition to his duties in the Sai Kung Detachment, he held the post of captain of the Pistol Unit of the Independent Brigade. Throughout the war, he made his name by moving around different districts in the New Territories and urban Kowloon, assassinating traitors and collaborators. The most daring case happened when a collaborator, Xiao Jiuru, a notorious interpreter for the Japanese military police, held his birthday party in a restaurant in urban Kowloon in March 1942. Liu and one other guerrilla soldier just walked up to him and shot him in the presence of all his guests. Not only did Liu kill him and leave safely himself, but he also calmly disarmed Xiao's two bodyguards and took away their firearms.

Another famous case that Liu was involved in occurred in December 1942. The Japanese army had set up an important checkpoint at the junction of Clearwater Bay Road and Fei Ngo Shan. This checkpoint was important to the Japanese because it controlled all the human and cargo traffic between Sai Kung and urban Kowloon. One day in December 1942, Liu and two other guerrilla soldiers walked right up to the Japanese captain who was in charge of a platoon of Indian soldiers who collaborated with the Japanese and shot him. Liu was able to carry out this daring operation, as he dressed as a Hakka woman and carried two baskets of vegetables, so the Japanese did not notice his presence. After Liu killed the Japanese captain, the Indian soldiers were in total disarray and did not put up any resistance. They were all captured by Liu on the spot. After a stern lecture from Liu, they were disarmed and released.

The whole Sai Kung district was so desolate and well covered by the guerrillas that they kept their radio transmitter and their mobile headquarters in either Chek Keng or Cheung Sheung for a long period. Both of these locations are neighbouring villages accessible within walking distance. But both could only be reached through steep climbs through village paths. By 1943, the East River Column had an elaborate and well-organized structure. In addition to the full-time soldiers who were organized into six different *duis* with a total strength of about 5,000, the paramilitary side had departments with duties such as logistics, intelligence, *minyun*, hearts and minds work, newspapers, radio station, propaganda, signals, reconnaissance, VIP protection, foreign liaison, medicine and field hospital and training.

According to Chen Daming, to succeed in establishing their base and to win the support of the local populace, particularly those in the New Territories who were known to be defiant and independent, the first priority of the guerrillas was to eliminate the bandits in the New Territories and the areas north of Deep Bay and Bias Bay. After the surrender of the Hong Kong government on Christmas Day 1941, it took a while before the Japanese established themselves in the New Territories. During the hiatus, many local bandits who used to operate in KMT-controlled areas in China moved south from Shenzhen to the New Territories. It was estimated that there were over twenty such groups each numbering 200 strong with rifles and machine guns in the New Territories. Some of them co-operated with the guerrillas out of respect for General Zeng Sheng, while some others not only robbed the villagers of their valuables but also demanded regular contributions from them, as a form of "protection money". Some villagers were even kidnapped for ransom.[5] The stronghold of the Hong Kong and Kowloon Independent Brigade was in Sai Kung itself. So to garner support from the Sai Kung villagers, bandits in Sai Kung were dealt with seriously in the first instance. As early as March 1942, a local bandit named Li Guanjic, who led a group of over sixty bandits, was executed in public in the Sai Kung area.

In Yuen Long and Tai Mo Shan, a notorious group of bandits led by Huang Murong used to collect protection money from the local people. Those bandits were also eliminated on their way to China at the same time. By the end of 1942, the column had a working understanding with every armed group on the seaboard of Mirs Bay. They controlled the waters of Mirs Bay, partly through their Marine Detachment, but also by employing some of the fishermen and pirates, for cash.

Another collaborator executed by the Pistol Unit led by Liu Jinjin was Wang Er, who was the head of the district bureau in Shataukok. Wang was notorious for ill-treating the local people in the district by curtailing the issue of their rice ration. The Pistol Unit discovered that Wang visited the Tai Po market twice a week. In May 1943, Liu and about ten soldiers waited for two days by Shataukok Road to capture Wang. After his capture, Wang was executed in front of his subordinates. Then Liu released Wang's subordinates and told them to report the execution to the Japanese.

Another case of such tactics was the assassination of Su An, a collaborator who rose to the rank of sergeant in the local police force in Yuen Long. Su ran a business in downtown Yuen Long. On the first day of his shop's operation in May 1945, he staged an opera troupe to perform as part of the celebrations. Lee Sheng, a captain of the guerrillas, and about fifteen of his teammates, camouflaged themselves as spectators in the audience. At the right moment, Lee walked up to Su and shot him point-blank. The team disarmed all of Su's bodyguards before they melted into the crowd.[6]

One such famous case happened in October 1943. A collaborator, Rin Kaiju, was taken captive while playing a game of mah-jong in Tai Po Market. Rin was of Taiwan descent, and being able to speak both Chinese and Japanese was an important asset to the *Kempeitai*. After his capture and execution, the Japanese had to mobilize nearly all the soldiers in the Kowloon District *Kempeitai* to conduct a search in Tai Po, Ho Chung and Nam Wai in Sai Kung. As a result, over eighty civilians were arrested and interrogated. The guerrillas' wide support from the local people could be gauged by the remark of Omura Kiyoshi, chief of the Special Branch of the Kowloon District *Kempeitai*, who said, "such suspects were normal and ordinary residents of the New Territories and at the same time were members of the Communist guerrillas. Their numbers were so large that it was very hard to deal with them. Usually we had to mobilize up to four or five companies of soldiers to deal with one such case", i.e. whenever one of the collaborators was captured by the guerrillas.[7]

The Japanese had a reasonably adequate intelligence network in the urban area, but they had to rely on collaborators almost entirely in the New Territories. As a show of force, the guerrillas executed a number of local collaborators who worked for the Japanese as interpreters or informers. Between early 1942 and 1944, three of the most important interpreters in Sai Kung were executed. Because the local villagers spoke a dialect different from Cantonese, the Japanese found it difficult, if not totally impossible, to obtain intelligence and co-operation in the area without such interpreters.[8]

Another collaborator, Chen Datou of Shek Pik Village, Lantau Island, met a similar fate. He pretended to be a sympathizer to the guerrillas throughout the occupation period. When the Japanese launched their sweeping search for the guerrillas in Lantau in late 1943 and early 1944, he became a turncoat and led the Japanese to Shek Pik Village, looking for the guerrillas. A few of the guerrillas were captured and executed. The Marine Detachment of the Independent Brigade sent out a special squad of sharpshooters to catch him. He was taken back to the brigade's base for interrogation, when he put up a stiff struggle. He was executed on the spot.[9]

# Debacle: The "Three-three Incident"

By 1943, the Japanese realized that they had a problem in the New Territories. After their raid in Wu Kau Tang, in Tai Po, they conducted extensive search-and-arrest operations in Sai Kung and Shataukok. In the Shataukok operation, the guerrillas were caught unawares and suffered one of their worst defeats. The members of the column called the defeat the "Three-three Incident", as it happened on 3 March 1943. Despite the fact that Japanese operations had been conducted in the Sha Lo Tung and Wu Kau Tang areas in the second half of 1942, the Political Commissar's headquarters were rather complacent. Instead of adopting the classic guerrilla tactic of being mobile, they stayed put in the village of Nam Chung in the Shataukok area for over a month, starting in January 1943. By then some Chinese collaborators who posed as *shuike* had already discovered the actual location of the Political Commissar's headquarters. On 3 March, nearly all the armed personnel moved west to Wan Shan. Huang Gaoyang, head of the Political Indoctrination Department, Chen Guanshi, cadre in charge of propaganda, a few Little Devils and most of the cadres under training were the only people at the base. At around 3:00 p.m., the Japanese unleashed two companies of soldiers and over fifty heavily armed *Kempeitai* and marched into Nam Chung. On the way, they arrested a local villager and forced him to lead the way. The guerrillas were so complacent that they were actually cooking their lunches while the Little Devils who were supposed to be on sentinel duty were called to do other errands. By following the smoke emanating from the cooking fire, the Japanese caught the guerrillas by complete surprise. The Japanese were discovered when they were a mere fifty metres from the guerrillas' base. Out-gunned and outnumbered, eleven of the most senior cadres were killed and four others were captured. Huang Gaoyang, the most senior and important of all the cadres, was seriously injured. But he escaped by rolling down the hill in Nam Chung. Luo Oufeng, captain of the Marine Detachment, lived in the village nearby and went to rescue Huang, who hid in Shataukok for months afterwards. Besides the casualties and the loss of weapons, the Japanese found documents that exposed the presence of some of the guerrillas who infiltrated into the District Bureaux and the *Kempeitai* barracks. Chen Yangfang and Chen Yongyou, who were identified in the captured documents, were executed. In the subsequent debriefing session, the Political Commissar's office made some tactical changes. The Political Commissar's headquarters was moved to Sai Kung, where better protection was available. The more heavily armed company was moved to Xiaomeisha, the village just north of the border, some twenty miles east of Shenzhen.

## Guerrilla Relations with the British and Americans (Second Part of the War)

One of the column's most significant contributions to the Allies' overall war effort in this area was their co-operation with BAAG intelligence gathering and other activities. But the co-operation and relations between the two were fraught with difficulties and obstacles. In the first place, nearly every operation launched or planned by BAAG had to be approved by Major General G. E. Grimsdale, the British Military Attaché in the embassy in Chongqing. The British were trying to avoid offending the KMT government at all costs, as the two nations were allies fighting on the same side. Also, the British did not enjoy a high standing in the eyes of the KMT government, because of their crushing defeat by the Japanese in Hong Kong and Southeast Asia. In July 1943, Ronald Holmes and his team of subordinates wanted to establish a shipping observation post on Sunset Peak, the highest point on Lantau Island. This post was of considerable strategic importance to the Allied forces, as from it they could watch the Japanese naval movements between Hong Kong and Guangdong through the Pearl River estuary. BAAG called it "the Sunset Plan". Part of the deal was that the British side had to supply a small quantity of arms and ammunition to the guerrillas for the post's protection. BAAG was prepared to send a team of twelve men and a leader to staff the post long term. At the same time, the Japanese realized the importance of the long-term location, so the military governor personally visited Mui Wo, Cheung Chau and Tai O in early June 1943. The Japanese commander in charge of Tsuen Wan interrogated villagers in the Sunset Peak area, Lantau, about the strength and presence of the East River guerrillas.

But as the British government had to work through the KMT garrison commander in Huizhou, one of Holmes's colleagues, Major E. D. G. Hooper, was sent to brief the KMT commander, General Ye, in July 1943. He made it clear to Ye that, in order to set up the observation post on Lantau Island, it would be necessary "to invoke the aid of the guerrillas in Sai Kung". The announcement came "like a red flag to a bull". The KMT general made the following comments to Hooper: "If the British Government are really allies of the Chinese Government, they should have nothing to do with the Communists. And if BAAG continues to have any contact with the Communist guerrillas, it will be the end of BAAG as they will be removed from Huizhou'." So the plan was aborted, despite the fact that the East River Column was willing and able to lend such help to the British. Hooper actually said "we may come to grief over this tricky problem" as BAAG "must have the goodwill and the help of the Communists in Sai Kung" if it wished to carry out its intelligence-gathering operation, and yet "this thing may lead to our undoing with the Chinese authorities". So the plan of setting up the observation post on Lantau Island had to be abandoned due to the KMT's objection. The KMT general said that he was prepared to assist the British in setting up the observation post in Da Peng Peninsula. Eventually, the post was set up on a mountaintop in Da Peng, under a scheme called the "Frigate Bird". In addition, Hooper reported that "Francis Lee Yiupiu is not very happy about the current situation either". Apparently on his way down to Huizhou he was got at by the intelligence officer of the KMT's 187 Division, who warned him that his activities in the Sai Kung area were dangerous and likely to get him into trouble with the Chinese government later on. Hooper therefore proposed to his commanding officer "either to break off all direct contact with the Communists in Sai Kung or to carry on as before, hoping from day to day that things will not come to a head". For obvious reasons, the contact and co-operation with the column was too important for BAAG's operation, so Hooper's second option was adopted.[10]

Another significant area of their work was the rescue of the American 14th Air Force pilots who parachuted into the Kowloon area of Hong Kong. Those rescued included Lieutenant W. Lefkoe, Lieutenant G. Laverell, Sergeant R. D. Shank, Sergeant H. Ellis, Lieutenant J. Egan and Second Lieutenant M. J. Crehan.

The one whose rescue was recorded in the greatest detail was Lieutenant Donald W. Kerr[11] from the 32nd Fighter Squadron, USAAF. On 11 February 1944, he led a squadron of twelve bombers and twenty fighter planes in bombing Kai Tak Airport. They encountered heavy resistance, and in an ensuing dogfight over Kowloon, Kerr's plane was hit. When the gas tank caught fire and he was injured, he parachuted and landed in an area one mile north of the airport. As this happened in broad daylight, the Japanese mobilized several companies of soldiers to capture him when he landed. He tried desperately to find a hiding place in a hilltop not far from Lion Rock. A little boy, Li Shi, one of the Little Devils, appeared and took him to a safe hideout. Subsequently, a female guerrilla, Lin Zhan, who spoke English, appeared at night and brought him food and warm clothing. Kerr was taken by Lin to hide in a cave in the Ma On Shan area for two weeks, during which Lin and Li brought him food and new bandages for his wounds. After two weeks, the guerrillas' captain, Liu Jinjin, appeared at night to move Kerr to a safer place. Finally, Kerr recovered from his injury and was escorted to Huizhou and then Free China, some six weeks after he was shot down. In Huizhou, he was handed over to BAAG, where he met with Major Ronald Holmes and told him the full story. Before he was escorted to KMT-held territory, he was taken to see Cai Guoliang and then General Zeng Sheng himself, who feted him. Cai went through great lengths to "convince him that the column was efficient, and they were on the right side in their dispute with the KMT, and that the column was most anxious to help the Allied war effort by supplying intelligence". Kerr was deeply impressed by the discipline of the guerrillas and the harsh and difficult conditions under which they operated. He promised to try to obtain for them badly needed medical supplies and other equipment when he returned to his air force base and to tell their story to his colleagues and the American people. Before he departed, Cai gave him a letter to General Claire Chennault of the 14th Air Force, suggesting that the force might consider posting a liaison officer with the column. Almost a year afterwards, Kerr sent a letter to the guerrillas, in which he said "China's heroic resistance is recognized by the whole world. We Americans take pride in fighting side by side with you. May we stand with you forever, in peace or in war". After he returned to his base, the 14th Air Force used his reports as teaching materials to train other pilots to seek help from the guerrillas if their planes crashed in enemy territory. [12]

The request for a liaison officer with the column was complied with by the US military authorities. In October 1944, an army officer from the Technical Services Department of the US Army, Merrill S. Ady, was posted to the column's headquarters for the purpose. Ady stayed on until 17 August 1945, when he was replaced by Lieutenant B. G. Davis, who stayed on till late September 1945.[13]

On 16 January 1945, the 14th Air Force launched one of its most daring and intensive bombing raids on Hong Kong. At 8:00 a.m., waves of a group of sixty bombers flew over repeatedly and bombed the urban area of Hong Kong Island and Kowloon. Out of the squadron of sixty planes, three were shot down by the Japanese. One of the pilots who was shot down was Lieutenant J. Egan, who had led a squadron of bombers to attack some of the Japanese military installations in Kowloon. His own plane was shot down and he parachuted into the waters of Mirs Bay. When this was discovered by the Marine Detachment of the battalion, Luo Oufeng, captain of the detachment, quickly mobilized some of the fishermen who were in the area to rescue him. It was a race between the Marine Detachment and some of the Japanese boats. It was fortunate that the two fishermen, Zhou Er and his son, knew the area well. So Egan was rescued onto their junk and hid on one of the small islands. Luo and his assistant, Huang Kang, then interviewed Egan with the help of their interpreter, Luo Rucheng. They hid on the small island for three days before they sailed to one of the fishing villages, Nam Ao. Egan was then escorted to the column's headquarters in Huizhou, by Luo Oufeng and Lee Guanlai, before he was sent to Free China.[14]

By 1944, as the guerrillas became more daring and active in their operations, the Japanese, in their desperation, arrested eighty civilians in Sai Kung for interrogation and torture. While they were being detained in the *Kempeitai* headquarters in Yaumatei in urban Kowloon, the guerrillas mounted an attack on the Japanese guard post at the Shatin railway tunnel in the early morning of 28 September. Not only were some Japanese soldiers killed and injured, but arms and ammunition were looted and carried away. In anticipation that the guerrillas would launch another attack on this strategically important site on 10 October, Chinese National Day, the Japanese had to deploy additional soldiers to staff the guard post.

However, the guerrillas launched a surprise attack on 17 October instead. On that day, they simultaneously bombed the railway siding and the dockyard in Hung Hom. The result was a Japanese gendarme and two Indian police were killed by the building materials brought down by the explosion. On 15 November, the guerrillas launched a daring attack on the Japanese barracks in Sheung Shui in broad daylight. The guerrillas sent one company of soldiers, who attacked the Japanese while they were changing shifts in the morning. One auxiliary gendarme and one auxiliary policeman were killed and one gendarme injured. Again, arms and ammunitions were looted. The Japanese commanding officer, Colonel Noma Kennosuke, was so furious that he considered it "a disgrace" that Japanese arms could be looted by "a band of guerrillas". He ordered Major Hirao Yoshio to recover the rifles "lost" "at all costs". The pressure on the subordinates was so great that Warrant Officer Omura Kiyoshi had to buy two rifles in the black market in Shenzhen to pacify the commanding officer.[15] In another daring incident the guerrillas moved right into the Mongkok Fire Station in urban Kowloon in April 1944 and captured the Chinese interpreter. Then, in early January 1945, the interpreter based in the army barracks at the border in Shataukok was captured. Both interpreters were subsequently executed.

The name "East River Column" was formally adopted at an inauguration ceremony held at a Taoist temple on Luofu Mountain, Huizhou, on 2 December 1943 as a branch of the Guangdong People's Anti-Japanese Guerrillas. On that occasion, a six-page bilingual manifesto was issued whereby the column openly declared that it accepted the Chinese Communist Party's leadership. The manifesto not only detailed the column's "victories" in its sabotage work in Hong Kong and South China, but also gave details of the Allies' victories in the other war theatres in the Pacific and Europe. On 22 February 1944, the female warriors of the column daringly displayed the same six-page manifesto in English and Chinese in some of the buildings in urban Hong Kong:

> The world war against the fascists has entered the final stage of victory, which is also the stage for the final struggle. This has been effected by the continuous victories of the Soviet Red Army, which is defeating Hitler's bandit troops on a wide front. It has crossed the Dnieper, pushing along towards the frontier. At the same time, the Anglo-American armies in Italy have scored one victory after another, and the fiercest bombing raids are being directed against Germany. Hitler's regime is simply crumbling, and the fate of the fascist nations is being thrown into the wide sea. Mussolini is overthrown, and Italy has gone one step further from her surrender to the active participation in the war on the side of the Allies. The guerrilla battles in southern France and Yugoslavia are developing. The unity of the Allies is manifested particularly in the Moscow Conference; it also declared a definite and fixed strategy. The first task is to overthrow Hitler, and use all possible means to shorten the war. Though the fascist elements in the

Allied nations have done their utmost to disrupt their unity, they have failed to succeed. The neutral nations Turkey, Sweden and Portugal all have taken steps unfavourable to Germany.

On the eve of this great international change, the fascist Japanese are feeling the sorrow of death already. In the Pacific, they are losing one battle after another. They are suffering heavy losses in officers and men. The counter-attacks of the Americans and Australians are just beginning, and the terror of defeatism is spreading throughout the entire Japanese army and nation. Tojo is planning to mobilize all resources for a decisive battle with Britain and America. But facts have shown that it will be a vain effort.

Our Guangdong People's Anti-Japanese Guerrilla Corps is the army of the young men in the East River Basin. Among us are members of patriotic parties and people belonging to no party; there are especially many patriotic returned overseas Chinese. We are all united irrespective of party, rank, thoughts and faith, and we have the common objective of fighting the Japanese and reconstructing our nation. Since the formation of our Corps, we have been enthusiastically assisted by the enlightened patriots. For five years, we have been dealing blows to the enemy and puppets in the region of Wai Tung Po (Huizhou, Dongguan and Bao'an). We have been reoccupying lost territories and have destroyed many puppet organizations. We restored the original conditions of the administration in the rural areas and have maintained order and peace in many localities. Education and production have been promoted by us, and we have done much relief work too. So far, we have been praised several times by the authorities of the War Zone. As soon as the Pacific War flared up, we marched towards Kowloon and Hong Kong immediately to disturb the enemy and to save the families of important Chinese officials from the clutches of the enemy. We have also saved people of the Allied Nations from the concentration camps of the enemy. Many cultural workers and well-known people have been saved by us too.

We are not alone; we are related to the Communist Eighth Route Army, the New Fourth Army, the patriotic parties and all the people of the nation in their bloody fight against the enemy. We are on the same front with the international anti-fascist fighters…In the past, our Guangdong People's Anti-Japanese Corps had only two battalions, and our activities were limited to a narrow area. However, after several years' fighting against the enemy and for our own defence, we have been hardened and have expanded our units. We are now engaging the enemy on the Huizhou, Dongguan and Bao'an Front, and penetrate even to Kowloon, and carry on our activities in the heart of enemy territory. Our men and guns have not been reduced in number, but have increased more than ten times. In order to cope with the circumstances, we have overcome difficulties, recovered our lost territories and will protect the life and properties of the people until we gain the final victory…

The manifesto, dated 2 December 1943, carried the names of Zeng Sheng, as commander of the East River Column of the Guangdong People's Anti-Japanese Guerrillas, Wang Zuorao, deputy commander, Lin Ping, political commissar and Yang Kanghua, director of the Political Department.[16]

On 13 April 1945, when the Japanese military government imposed a complete blackout for fear of the Allies' bombing, the guerrillas of the Urban Detachment moved into the heavily populated areas in Shaukiwan and the Taikoo Dockyard on Hong Kong Island and Austin Road in urban Kowloon. They then distributed some 3,000 copies of a shortened version of the manifesto in shops and tenement buildings. Two days later, ten copies of an open letter titled "An Open Letter to Hong Kong/Kowloon Compatriots" were displayed at probably the busiest part of Hong Kong Island, the entrance to the Central Market, Queen's Road, Central. On 21 April, propaganda pamphlets were distributed in the Yaumatei area in urban Kowloon. Subsequently, a propaganda newspaper called *The Underground Fire* was launched in urban Kowloon. The newspaper was again repeatedly displayed in some prominent buildings in the busiest part of Hong Kong Island and in Kowloon. Not only did the newspaper give details of the guerrillas' activities, it also openly mobilized the workers in Kowloon and Whampoa docks to sabotage the shipping repair work in the two docks.

By mid-1943, when the tide of war was turning against the Japanese in the Pacific, the Hong Kong and Kowloon Independent Brigade was getting so confident and daring that they made use of the system of "District Bureaux" created by the Japanese to form their own underground government. Those who were selected to serve as village leaders or village representatives, whose main duties were the distribution of rice rations and other rations for the Japanese, were mobilized to form into "village offices". They designated various departments of administration, finance, village hygiene and militia to work closely with the guerrillas. The first village in the New Territories to form an underground government was Nam Chung, Luk Keng, near Shataukok. This village, over 200 households with a total population of about 1,500, formed such an underground government in June 1943.

This new underground government assisted the guerrillas in obtaining food supplies and operated an intelligence network for the guerrilla soldiers. But it attracted the *Kempeitai*'s attention. The two village representatives, Chen Binliang and Zhang Cai, were closely monitored and watched.

By late 1944, it was obvious that the Japanese were suffering heavy losses in various parts of the Pacific. Consequently, some of their experienced soldiers stationed in the New Territories were deployed to various regions outside Hong Kong. The guerrillas seized the opportunity to form an underground government.

As a first step, the guerrillas selected Sai Kung, Sai Kung Market and Hang Hau to launch their new venture. The three were formed into a "Joint Defence

Council". Representatives who were invited to serve in the council were selected according to the United Front Policy adopted in other parts of China occupied by the Communist Party. One third of the representatives came from the communists, one third from sympathizers and the last third from "neutral" elements.

One of the policies adopted by this underground government was a moderate form of land reform that followed closely what was adopted in interior China, under the Communist Party's occupation. They wanted to win the hearts and minds of the poor peasants while not hurting the landlords. The measure adopted was called the "Two-five Rent Reduction". The then-prevailing land rental levied by landlords was that the crops harvested annually were split seventy percent to thirty percent between the landlords and the tillers, with a hidden clause that the tiller must make up a certain amount to the landlord, should there be a crop failure or during a bad harvest. But the guerrillas considered this practice harsh and excessive. What was proposed was a share cropping basis of fifty-fifty between the two parties. The reduction in rental provided an incentive for the tenant peasants to work harder, thus increasing productivity. The effect of this measure was that in most cases, the landlord could expect to reap the same level of rental as before, only one year after the introduction of this new measure. Generally, most landlords welcomed this policy. After the introduction of this policy in Sai Kung, it was introduced to Yuen Long.

In the winter of 1944, the guerrillas invited Yuen Long and Tsuen Wan rural leaders to a discussion. The result was that a "People's Consultation Association" was formed in Yuen Long in February 1945, followed by the introduction of the Two-five Rent Reduction practice.

In spring 1945, an identical "association" was formed in Tung Chung, Lantau Island. Almost immediately after the formation of the association, the "Two-five Rent Reduction" was adopted.[17]

General Zeng Sheng, Commander of the East River Column with his wife, Ruan Qunying, in Pingshan, Bao'an, 1939.

Wong Mo Ying Catholic Chapel, North Sai Kung, New Territories, Hong Kong. The Hong Kong and Kowloon Independent Brigade of the East River Column was founded here on 3 February 1942.

A banner given to Lt. Donald W. Kerr by the East River guerrillas in Huiyang in 1944. It was presented to the veterans of the column when David Kerr visited them in Hong Kong on 11 August 2008.

A banner presented by General Sir Neil Ritchie to the people of Sai Kung, New Territories, Hong Kong that extol their loyalty and help given to the Allied soldiers during the war.

Soldiers of the Hong Kong and Kowloon Independent Brigade on the move in North Sai Kung, New Territories, Hong Kong in 1943.

Young soldiers of the East River Column.

Jiang Shui, leader of the Shataukok Detachment, 1943.

One of the three landing crafts of the US 7th Fleet used for the repatriation of some of the East River Column soldiers to Yantai, Shandong on 30 June 1946.

Lieutenant Donald W. Kerr of the US 14th Air Force, whose plane was shot down by the Japanese during a bombing raid over Kai Tak airfield on 11 February 1944. Kerr was rescued by the East River Column soldiers. The picture was taken when he posed with his wife in 1946.

General Zeng Sheng (left), General Wang Zuorao (middle) and Yang Kanghua, Political Commissar. The picture was taken in Bao'an, near the embarkation point of Shayuchong, on 27 June 1946. All three wore KMT army uniforms and designations to show that they were soldiers of the Allied forces.

At the ceremony where the banner was presented, held outside the Sai Kung Chamber of Commerce, on 12 April 1947. Front row: second from left is James Wakefield, District Officer, South, New Territories Administration. Third from left is John Barrow, District Commissioner, New Territories Administration of Hong Kong Government. Next to John Barrow is Li Shiu Yam, Chairman of the Chamber. He met K. M. A. Barnett in 1945 during the Military Administration. Next to him in the middle is General Sir Neil Ritchie.

Luo Oufeng, leader of the Marine Detachment of the East River Column.

A fishing boat used by the Marine Detachment of the column.

臨時復員証

中共廣東武裝人員

根據三人會議代表團之調處，本隊武裝人員除二千四百名由美艦運至山東集中外，餘概進行復員，並經委員長廣州行營代表王衡少將予以決不歧視之保証。茲有

劉輝同志是本部人員，經核准復員回廣東省予慰解，望沿途軍警給予保護，該員藉貫地方政府給予安居就業。

特此證明

右發

中共廣東武裝人員 劉 輝存軋

中共武裝人員代表 曾 生

中共武裝人員代表 林 平

附註：此臨時復員証一俟全國復員問題解決後，當另換發統一的新証。

000052

A Demobilization Certificate issued to an East River Column soldier who did not join the repatriation party to Yantai, Shandong on 30 June 1946.

Some of the political and literary figures posed for a picture on Repulse Bay Beach, Hong Kong, shortly before the war broke out. The old lady in the middle is He Xiangning, mother of Liao Chengzhi.

Huang Zuomei, head of the International Liaison Department of the column, posed outside the White Hall, London, in 1947.

General Zeng Sheng (middle) visited Sai Kung, New Territories, Hong Kong in August 1984. The author is on the left. Chung Pun, chairman of the Sai Kung Rural Committee, is on the right.

Luo Oufeng, leader of the Marine Detachment of the column, revisited the Wong Mo Ying Catholic Chapel, North Sai Kung, New Territories, Hong Kong with some veterans, in August 1997.

C. H. Tung, Chief Executive of the Hong Kong SAR Government, placed a list of the names of martyrs of the column in the Memorial Hall of Hong Kong City Hall on 28 October 1998. It was the ninth day of the ninth lunar month, a traditional day of mourning for the dead. Luo Oufeng stands next to Tung.

*Nanfang Ribao* article dated 10 August 2008 that features Donald W. Kerr's son, David Kerr who came to China to thank the soldiers who rescued his father.

David Kerr (middle), on his visit to Hong Kong on 11 August 2008 with Zeng Fa (left), second in command of the Shataukok Detachment of the column.

# 5 The Hour of Victory

## The Collapse of Japan: The East River Column Fills the Vacuum

On 16 July 1945, US President Harry Truman, British Prime Minister Winston Churchill and Soviet leader Joseph Stalin held a conference in Potsdam, Germany. The aim of the conference was to map out their various areas of interest in Europe and Asia. The Americans by then had successfully detonated the first nuclear device in New Mexico. They were still anxious, and urged the Russians to enter the war with Japan in Asia as a means of saving lives. On 26 July 1945, the US, Britain and China issued the Potsdam Declaration that demanded the Japanese government "unconditionally surrender or face prompt and utter destruction".

Although Japan was in a hopeless position concerning the war, the Japanese government was playing for time. It made a desperate effort to persuade the Soviet Union to continue being neutral, by sending Ambassador Sato to meet with the Russian foreign minister to pursue the idea. Sato got the cold shoulder from the Russians. In fact, the Russian government had declared the treaty of non-aggression between the countries void as far back as 5 April 1945.

Finally, the Americans dropped the first atomic bomb in Hiroshima, on 6 August. Two days later, the Russians entered the war and thoroughly defeated the crack Japanese army in Manchuria. On 9 August, the second atomic bomb fell on Nagasaki. On 15 August, the Japanese emperor issued an imperial rescript to end the war. In Hong Kong, the Japanese emperor's rescript was read out — first in Japanese and then in Chinese — on a public announcement system in the busiest part of the city, outside the Gloucester Hotel. As it was obvious that the Japanese government's surrender was imminent, Chiang Kai-shek, as the commander-in-chief of the China war theatre, issued the following three directives to all his armed forces in China:

1. Armed forces within the "liberated areas", i.e. those occupied by the Communist armed forces, to stay, *in situ*, pending further directives to be issued by him.

Communist forces must not deal with the Japanese and the quisling forces directly;

2.  KMT armed forces should actively proceed to attack Communist-controlled areas in accordance with whatever original plans; and

3.  Quisling soldiers were directed to maintain law and order in their respective areas of control. They were directed not to surrender to the Communist armed forces.

However, after the Japanese government formally announced their surrender, General Zhu De, as the commander general of all the Communist armed forces in China, rebutted Chiang's directives by sending him a telegram with five demands on 16 August. They were:

1.  In accepting the surrender from the Japanese and quisling troops, I request that you consult me so that a consensus on this issue can be reached;

2.  Within liberated areas and those areas occupied by the Japanese nearby, all Anti-Japanese People's armed forces, i.e. Communist armed forces, have the right to deal with the Japanese to accept their surrender, confiscation of their weapons and equipment, in accordance with the terms of the Potsdam Declaration;

3.  All the People's Anti-Japanese armed forces in liberated areas and those in Japanese-occupied areas have the right to participate in all the surrender ceremonies organized by the Allied forces and have the right to handle all the matters after the ceremony;

4.  You should stop the civil war forthwith; and

5.  You should abolish the one-party dictatorship in the country at present and convene an all-party conference to set up a coalition government.

Concurrently, General Zhu De issued a general order to the Communist forces and units of the East River Column, particularly the soldiers of the Hong Kong and Kowloon Independent Brigade, to advance on the nearest Japanese units and demand the Japanese soldiers surrender. Failing this, East River guerrillas were directed to eliminate the enemy soldiers by force. The main body of the Hong Kong and Kowloon Independent Brigade was directed to move from Danshui, in the Mirs/Bias Bay hinterland, to Yuen Long, New Territories.

Zhu De was one of the most colourful persons who had been involved in the rise of the CCP at an early stage. Born in Sichuan in 1886, he received military training at the Yunnan Military Academy. He joined Sun Yat-sen's Tong Meng Hui and later the KMT. Following detoxification from his opium addiction in Shanghai, he went to Europe and studied in Göttingen, Germany. He met Zhou Enlai in Berlin and joined the CCP in Europe. He was one of the few who planned and staged the Nanchang Uprising on 1 August 1927. Subsequently, he joined Mao in Jinggangshan, the mountainous retreat in Jiangxi Province, and took part in the Long March.

On receiving Zhu's order, General Zeng Sheng personally led a group of 1,300 soldiers, marching from their headquarters in Luofu Mountain, about 50 kilometres north of Shenzhen, into the sparsely populated areas in north Guangdong to set up bases, push out the weaker units of KMT soldiers and, more importantly, stage summary executions of quisling soldiers and collaborators of the Wang Jingwei regime. In keeping with the classic guerrilla war tactic, they tried to occupy as much of the countryside as possible so they could operate at ease among peasants. Another team, led by the column's political commissar, Lin Ping, moved south along the Kowloon-Canton Railway and captured important towns like Dongguan, Zengcheng, Boluo and Huizhou. On 11 August, Cai Guoliang of the Hong Kong and Kowloon Independent Brigade led a company of soldiers into various important market towns in the New Territories, Hong Kong.[1] They went first to Yingde, in north Guangdong and quick-marched and crossed the border into the New Territories.

Fang Lan, the leader of the Urban Detachment, led a group of about ten soldiers into the Japanese military barracks in Chatham Road and the shipyard in Hung Hom at 6:00 a.m. on 16 August. The Japanese captain had heard of the Japanese emperor's proclamation of surrender the previous day, so he led his company of soldiers in an escape from the barracks the previous night. Only a few of the quisling soldiers and their weapons were left. Fang Lan and her team confiscated fifty rifles, motor car spare parts and telecommunications equipment.

In Yuen Long, a team under the command of Yang Jiang moved into the Hung Shui Kiu area and demanded the Japanese capitulate. As a result, at least one officer, three Japanese army soldiers and 100 puppet soldiers surrendered. They then handed over 200 weapons.

In Shataukok, the Japanese initially resisted but eventually were disarmed. They handed over not only weapons but also other materials such as food items, textile goods and pharmaceuticals. There was such an abundance of these goods that it took the guerrillas a whole week to transport them to their headquarters north of the Shenzhen River. In fact, they had to distribute some of the surplus items to the local populace. But by then, many Japanese soldiers realized that they were facing a lost cause: some soldiers who were unfortunate enough to be found by the local people outside the barracks were actually beaten to death. It was a situation of every person for him- or herself, and many soldiers made their way to the urban areas in isolated groups of twos and threes.

In Fanling, a team of about fifty soldiers led by Zeng Fa, second-in-command of the guerrilla unit in Shataukok, advanced on the Japanese barracks in Lung Yeuk Tau and demanded the captain surrender. The Japanese stalled in their reply and escaped to the urban area at nightfall. Eventually, Zeng Fa and his soldiers helped themselves to the goods inside the barracks — so much food and pharmaceuticals that it took Zeng more than ten days to transport these goods across the border to Huizhou. Along the way, Zeng distributed quite a lot to the local populace.[2]

In Sai Kung, the Japanese refused to recognize the legitimacy of the guerrillas as Allied soldiers. A team commanded by Zhang Xing exchanged fire with the Japanese, resulting in casualties on both sides. Eventually, the Japanese escaped to urban Kowloon at night. The guerrillas occupied the Japanese barracks and then staged a celebration with the local people.

On 20 August, a Japanese military police captain, together with six of his men in Fanling, discovered that they had become isolated, as they could not establish contact with their commanding officer in the district. Threatened by the nearby guerrillas, the captain took his men and weapons and walked all the way to Shataukok to surrender to the guerrillas there.

However, in the Island District, the situation was quite different. The Japanese presence had been relatively weak there, and the local garrisons were out of touch with developments elsewhere. During the entire occupation period, they seldom visited places such as Cheung Chau and Lantau Island. However, on 21 February 1945, a group of about eighty Japanese soldiers were stationed in Mui Wo, Lantau Island. They forced the local people to dig caves and tunnels in the surrounding hills. These were foxholes and were meant to be a defence measure against the invasion that the Japanese fully expected the Allied forces to launch.

In the beginning, the local villagers who were forced to work on these projects were each given 1.5 catties of rice each day, but this amount was reduced to only 0.75 of a catty in May. The treatment meted out to the villagers was so cruel that they were left to spend nights in the hills without any facility for board and lodging. Large numbers were so ill and weak due to malnutrition and ill treatment from the hands of the Japanese that the Japanese had to bring in a fresh supply of labourers from urban Kowloon.

Towards the end of May 1945, the first group of Japanese soldiers was replaced by another company of about eighty men commanded by Second Lieutenant Saito, assisted by Sub-Lieutenant Matsumoto. In late May 1945, Saito and his company were ambushed by the guerrillas in the hills behind Mui Wo when the Japanese soldiers were travelling from Tung Chung to their barracks in Mui Wo, after Saito and his company went on a routine patrol of the area. During a brief conflict, Saito and four of his soldiers were killed. The guerrillas withdrew but suffered no casualties. The digging of caves and tunnels continued right up to the afternoon of 18 August, despite the Japanese surrender to the Allied forces three days previously.

On 18 August, a guerrilla unit commanded by Chen Liangming, with Political Commissar Wang Ming and Chen Man, led a group of about fifty soldiers and occupied a high vantage point in the hills in Mui Wo overlooking the Japanese barracks. They demanded the Japanese surrender. Lieutenant Kishi Yasuo, commander of the company, refused. Another company of guerrilla soldiers, led by Qiu Qiu, occupied the hills behind the barracks and launched a full-scale attack on the following day. The end result was that over twenty Japanese and quisling soldiers were killed in action. The guerrillas also suffered a few casualties and deaths, including that of the company leader, Chen Yao. The battle took about an hour or so before the guerrillas withdrew into the hills behind Mui Wo. When the battle was over, the Japanese sent detachments into the villages of Pak Ngan Heung, Chung Hau, Tai Tei Tong and Luk Tei Tong behind the main rural township of Mui Wo.

## Massacre after VJ Day

There was an indication that, despite the Japanese government's surrender, the Japanese soldiers were still in control of much of the territories and could do whatever they liked. They arrested every man, woman and child they could find — about 300 in and around the Mui Wo area. During the process, shots were fired indiscriminately: a girl was wounded in the head, a woman who was gathering grass for fuel on the hillside was killed, and a woman domestic worker, employed by Yeung Siusang, was killed. Yeung's granddaughter, a child of about five years of age, was also shot in the head and the chest when she happened to be walking by. Yeung was one of the better educated and more affluent villagers, as he had primary education and had worked as a seaman before the war. With his savings, he had managed to buy some land and operate a grocery store in Mui Wo. He was looked upon as a village leader among the people, who were mostly poor peasants and fishermen.

The wife of another villager, Fan Fook, was dragged out of bed by the Japanese soldiers and apparently died of a heart attack outside her own house. Lieutenant Kishi accused the people of the four villages of being "responsible for the guerrillas' attack. Therefore they had to pay a price". Two village elders, Lam Sau and Tsang Fuk, were arrested and severely beaten. Kishi then beheaded them on the beach without trial or questioning. By nightfall, the 300 innocent civilians were grouped together and guarded by Japanese soldiers with machine guns. In the evening, Kishi commenced to beat and torture them using a variety of means, including water torture.

On 21 August, Sergeant Uchida arrested two innocent villagers, So Powa and Leung Tungcheong, and executed them after they had been beaten severely. In the afternoon of 22 August, another detachment of Japanese soldiers was sent to the village of Ngau Ku Long, where they captured some villagers, including Lam Tsan, who was shot on the spot. They then stripped everything of value in the village before setting fire to two of the houses. Another villager, Lam Kuen, who was brought back to the beach in Silver Mine Bay, was beheaded. The Japanese raided Ngau Ku Long Village again on 23 August, and burned all the houses in the village. A villager, Lam Poontai, was wounded but still mobile, and asked two fishermen in Mui Wo to take him to Kowloon for treatment. Unfortunately, the party of three were intercepted by the Japanese before they could board the fishing boat, taken away and apparently executed.

Early next morning a sampan was commandeered, and two fishermen and a local villager were forced to carry several Japanese soldiers, one of whom had been wounded, to their regimental headquarters in Tsuen Wan. The sampan never returned, and the three civilians were thought by the village elders to have been killed and the sampan burned.

Subsequent to the massacre, the Japanese commander visited the families of the 300 detained villagers and demanded the family of each provide three catties of chicken and pork before the prisoners could be set free. On the evening of 25 August, he demanded additional contributions of peanuts, taro, eggs and other foodstuffs, before all the prisoners were set free on 26 August. Such demands were very harsh at a time when the entire territory was still in a state of confusion and chaos, and the people were facing such shortages of their own. After the people supplied the food items, the Japanese then left Mui Wo by motorized junk.[3]

The end result was that several of the villages were burned to the ground and some of the civilians just disappeared. It was not possible to ascertain, with any degree of accuracy, the actual number of people killed by the Japanese. It was only after British Military Intelligence staff and K. M. A. Barnett visited Mui Wo in late September 1945 that village elders, Lam Chun, Chau Taipo, Tsang Lin, Wan Cheung and Tsang Laifook, came forward and filed a detailed report to Brigadier David MacDougall, the chief civil affairs officer, on 27 September. This group of village leaders were then taken to the Japanese prisoner of war camp in Shamshuipo and identified the culprits on 4 December.[4]

At a war crimes trial held in March 1946, Lieutenant Kishi's defence was that he had been ordered by his commanding officer to "maintain a state of defence and security until the landing of Allied forces". Since they had been attacked by the guerrillas, they only counter-attacked in self defence. Kishi also revealed that, in addition to the various Japanese soldiers killed in the battle, two privates, Nodamura and Kinoshita, were missing and never found. He implied that they had been captured by the guerrillas and secretly executed.[5]

Both Kishi and Uchida were sentenced to death at the end of the trial. They were executed by hanging at the Stanley Internment Camp, six months after the sentences were handed down.

In the meantime, the news of the guerrillas' attack in Mui Wo spread to Cheung Chau. A company of Japanese soldiers stationed in Cheung Chau immediately retreated to the urban area. Three Japanese soldiers and about fifty quisling police who were poorly armed were left stranded on the island. Before the armed guerrilla soldiers arrived, two underground agents of the guerrillas talked the police into surrendering and handing over their weapons. Once the police were relieved of their arms, the same group of guerrillas who had attacked the Japanese in Mui Wo, led by Chen Man and Political Commissar Wang Ming, sailed triumphantly into Cheung Chau on 25 August. A mass meeting of over 1,000 people was held. The guerrillas functioned as the local government and provided a rudimentary police force by patrolling the island. A self-defence team among the island's fishermen was formed. They then confiscated the property of all the Japanese and collaborators on the island.[6]

The overall result was that the guerrillas disarmed over 500 Japanese and puppet soldiers and forced them to surrender. In the process, they killed over fifty Japanese soldiers and confiscated over 400 rifles, 20 machine guns, 5 light cannon and other ammunition.

## Political Background to the Column's Moves

In the city itself, the situation was different. The British government was well aware that Chiang Kai-shek was keen to regain the Colony of Hong Kong as a piece of Chinese territory lost to the Imperialists as a result of three "unequal treaties". Therefore, a Hong Kong Planning Unit was formed in 1943 in London, as a core of the future Civil Administration Unit to administer Hong Kong once it was recaptured from the Japanese. After the American Air Force dropped the second atomic bomb over Nagasaki, it was clear that the Japanese government's surrender was imminent. So the British government was determined that a message be relayed to Franklin Gimson, the colonial secretary, to assume the administration of Hong Kong once he was released from Stanley Internment Camp. On 11 August, a message was relayed from Sir Horace Seymour, the British ambassador in Chongqing, to Lindsay Ride, commandant of BAAG, through John Reeves, consul general in Macau, to tell Gimson to provide a token British presence in Hong Kong. BAAG was the only British unit near Hong Kong, as it had a forward post in Enping, about 100 miles north-east of Hong Kong in the Pearl River Delta.

Two days later, the Foreign Office in London sent a second message to the British Embassy in Chongqing to instruct BAAG to deliver the following message to Gimson:

> His Majesty's Government considers that on capitulation Japanese may release you and other officers to assume authority. I am directed to inform you that under such circumstances you have full assurance of HMG support and following instructions (a) and (b) are sent by them for your guidance.
>
> a) Policy of HMG is to restore British sovereignty and administration immediately. For initial period it is proposed to establish military administration as soon as duly authorized by Commander British or Allied or Naval Force can reach the Colony.

b)  It is open to you to assume administration of the Government under power which you have in absence of Governor under existing Letters Patent. Your duties will be to act accordingly with full support of HMG until such time as Force Commander as stated (a) above arrives with authority to establish Military Administration. You should communicate by telegraph requesting Secretary of State for Colonies for confirmation authority of any British or Allied officers on arrival of such officer to Hong Kong and with officer concerned. You should await specific authority from Secretary of State for Colonies before formally handing over.

The message was sent by telegraph to BAAG's forward post in Enping, north of the Portuguese colony of Macao, in the Pearl River Delta. The instructions from the British government were that the message was to be delivered to Gimson by hand.

Y. C. Liang, a BAAG agent who was based near Macao, personally took the message inside a sealed envelope to Gimson in the camp in Stanley. Liang was accompanied by two Macao Portuguese, Roger Lobo and Dr. Eddie Gosano, on this important mission. Gosano had adopted the code name "Phoenix" in the BAAG underground agent establishment. Initially, both Portuguese were hesitant in taking on such a risky mission. Liang not only gave them the assurance of safety but, in addition, provided four armed guards who were members of the triads in Macao. All three masqueraded as fishermen and went on the hazardous trip, their motorized junk breaking down three times between Macao and Hong Kong. Roger Lobo was the son of Dr. Pedro Lobo, the secretary of economics in the Macao government and concurrently a prominent entrepreneur. Liang was a clerk employed in Dr. Lobo's firm. Gosano had been a medical practitioner in Hong Kong before the war and had looked after some of the prisoners of war after the British surrendered on 25 December 1941. As Portugal was a neutral country during the war, he was allowed to go to Macao a few months after the British surrender, where he continued to practise medicine.

When the party of three arrived in Hong Kong, Gosano was directed separately to contact Dr. Selwyn-Clarke, director of Medical and Health Services before the war. Selwyn-Clarke had been allowed by the Japanese to stay outside the internment camp for some months to look after the sick and the starving population, before he was finally incarcerated.[7] The reason for contacting Selwyn-Clarke was that the British government and, for that matter BAAG, were fully aware of the prisoners' serious health conditions due to malnutrition and torture. For the same reason, Admiral Sir Cecil Harcourt's fleet was allowed to be detached from the US 7th Fleet so they could speed to Hong Kong as early as 30 August, offering help and rescuing the prisoners.

Who actually gave the order to the party of three is a mystery, even today. Initially, Ride resisted the idea, using the excuse that it "would take days or even weeks" to travel to Hong Kong under such circumstances. Furthermore, he did not want to "endanger his men". According to both Lobo and Gosano, all they knew was that they had to "deliver" an envelope to Gimson. What was inside and the significance were unknown to them. On arrival in Hong Kong, they landed at the waterfront in Kennedy Town. Before making their way to Stanley Internment Camp, they walked all the way to relay the news to Sir Robert Kotewall at his residence on Kotewall Road, as he had been the senior unofficial member of the Executive Council before the war. The reason why the two went to Kotewall first is also a mystery, as Ride was against the idea of his staff meeting Kotewall, considered a "collaborator" with the Japanese. Kotewall, however, probably had heard of the Japanese military setback and knew that the Japanese occupation of Hong Kong would soon come to an end, so he had declared that he was on "sick leave" from all official duties, beginning 1 August until further notice. He was not too keen to meet with the mission and so directed the three to go to see Man Kam Lo, the son-in-law of Robert Ho Tung. Despite being Eurasian, he was always looked upon as a representative of the Chinese community. As most of the Japanese were demoralized, the three just walked to the affluent Gloucester Hotel, after Liang completed his mission, without encountering any difficulties, and stayed there until the arrival of Sir Cecil Harcourt.

Having received the letter from the British government delivered by Liang on 23 August, Gimson confronted the Japanese commandant at the Stanley Internment Camp and demanded transport so that he could travel to the City of Victoria, Hong Kong. Before the Japanese could respond to his demands, Gimson met up with Sir Atholl MacGregor, the chief justice who had been interned in the same camp. He then took the oath of office, in the presence of the chief justice and a few pre-war executive council members who also had been interned. Thus, Gimson appointed himself the officer administering the government of Hong Kong. Postmaster General Gwynn-Jones was directed to send out signals from the then Hong Kong radio station ZBW for help, in the name of "Mr. Franklin Gimson, the Acting Governor of Hong Kong".

Gimson then left Stanley Internment Camp and met with two senior military officers who were kept in the Shamshuipo Camp on the other side of the harbour, on 18 August. Captain D. Heath, Royal Artillery, and Lieutenant A. MacGregor, Royal Scots, were sent to liaise with the Japanese in the city to set up temporary government headquarters. As the Hongkong and Shanghai Bank building in Victoria was occupied by Japanese civilian officials, they moved across the road and occupied the French Mission building at Battery Path, to set up temporary Hong Kong provisional government headquarters. They then hoisted the Union Jack.

In fact, as early as 13 August, the Admiralty sent instructions for the Royal Navy to re-establish British sovereignty in Hong Kong. Admiral Bruce Ramsey, commander-in-chief of the British fleet, was told to despatch a force to Hong

Kong as soon as possible. But the British fleet was integrated, for operational reasons, into the much larger United States Pacific fleet. The Americans were not too keen to play any part in the recovery of a colonial territory, so there was a long exchange of signals, and the Americans were reassured that this move "was unrelated to any British proposals concerning Hong Kong".[8] Finally, Admiral Sir Cecil Harcourt was directed to command a fleet of twenty-four Royal Navy ships to set sail for Hong Kong from Subic Bay, the Philippines, to take the surrender of the Japanese and to rescue prisoners of war and internees. His fleet included two aircraft carriers, HMS *Indomitable* and HMS *Venerable*. In addition to the sailors and soldiers of the 3rd Commando Brigade, there were 3,000 personnel from a Royal Air Force construction unit. Harcourt, who was in his early fifties, was a career Royal Navy sailor. Short of stature, he was popular among his men. Having no experience or background knowledge of Asia and China in particular, he referred to every Chinese as a "Chinaman", without intending or realizing that it could cause offence.

Then on 29 August, a fighter plane, supported by several Grumman Hellcats, landed at Kai Tak Airport to pick up a Japanese naval officer and take him to Admiral Harcourt's flagship, the aircraft carrier HMS *Indomitable*, to map out the final details of the British forces' entry into Hong Kong. On 29 August, Gimson issued the following communiqué to the people of Hong Kong:

> Rear Admiral Harcourt is lying outside Hong Kong with a very strong fleet. The Naval Dockyard is to be ready for his arrival by noon today. Admiral Harcourt will enter the harbour having transferred his flag to the cruiser *Swiftsure,* which will be accompanied by destroyers and submarines. The capital ships will follow as soon as a passage has been swept. The fleet includes two aircraft carriers, the *Indomitable* and the *Venerable*, the battleship *Anson* and the cruiser *Euryalus*.

Duncan Sloss, vice-chancellor of the University of Hong Kong, who was also being held in Stanley Internment Camp, was appointed publicity officer by Gimson and held a press conference. Through Sloss, Gimson found Chan Kwanpo, a lecturer of Chinese at the university, who translated the communiqué into Chinese. Chan was one of the few academics who were not incarcerated during the war. Since late 1938, he had been the Chinese secretary in Madam Soong Ching-ling's China Defence League. The message was then relayed to the editor of *Wah Kiu Yat Po*. Chan then organized the two Chinese newspapers, *Wah Kiu Yat Po* and *Heung To Yat Po,* to issue extra editions.[9]

Before the arrival of Admiral Sir Cecil Harcourt, the Hong Kong and Kowloon Independent Brigade was the only military force in control in the territory. They took the opportunity to stage war crimes trials against local bandits and collaborators. It was a sign that the guerrillas were keen to show to the Japanese and to the world that they were part of the Allied forces. British intelligence suggested that the

East River Column's intention was to capture the entire territory of Hong Kong and use it as a base to repel the KMT forces in the area. Another possibility was that they wanted to hand over the city to the British, with consequent prestige and bargaining power.

General Zeng Sheng, in his capacity as the commanding general of the Guangdong People's Anti-Japanese Guerrillas Headquarters, actually sent a notice, in Japanese and English, to the "Japanese Army unit defending Hong Kong and Kowloon", two days after the Japanese government surrendered to General Douglas MacArthur in Tokyo on 2 September 1945:

> 1. On the 2nd of September the Japanese Army signed the formal surrender to the Allied countries. In accordance with their undertaking the Japanese Army should lay down their arms to us.
>
> 2. When you have laid down your arms, you will be properly treated according to the procedure for those who surrender.
>
> 3. If you do not surrender wherever you are, you should immediately concentrate yourselves in Kowloon, Canton (Guangzhou) or Waichow (Huizhou).
>
> 4. In case of doubt as to any other matter, please send your representative to my H.Q. to clear up the doubt.
>
> 5. I will issue orders to my men to cease fire during the period of such discussion between us. If you do not obey the surrender order, and plunder people's property to the detriment of good government, my men will not be given the ceasefire order.[10]

## The British Restoration: A New Partnership with the East River Guerrillas

When Admiral Sir Cecil Harcourt eventually arrived, a military government was set up by a proclamation issued on 1 September. The next day, Admiral Harcourt was appointed commander-in-chief and head of the military government. By another proclamation, Gimson was appointed lieutenant-governor. Some pre-war local leaders were appointed members of provisional executive and legislative councils. David MacDougall and John Keswick, two people who previously had worked in Hong Kong and had important connections there, were in Madras, India, when the Japanese announced their surrender. They flew from India to Hong Kong, arriving on 7 September.

On arrival, MacDougall was appointed chief civil affairs officer, which carried the rank of brigadier in Harcourt's military government. Keswick was directed by Lord Louis Mountbatten to liaise between his headquarters and General Carton de Wiart, the British prime minister's military representative in China. Because of

Gimson's unstable health after years of incarceration, it was MacDougall who did most of the work. In fact, not long after MacDougall's arrival, Gimson and some of his senior colleagues were sent home for recuperation leave. In one of his reports to the Colonial Office, MacDougall spoke in glowing terms of "the sterling work done by a nucleus of only 27 civilian officials, two of them pre-war Cadet Officers (Administrative Officers), who came out of the internment camp in Stanley to man the civilian section of the Military Government", under Sir Cecil Harcourt.[11]

Thirteen days after Harcourt's arrival, there arrived the 3rd Commando Brigade (comprising Brigade HQ, 1st and 5th Army Commandos, 42nd and 44th Royal Marine Commandos, and Royal Marine Signals and Engineer Units), commanded by Brigadier C. R. Hardy. Hardy was assigned to patrol and police the New Territories as much as possible. The urban area was policed by a few young naval ratings. Overall, the whole territory was in a state of lawlessness with rampant looting and gunfighting. A much more important consideration, however, was that the British were determined to establish their claim of sovereignty. The two administrative officers were given military ranks in the military government and were assigned some unusual duties. The military governor, on MacDougall's recommendation, appointed K. M. A. Barnett to the 3rd Commando Brigade and gave him the rank of captain, Royal Artillery and concurrently civil liaison officer (Kowloon and New Territories) under Brigadier Hardy, Lieutenant-Colonel Jack Churchill and Major Tony Pigot, Royal Marines, brigade major of the 3rd Commando Brigade. Another official, John Barrow (the district officer, north, New Territories, before the war) was given the rank of lieutenant, and he and Lieutenant G. Howarth, Royal Marines, were appointed MacDougall's assistants. All of them worked in an office on the mezzanine floor of the Peninsula Hotel in urban Kowloon and travelled daily to the New Territories.

John Barrow's area of responsibility covered the north-east part of the New Territories, an area that runs roughly from Lin Ma Hang and Tai Po eastward. He worked closely with the commandos who were stationed around Fanling. Howarth and Barnett's areas of responsibility covered Yuen Long, Tsuen Wan, Tuen Mun, Sai Kung, Clearwater Bay Peninsula and all the islands. During the few weeks until the setting-up of the Civil Affairs Office under David McDougall, Barnett and Barrow had no regular civilian staff to support their work. They were the only senior British presence in the whole of the New Territories until the arrival of a skeleton staff of Hong Kong police, twelve months after VJ Day. During this period, both Barnett and Barrow had to report at least weekly to the Kowloon garrison conference and the chief civil affairs officer.[12]

As both of them spoke Hakka, one of their first duties was to go to the New Territories and establish contact with various rural leaders. During the war, the Japanese had removed all the boundary stones, so with the rural leaders' help, Barnett and Barrow reinstalled the boundary stones at the border in Shataukok, as a symbol of British sovereignty over the whole territory.

Initially, Barnett had to deal with the KMT troops who were stationed at the border. He encountered a stiff and less than cordial attitude from the troops. They also tried to establish contact with the East River guerrillas. Since there were so few British armed personnel available, Barnett and the guerrillas virtually were in charge of the whole New Territories land mass and outlying islands. In some of the out-of-the-way locations such as Tai O, Japanese soldiers were disarmed only as late as the end of November 1945.

It was a pragmatic move for the military government to contact the guerrillas: they were the most organized and effective armed force on the ground and, hence, were asked to provide police support. It was Barnett who made his way into Sai Kung together with Lieutenant Hiram Potts of the 3rd Commando Brigade Engineers to open the first stage of a barely passable village path that was later named Hiram's Highway. Barnett later recalled fondly his first-hand experience when they arrived at the junction of Clearwater Bay Road and the unpaved country path leading down to Sai Kung. Initially, they discovered a few boulders that were as large as half a military lorry, blocking the unpaved village path. The local villagers told them that these were the result of the sabotage work left by the East River Column guerrillas. When the army engineers suggested the use of dynamite, Barnett stopped them. Because of his excellent command of the dialect, he managed to find — through the rural leader Lee Siuyam — a local stonemason who was old and weak. Armed with only a hammer and a chisel, the stonemason managed to break open the boulders within a few minutes, by working along the grain of the stones.

As directed by Brigadier Hardy, Barnett also made his way to Cheung Chau and Lantau Island, together with some of the BAAG agents — Dr. Paul Wilkinson, Lieutenant-Colonel, RAMC; Arthur Pittenhigh, a former marine police inspector; and Corporal Saunders of the Commandos — to assure the local people that there was a functioning Hong Kong government in the city itself.

In late 1945, Barrow went from village to village and assisted some of the guerrillas —mostly apolitical peasants — to return to their own villages on both sides of the border. Except for a nucleus of Communist Party members and cadres, most of the guerrilla soldiers did not want to be bothered with any political ideology and the impending civil war between the KMT and the CCP. They simply wanted to return to their own hometowns and continue their lives as before. Therefore, John Barrow, together with the military government, obtained a small warship from the Royal Navy and escorted some of them — still carrying weapons — to the Chinese territory north of Dapeng Bay. The British military accorded them the full protocol of those on the side of the Allies. Before they sailed, Major General Francis Wogan Festing reviewed them in a parade as regular soldiers.

When I interviewed Barnett some forty years after VJ Day, he was still full of praise and admiration for the soldiers of the East River Column. He was dismissive of my remarks about "the Communist guerrillas" by saying that these were "the real sons and daughters of Hong Kong who took up arms to defend their homes. Their courage and sacrifice were admirable. The Communists only provided leadership and organization skill". According to him, there were two lots of Chinese soldiers operating near the border. The KMT occupied the area from Man Kam To to the west and in his opinion did not do any fighting during the war. After VJ Day, they were mostly interested in looting. The other group was the Hong Kong and Kowloon Independent Brigade of the East River Column. Despite their Communist ideology, this group co-operated with the British officials courteously and reasonably. For nearly nine months following VJ Day, armed forces of the central government and Communist soldiers, regular or otherwise, were involved in incessant skirmishes all over China. For example, MacDougall, in one of his weekly intelligence reports sent to the Colonial Office, mentioned that, on 18 September, a group of over 300 irregular KMT soldiers appeared in the Fanling area. Their excuse was that they were retreating from the Communist guerrillas in south China. Their leader was met by a British officer who requested they return to China, informing them that they would be disarmed if they re-entered the New Territories. Before the group retreated, two of their liaison officers were allowed to proceed to call on Sham Chit-son, a KMT official based in urban Kowloon.

In addition, there was the "Gambling House Gang", armed with hand guns and sub-machine guns. These were the gangsters, some 3,000 strong, who had been commanded by Wang Tuck-ming and employed by the Japanese to maintain law and order in exchange for the right to operate casinos during the occupation. After the departure of the Japanese, these gangsters offered the same service to the British authorities, under the same terms as they enjoyed with the Japanese. However, the British courteously refused their offer. As the gangsters outnumbered the available number of police by an overwhelming ratio, they were disarmed only by the authorities offering them 5 million yen as a reward for their co-operation.

Another group who posed a serious threat to overall law and order were the triads. It was estimated that there were as many as 60,000 of them when the Japanese attacked Hong Kong in 1941. Again, they had been employed by the Japanese during the occupation period. On VJ Day, many were heavily armed, as some of the Japanese soldiers had indiscriminately given away their small arms. Approximately 7,000 unregistered arms were in the hands of these gangsters.

Barnett was deeply impressed by the discipline and conduct of the East River guerrillas who were occupying Shataukok.[13] Despite their strong national and patriotic feelings, the guerrillas co-operated fully with the British military forces. Admiral Harcourt's sailors and marines from the 3rd Commando Brigade, Royal Marines, numbered a mere 1,000 in a city with a population of some half a million — a population that had been ruled brutally for nearly four years. Besides the re-establishment of a British administration, one of its many urgent tasks was to secure a food supply to feed the population. In addition to nearly 600,000 civilians, there were over 21,000 Japanese prisoners of war, 2,700 of whom required hospitalization and medical care.

Another sensitive problem was the collaborators. Many local community leaders who had advised the Hong Kong government pre-war worked, in one way or another, with the Japanese military governor during the occupation, either voluntarily or through coercion. Acting on intelligence supplied mainly by BAAG underground agents, the British arrested forty-one people as collaborators.

During this period, MacDougall had to tread a delicate path. The overall situation in the territory could only be described as unsettled, chaotic and precarious. While the British had a barely functioning military government in the city, there were large numbers of regular KMT soldiers camping inside urban Kowloon. They had been brought to Kowloon with US military transport on their way north to stake claims (in competition with the CCP) on various cities. Flags of Allied nations were on display in the city. But, as MacDougall reported, there were four times the number of Chinese flags as British flags, up to the end of 1945.[14] Law and order was barely maintained; pirates operated within the territorial waters of Deep Bay and Mirs Bay, so passengers who sailed for even the short distance from Bao'an to Yuen Long were robbed. There were gunfights between rival gangs, even in the streets of urban Kowloon. All sorts of characters from China who claimed to represent various branches of the central government, including the Blue Shirts, muscled their way into Hong Kong. Major General Pan Huaguo, who had been present at the surrender ceremony, stayed on for a few months as the head of the Chinese military delegation. Another KMT general, S. K. Yee, also arrived; he was senior aide to General Dai Li, the notorious and much feared head of the Secret Service of the central government. As he was a full general, he outranked General Pan and claimed that he officially represented the central government.

While the main body of the Hong Kong and Kowloon Independent Brigade of the East River Column left the territory and moved north of the border in September 1945, there were isolated pockets that were not eager to depart and were hiding in places such as the hills near Shataukok, Lantau Island and urban Kowloon, until 8 November 1945. There were also other people who claimed to be soldiers of the brigade who demanded protection money from shops and cinemas in urban Hong Kong and Kowloon. The military government could not verify their claims and credentials. The commandos had to carry out a search in Lantau, particularly in the Tai O area, to round up stragglers and collect arms and equipment the guerrillas intended to hide. Some of the local bandits who once operated on the periphery of the brigade or those who claimed to be members of the brigade certainly did not retreat. Some actually resorted to robbery and collection of protection money from small shops and cinemas in urban Hong Kong. Up to May 1950, several ex-guerrillas resorted to extortion. Some were involved in a series of hand-grenade-throwing incidents in shops and cinemas. But armed with the powers under the *Emergency Ordinance*, the police managed to apprehend most of them. After trials in the High Court, the culprits were executed.[15] One senior cadre of the column's headquarters told me that he was not at all surprised that there were such unsavoury types among them, as there were six detachments and the headquarters had little control over them. Indeed, the detachments had not always been careful when recruiting their soldiers during the war.

Despite all the difficulties of politics and law and order, the military government's record in other areas was impressive. Electricity was restored to most of the urban areas on 10 September 1945. Hong Kong currency was declared the only legal tender on 14 September, in place of the Japanese military yen. Two days after the Japanese formally signed the document of surrender on 16 September, night curfew was cancelled — the first time since February 1943. As unemployment was rife while public hygiene had been left unattended during the last years of the Japanese occupation, the military government employed over 20,000 workers to do a massive cleanup of the streets and the underground drains of the city. Because of the shortage of Hong Kong currency, these workers were paid half in cash and half in kind. After nearly four years of ill treatment and starvation, such an arrangement did not cause any dissatisfaction to either party.

In fact, of the 1,000 Royal Marine Commandos, only 450 were on active patrol to do regular police duties; the remaining 550 had to handle administrative, medical and transport duties. As the guerrillas were the only military force on the Allied side present in the territory, the British military government had to deal with and negotiate with them on a number of issues. The guerrillas were represented by Major Yuan Geng, Major Huang Zuomei, Political Commissar Huang Yunpeng, Luo Rucheng (second in command to Yuan Geng) and Interpreter Tan Gan. At the negotiations, the guerrillas raised the following six points:

1.  The British should offer protection to members of the brigade who were on the casualty list and who could not be repatriated with the main brigade on 28 September 1945;
2.  A liaison office should be set up in Hong Kong, initially to organize the repatriation and then to maintain liaison with the Hong Kong government;
3.  The Marine Unit of the brigade should not be repatriated together with the main body, as the unit had to organize other transport duties;
4.  The British should agree that "people in Hong Kong and Kowloon" had the right to organize their own self-defence units;
5.  The brigade should set up a relief and rehabilitation unit after the war and the British would render it assistance; and
6.  The British should not enter the brigade's area of control without prior consultation.

The British agreed with most of the items. Initially, the column's Liaison Office was set up at 172 Nathan Road, in the heart of urban Kowloon. In fact, this address was selected because it was close to British military headquarters. Yuan Geng was appointed head of the office, and Huang Zuomei, Tan Gan, and Lee Chong were the staff.[16]

Yuan Geng was actually the pseudonym of Ouyang Rushan, who was born in Bao'an in 1917. He graduated from Guang Ya School in Guangzhou in 1936 and then enrolled in a KMT-operated military academy, where he received training in artillery and communication. He secretly joined the CCP in March 1939. In November of the same year, he joined the guerrilla column led by Zeng Sheng. As he was relatively well educated, he was assigned to head the International Liaison and Intelligence Unit of the East River Column throughout the war.

At the request of the military government under Harcourt, some of the guerrilla soldiers in the New Territories were organized into four self-defence teams to provide constabulary duties in towns such as Sai Kung, Yuen Long, Shataukok and Sheung Shui. Various experienced soldiers such as Zhang Xing (Sai Kung), He Fa (Yuen Long), Deng Mao (Sheung Shui) and Huang Guanyu (Shataukok) were appointed to head these teams. Each team was set up to command six units of four persons each. The British military government called them the "village guards" and provided them with arms and ammunition. Initially, the agreement was that these teams would be on duty for only five months, beginning September 1945. At the request of the British, however, these teams remained on duty until they were disbanded in September 1946, when regular Hong Kong police and British soldiers took over. The spirit of co-operation between the two sides was so harmonious that the British set up a temporary medical clinic in Tai Po Market, near Hong Lok Yuen, for the sole purpose of helping the guerrillas. From December 1945 until the end of February 1946, over 300 members of the brigade were treated in the clinic. General Zeng Sheng readily acknowledged that many casualty cases who had suffered for long due to the unavailability of proper medical care were well looked after by the British medical staff.[17]

Except for a handful of staff who managed the Liaison Office, which eventually changed into the local branch of the Xinhua News Agency, and a few thousand who were demobilized, the main body of the Hong Kong and Kowloon Independent Brigade moved out of Hong Kong into the areas north of the Shenzhen River. Announcing their farewell to the "compatriots in Hong Kong and Kowloon" on 28 September 1945, they issued the following notice in the media and distributed it as handbills in the urban areas:

> An announcement on the East River Column Hong Kong/Kowloon Independent Brigade's withdrawal from Hong Kong, Kowloon and the New Territories.

China's Anti-Japanese war and the Anti-Fascist war are now concluded with victory. Our people in Hong Kong and Kowloon have now been liberated from the cruel yoke of the Japanese bandits.

We can recall that when we first established our Brigade when the Japanese occupied Hong Kong, our aim was to defeat the Japanese aggressors. Under the leadership of the Chinese Communist Party in the last three years and eight months, we have taken great risks, and suffered great sacrifices. We have rescued Allied personnel, eliminated local bandits, sabotaged the work of the occupying force and protected the people's interests. Throughout our struggle, we have witnessed the people's loyalty to the motherland and their extreme hatred of the enemy. In the last three-odd years, the people's help and support given to us have been ever increasing despite their suffering from the cruel persecution of the Japanese bandits. Today, it is time for the whole world and for China to undertake peaceful reconstruction. Under such circumstances, we have been ordered by our Headquarters to withdraw from Hong Kong, Kowloon and the New Territories. In the meantime, we discovered that there are hoodlums and gangsters who pose as members of the East River Column in committing fraud, armed robberies and demanding ransoms. Their aim is to tarnish our Brigade's reputation. This is why the people of Hong Kong should be more vigilant in the future. They should improve their self-defence abilities and eradicate all sabotage work done by the gangsters, bandits and reactionary elements. Our Brigade hereby solemnly declares that, from the date of the announcement, we shall completely withdraw.

Farewell, our beloved Hong Kong compatriots. Today, we shall depart from Hong Kong. But our care and concern about your happiness and liberty remain as before. You have experienced a long period of suffering. We hope that the Hong Kong Government shall give you adequate relief, to assist you in rebuilding your businesses and improve your livelihood. We hope that your glorious struggle will earn well-deserved respect from the international community.

Today we shall withdraw. But our hearts are with you forever.

Huang Guanfang, Leader of Hong Kong and Kowloon Independent Brigade
Huang Yunpeng, Political Commissar
28 September 1945

In the immediate post-war period, however, peasants, industrial workers and shopkeepers who had served with the East River Column, having been demobilized, faced a bleak future. Just as in pre-war times, it was hand-to-mouth subsistence farming in the countryside, and cities faced shortages of every kind. Overcome by poverty and unemployment, some of them who were not regular soldiers moved into the city, looking for jobs and assistance. They were in such dire straits that Huang Zuomei set up the East River Rehabilitation and Relief Committee in Kowloon. Others formed a Seamen's Welfare Society in Kowloon, which found seafaring jobs for unemployed veterans.

According to one report, as many as 5,000 to 6,000 demobilized soldiers and their families from the East River Column were stranded in Hong Kong and needed help and relief. In a long letter addressed to Hilda Selwyn-Clarke dated 14 March 1946, Huang complained to the British government that some units of the Royal Navy harassed units of the East River Column's marine units in the waters of Bias Bay and Dapeng Bay at the instigation of the central government of the KMT regime. In great detail, Huang cited the good work of the Hong Kong and Kowloon Independent Brigade's co-operation with the Allies and, in particular, their work in rescuing Allied soldiers during the war. The gist of the letter was that, following the Allies' victory and the guerrillas' present engagement in civil war with the central government, the British should at least stay neutral and not engage in unfriendly actions against the guerrillas. A more important message in the letter was that members of the Independent Brigade were "the sons and daughters of Hong Kong who have rendered great sacrifice". Since they were suffering under such difficult circumstances, would the British government offer some help.[18] Hilda Selwyn-Clarke immediately contacted Sir Herbert Philips of the Far East Division of the Foreign Office. At the same time, she contacted Mr. James Callaghan, MP, who had some East Asian experience during the war. It was evidently a contentious issue for the Foreign Office. While acknowledging that Hilda Selwyn-Clarke's argument had "considerable force" in that the East River Column's service "ought not to be overlooked", it had the lingering worry that it was a "Communist organization" and that the central government, with whom the British government had formal diplomatic relations, "would not be sympathetic" should the British give any form of recognition to the column. A half-hearted suggestion was made that some "publicity be given in the United Kingdom press" to the assistance rendered by the column. The issue of material assistance was "out of the question". Before a formal reply was given to Hilda Selwyn-Clarke, the whole matter was passed on to MI9 of the War Office and the Colonial Office. Therefore, there were extensive consultations between Colonel L. T. Ride, former commandant of BAAG, MI9 of the War Office, the Colonial Office and the Foreign Office, before the British government responded. Prompted by members of the China Campaign Committee and Hilda Selwyn-Clarke, questions were asked by Mr. James Callaghan, MP, in the House of Commons on 26 June and 10 July 1946, as to whether the British government was to "extend some form of recognition for their services during the Japanese war" and "what arrangements are being made to aid and succour the East River Guerrillas and their families".

## Post-war British Goodwill to the Column

The British government, however, was facing a delicate and difficult situation. They readily acknowledged the fact that "all escapees and evaders in the Hong

Kong area owed their lives to the efficiency and help of the East River guerrillas" and that they were "the most anti-Japanese of all the Chinese organizations in South China".

Huang Zuomei, in particular, was considered "an agent" of BAAG and, therefore, was recommended, through the commander-in-chief in India, for the award of a King's Medal for Courage during the war and a decoration of MBE after the war. He was also the only member of the East River Column who was invited to participate in the victory parade in London, in May 1946. However, the British government had formal diplomatic relations with the Chinese government, led by the KMT.[19] The hope was that the newly appointed minister of defence in the central government, General Bai Chongxi, a native of Guangxi, was less likely to be hostile to any move taken by MI9 on the recommendation of BAAG, because of the good relations between BAAG and General Bai. Ride was well known to General Bai in Guilin during the war years. At one time, the BAAG in Guilin actually had operated from General Bai's house, before it moved to its own office in late 1942.

Finally, in order not to offend the existing government in China, the British government stated in the reply to Mr. Callaghan that "the Guerrillas had been duly recompensed for the expenses they incurred in helping Allied nationals who escaped Hong Kong", which was "in accordance with our practice in Europe" and that further help in this context was "inappropriate". In fact, the most important part of the reply was that "His Majesty's Government desire to take this opportunity of expressing their appreciation of their services rendered by the East River Column, as well as other Chinese organizations in assisting persons escaping from Hong Kong". In fact, after the departure of the main body of guerrilla soldiers to Yantai, Shandong, on 30 June 1946, various forms of assistance had been rendered to some of the soldiers. Quite generous monetary awards had been handed out to villagers in the New Territories, many of them members of the East River Column who had played a part, however small, in helping Allied soldiers who escaped. It was also stated that some of the staff of BAAG, though demobilized, had been employed in the Civil Administration in Hong Kong and continued to help the guerrillas in Hong Kong. Members of MI9 who had been operating from Singapore since VJ Day also continued to help. In a letter of reply to the Foreign Office, Colonel S. L. Derry of MI9 said that he personally would contact the Honours and Awards Committee in London to find out the latest situation on Huang Zuomei's decoration.

On 15 February 1947, the Public Relations Office (as it was known then) of the Hong Kong government issued a communiqué that the supreme commander of the Allied forces of the Southeast Asia Command, acting on the recommendation of the District Commissioner, New Territories, Hong Kong, has decided to grant awards and decorations of various kinds to forty-nine villagers and fishermen in Hong Kong. Most of these recipients had been connected with the Hong Kong and Kowloon Independent Brigade in one way or another during the war years.

They were extolled for "their gallant services in the Allied course, during 1941–45, neither influenced by hope of reward, nor deterred by fear of reprisals..." A long silk banner was presented to the Sai Kung Chamber of Commerce by a representative of the commander of British forces, Hong Kong, General Sir Neil Ritchie, on 12 April 1947, thanking the people of Sai Kung for their services in assisting Allied soldiers in their escape through the area. At the ceremony, John Barrow, who by then had been appointed district commissioner, New Territories, was also present. He had assisted some of the ex-guerrillas in finding seafaring jobs in ocean liners. Eventually, quite a few of them settled in various cities in Britain and in Europe. Ex-guerrillas settling in London eventually founded the Gong He Association, i.e. Republican Association.

In total, fifteen groups of people were given generous monetary and other awards. They were:

1. The people of Po Toi O and Hang Hau were awarded HK$800 and HK$2,000, respectively. Certificates of Merit were awarded to Cheung Honleung, So Shauyung, Wong Kamshau, So Honping, Fan Yunggan and the next of kin of Yam Taimui. Yam had been executed by the Japanese for working with the East River Column and helping two British prisoners of war who escaped.

2. The people of Ta Ho Tun were awarded HK$1,200. The money was used to provide a well in Ta Ho Tun since there was not yet potable water from water mains. Certificates of Merit were awarded to Lo Pakyuk, Yau Fo, Yau Yung of Nam Wai and Lee Yau of Tso Wo Hang.

3. The people of Sha Kok Mei Village were awarded HK$2,000. Lee Yicksheung and Lee Shau were awarded Certificates of Merit.

4. The people of Sai Kung Town were awarded HK$2,000. Koo Tinnam, a rank and file guerrilla of the Hong Kong and Kowloon Independent Brigade, and Cheung Maushau, a school teacher of the Sung Tsun School, were awarded Certificates of Merit.

5. The people of Shan Liu Village were awarded HK$1,200.

6. The people of Lin Ma Hang Village, Fanling were awarded HK$2,000. Yip Tingchuen, Yip Wongkiu and Cheung Ahtik were awarded Certificates of Merit.

7. The people in Wun Yiu Village, Tai Po, were awarded HK$800. Ma Sailim, Ma Saifan and Ma Sainam were awarded Certificates of Merit.

8. The people in Siu Lek Yuen Village, Shatin, were awarded HK$800. Choi Shiulun and Choi Sang were awarded Certificates of Merit.

9. Ng Yiucheung of Tai Wai was awarded a Certificate of Merit.

10. The people of Hok Tau Village, Tai Po, were awarded HK$2,000. Tang Hingyuen was awarded a British Empire Medal.

11. Major Liang Yongyuan of the column, who personally helped David MacDougall escape through the enemy lines in 1941, was awarded the King's Medal for Courage.

12. The people of Chek Keng Village, Sai Kung, were awarded HK$1,200. Chiu Sunhay, Chiu Pinghay and Chiu Linshing were awarded Certificates of Merit. The people of Tai Long were awarded HK$1,200. Chan Ho, Ting Kiu and Chan Shing were awarded Certificates of Merit. The people of Cheng Sheung were awarded HK$800. Wong Chuenfat and Wong Fook were awarded Certificates of Merit. The people of Pak Tam Chung were awarded $800. Wong Lungkwong was awarded a Certificate of Merit. The people of Ko Tong, Sai Kung North, were awarded HK$800. Wong Yantai was awarded a Certificate of Merit. The people in Ping Tun Village, Sai Kung, were awarded HK$800. Cheung Ahmei was awarded a Certificate of Merit.

13. Lee Wingkwong of Sham Chung Village, Sai Kung, was awarded a Certificate of Merit and a cash award of HK$2,500 for helping and providing a hiding place for Professor Gordon King of the University of Hong Kong, who escaped through the village in February 1942.

14. Cheung Tin, Cheung Hungchuen, Cheung Tohei, Cheung Lam, Cheung Ahho and Chung Fookshing, all fishermen from Shaukiwan, were awarded Certificates of Merit and a total cash award of HK$2,000 for helping Superintendent W. P. Thompson, who escaped from Stanley to Cape Collinson.

15. The people of Tong Fuk Village, Lantau Island were awarded HK$1,500 for having helped some of those who escaped from Stanley.[20]

Shortly after VJ Day, despite the issuance of the statement by the column to the "compatriots in Hong Kong and Kowloon" on their departure, the Central Committee of the CCP realized the importance of Hong Kong as a base for their United Front work with the left-wing elements of the KMT and other neutral elements. In a telegram sent by the Guangdong Provincial Committee of the Party to the Central Committee, it requested the Central Committee's endorsement of working with and supporting Cai Tingkai, Li Jishen and He Xiangning in south Guangdong and, particularly, in Hong Kong. In a telegram sent by the Central Committee to Lin Ping in Hong Kong, dated 27 August 1945, the Central Committee specifically directed that experienced cadres of the column set up their organization to handle its "work in the city". Another part of the directive was that the work of the United Front with senior political leaders of the neutral elements and the left-wing faction of the KMT must clearly be segregated with a separate leadership structure. Huang Guanfang and Liang Weilin were assigned these duties with the KMT. Liang was one of the best-educated cadres of the guerrillas, as he had graduated from Waseda University, Japan, in the 1930s.

After the column's repatriation to Yantai, Shandong, in June 1946, the Liaison Office was renamed the Hong Kong Branch of the Xinhua News Agency, headed by Huang Zuomei and subsequently by Qiao Guanhua and his wife, Gong Peng, in 1947.[21]

# 6 Civil War and Repatriation

## Nationalists Versus Communists: The Worsening Conflict

After the surrender by the Japanese, both the KMT and the Chinese Communist armed forces raced to move into areas in north China, particularly Manchuria, which had been occupied by the Japanese during most of the war years.

With assistance from the US, KMT forces were airlifted to important cities in the north such as Shenyang and Qingdao. At the same time, there were intermittent local skirmishes between the KMT and the Communist forces, mainly in the northeast and Shandong, but also in Guangdong and Hainan Island.

Pressure came from independent political parties, such as the China Democratic Union and the Revolutionary Committee of the KMT. The latter was a left-wing faction of the KMT headed by Soong Ching-ling and He Xiangning. Chiang Kai-shek wished to show that he was prepared to negotiate with the Communists and loosen his firm grip on the whole country. Therefore, on 14, 20 and 24 August, he sent telegrams to Mao Zedong in Yan'an and invited him to Chongqing to "talk on all outstanding issues, both domestic and international". Patrick Hurley, the American ambassador, accompanied by General Zhang Zhizhong, flew to Yan'an on 27 August. Mao, accompanied by Zhou Enlai and Wang Ruofei, then flew to Chongqing on 28 August. After having talked face to face with Chiang, mainly on general issues like the future relationship between the two political parties, they delegated the actual detailed negotiations to Zhang Qun and Wang Shijie, representing the KMT, and Zhou Enlai and Wang Ruofei, representing the Communists.

Negotiations started on 29 August, when the KMT side declared that they were "willing to hear the views of the Communists" and concurrently that "they were not going to start a civil war" — hence the need for "real negotiations".

The actual negotiations began on 4 September, when the KMT tabled their proposals. They included:

1. Communist armed forces should be rationalized and reorganized into a total force of no more than 12 divisions;
2. The legitimacy of liberated areas, i.e. Communist-controlled areas would not be recognized;
3. The National Defence Commission would be reorganized into a political body with participation by all political parties; and
4. The original National Assembly would be retained.

Negotiations between the two sides went back and forth from 8 to 15 September, as both refused to give way on difficult issues, e.g. the retention of the agreed strength of armed forces on both sides and the number to be demobilized. Finally, General Patrick Hurley mediated, and the Communists made a major concession. Zhou Enlai agreed to reduce the total strength of the Communist forces to no more than 20 divisions, while the central government would maintain a total strength of 120 divisions. Zhou further agreed to repatriate soldiers based in liberated areas in Guangdong, Zhejiang, Jiangsu, Jiangxi, Hunan, Hubei and Henan to north Jiangsu, north Shandong and Anhui.

Further meetings were held between 27 September and 5 October. The question of convening a National Political Consultative Conference was getting closer, and the thorny issue of demarcation of liberated areas and the ultimate strength of armed forces remained unresolved, so both sides agreed on 8 October to sign a tentative agreement on a "Summary of negotiation". This so-called agreement merely confirmed the minutes of the negotiations so far. It was signed on 10 October between Zhou Enlai and Wang Ruofei for the Communists, and Wang Shijie, Zhang Qun, General Zhang Zhizhong and Shao Lizi for the central government. The twelve points covered in the agreement were:

1. In view of the need to embark on a policy of peaceful reconstruction in the country, both sides agreed to be united and embark on a long period of co-operation under Chiang Kai-shek's leadership, refrain from civil war and build an independent, free and strong new China, and thoroughly implement Sun Yat-sen's policy of the Three People's Principles.
2. On the political front, both sides agreed to introduce the rule of law, and convene a political consultative conference of all political parties.
3. The National Assembly was referred to as the Political Consultative Conference.
4. Both sides agreed that the people should have freedom of belief, speech, publication and assembly. The existing constitution should be suitably amended so that such rights would be enshrined.
5. The Communists requested that the central government should recognize the legal and equal status of all the political parties. The central government acknowledged that all political parties were equal before the law.

6. Both sides agreed that the central government should abolish the power of arrest and punishment enjoyed by government bodies other than the judiciary and the police.

7. The Communists requested that all political prisoners other than traitors be released. The central government agreed that it was prepared to release them.

8. On the question of autonomy in some districts, both sides agreed to implement such a policy and to organize elections at the municipal level.

9. On the question of nationalization of armed forces, the Communist side agreed to reduce its armed forces from twenty-seven divisions to twenty divisions. Soldiers in eight liberated areas in Guangdong, Zhejiang and Jiangsu should be demobilized as much as possible. Those not demobilized should be repatriated to north Shandong and Anhui. The areas to be occupied should be the subject of a further proposal from the Communists. To pursue this end, a commission of three should be formed to deal with the details.

10. On the question of local government in liberated areas, the central government emphasized that laws promulgated should be applied universally within the whole country. What the Communists proposed was not acceptable. Both sides agreed that this issue should be the subject of further negotiations.

11. The central government agreed that traitors, collaborators and puppet soldiers be dealt with according to existing legislation.

12. On the question of the Communist demand to participate in surrender ceremonies and the demarcation of areas, the KMT agreed to consider such demands only after the Communist armed forces agreed to abide by orders issued by the central government.

The agreement, known initially as *Huitan jiyao*, was signed on 10 October and released in full to the public on 12 October. It was then known as the Double Tenth Armistice Agreement.[1]

Mao, accompanied by Zhang Zhizhong and Wang Ruofei, then returned to Yan'an by air. It was obvious that the so-called agreement was only based on vague general principles but not on specifics, particularly in areas such as the control and administration of the Communist armed forces and the liberated areas. Zhou Enlai stayed behind in Chongqing to negotiate the remaining unresolved issues.

The central government team was again represented by Zhang Qun, Shao Lizi and Wang Shijie. The Communist side was led by Zhou Enlai and Wang Ruofei. The KMT raised three priority items:

1. Rail traffic to be restored;

2. Communist forces to retreat out of railway precincts and issue of status quo in liberated areas; and

3. General Ye Jianying, chief of staff of all the Communist forces, to join the separate negotiations held by a military committee. The negotiations were to

deal with demobilization of the Communist armed forces and their areas of occupation.

While the negotiations were taking place, intense battles were being fought, both sides deploying combatants of up to divisional scale in north China, in the Tianjin area, Suiyuan and in the East River areas in Guangdong. Faced with some military setbacks mainly in the north, the KMT proposed the following six points for further negotiations:

1. Armed forces from both sides to remain *in situ* in their respective areas of occupation.
2. Communist forces who occupied some of the railways to withdraw to a distance of ten kilometres from the railways. The central government should send in only a police force to occupy such areas.
3. Representatives from the National Assembly and other neutral elements should organize bodies to monitor such withdrawal.
4. The central government agreed to consult the Communist side, should it need to transport armed forces through such railway routes as mentioned.
5. Both sides agreed to find a solution to the issue of the Communist armed forces' bases and their demobilization within one month.
6. A National Consultative Conference to be convened forthwith.

While the KMT was stalling, Zhou Enlai worked patiently with the independent and neutral elements, for example, the China Democratic Union. By 22 December, General George C. Marshall, as special envoy of US President Harry Truman, arrived in Chongqing. His task was to mediate between the two parties and prevent a civil war. As a consequence, both sides resumed negotiations on 27 December. In the process, the Communists made a major concession by agreeing that their soldiers in seven liberated areas — Guangdong, Zhejiang, south Jiangsu, south Jiangxi, Hunan, Hubei and Henan — should retreat from their bases and move to north China, particularly the north-east and Shandong. Finally, on 5 January 1946, a formal armistice agreement was reached by both parties and signed on 10 January. It stated that:

All armed forces under the central government and those under the CCP, including regular soldiers, militia and guerrilla soldiers, should abide by the following orders:

1. All armed hostilities to cease forthwith.
2. Except for those activities such as demobilization and transfer replacement previously agreed upon, all military deployment should cease.
3. Sabotage and obstruction of all transport links should cease.
4. To implement the ceasefire agreement, a Military Mediation and Implementation Commission should be established in Beijing. Members

of the commission should come from the central government, the Chinese Communist Party and the American government. All directives issued by the Commission should be based on the unanimous decisions of the three members. Such directives should be issued in the name of the chairman of the Military Mediation and Implementation Commission.

The following four terms were appended to amplify the armistice:
1.  Term No. 2 on military deployment is not applicable to the central government's demobilization activities currently undertaken in areas south of the Yangtze River.
2.  Term No. 2 is not applicable to the central government's armed forces' move to the nine provinces in the north-east to re-establish national sovereignty in such places.
3.  Reference to transport links is also applicable to postal links.
4.  Any central government troop deployment and movement as agreed should be reported to the commission daily.

The three members of the commission created under Term 4 were: General Ye Jianying, Communist; Zheng Jiemin, central government; and Walter S. Robertson, the US Chargé d'Affaires. Four military aircraft were provided by the Americans to fly low over various mountainous areas in Hunan and Hubei to distribute the ceasefire order in the form of handbills. Eight separate field teams, comprising military officials from the three sides, were formed and sent out to all areas of conflict such as Jinan, Xuzhou, Datong, Zhangjiakou and Guangzhou. It was obvious that neither the KMT nor the CCP were sincere in their negotiations. Whatever they agreed on on paper was difficult to implement on the ground. The priority on both sides was to retain as many soldiers as possible and to grab as much territory as possible. As the regions in north China were rich in resources and strategically important, both sides were keen to occupy as much land in north China as possible. Therefore, the situation in Guangdong, where there were fewer combatants on both sides, was not the focus of their attention and became a sideline in the overall situation.

Field Team No. 8 was assigned to deal with the intermittent conflict in Guangdong and Hainan Island. It was headed by Colonel Paul Miller from the US Army. Major General Fang Fang representing the East River Column, and Major Huang Weiqin representing the KMT. When Fang negotiated with the military government in Hong Kong before the Hong Kong and Kowloon Independent Brigade's departure from Hong Kong on 28 September 1945, he was no more than a major. But in order to convey a sense of equal standing with the KMT side in the negotiations, he was quickly promoted to the rank of major general.

Throughout the war years, there had been no regular Communist armies in Guangdong. The armed forces were entirely native guerrillas. In fact, some of them, like the Qiongya Guerrillas, had been operating in Hainan Island from as early as 1927.[2]

However, the soldiers from the Hong Kong and Kowloon Independent Brigade of the East River Column who were evacuated to areas north of the Hong Kong border faced incessant hostilities from the KMT regular armed forces, beginning as early as October 1945. In one of the many skirmishes that occurred barely thirty miles north of Shenzhen, it was reported that 100 guerrillas had been killed and over 30 seriously injured. Many were transported by the brigade to a hospital in urban Kowloon for treatment.[3] Another incident reported was that the local KMT commander had deployed nearly 500 quisling troops who had surrendered to the KMT, to attack some of the villages in Bao'an where the East River Column had once been based. In addition to the killings, houses were torched, and over 700 innocent civilians had to flee across the border, ending up in Hong Kong as beggars and unskilled labourers. Media who were pro-KMT portrayed these people as "refugees" who had come to Hong Kong because of the "serious drought" in Shenzhen and Bao'an.[4]

At the same time the supreme commander, Chiang Kai-shek, directed the garrison commander in Guangdong, General Zhang Fakui, to convene a Guangdong and Guangxi Pacification Meeting with the commanders of the two provinces in Guangzhou from 20 October to 30 October 1945. The order from Chiang was that "Communist bandits" in the two provinces be totally eliminated within two months. Publicly, Zhang Fakui refused to recognize the guerrillas as bona fide soldiers who fought during the war. They were branded merely "local bandits". Three divisions of soldiers were mobilized by Zhang Fakui to round up and attack the East River guerrillas in the Dapeng Peninsula north of Mirs Bay.[5] In order to do this job in earnest, soldiers of the American-equipped New First Corp, under General Sun Liren, were sent to the East River area to assist local Guangdong forces. Up to 2,000 from this corps were unleashed in Communist-controlled areas in Huiyang on 27 December 1945. Eight warships from the central government were also sent from Hong Kong territorial waters to attack the Marine Detachment of the column in Dapeng Bay.[6]

From as early as 15 January 1946, the day after the armistice in the entire country came into effect, up to five divisions of KMT troops launched attacks in liberated areas in ten market towns, including Liaobu, Dongguan, Pingshan and Longgang. By mid-January, they aimed to clear out all guerrillas in Shenzhen and the neighbouring fishing village on the coast. Shayuchong was raided repeatedly. By 15 January, the strategically important coastal town of Yantian was attacked. Preceding the attack, the KMT forces had distributed propaganda handbills to warn all "young men and women" who were not pro-central government to surrender or face "serious consequences". A number of East River Column soldiers were based in the border town of Shataukok, using it as a safe sanctuary because they could move south into Hong Kong with ease. The KMT forces fully realized their objective and threatened to attack Shataukok on 16 January. Faced with a superior force, both in personnel and weaponry, the column had to withdraw by dispersing its soldiers into the mountains nearby.[7] On 6 February, one full company of KMT soldiers of the First Corps attacked Shataukok, but most of the East River Column's regular combatants had already retreated. When the East River Column had fewer than fifty armed militia present, the KMT soldiers moved in with ease. Most of the casualties were innocent civilians. The KMT troops occupied Shataukok for two days, without finding the main body of the column, and then moved east to Xiaomeisha, the fishing village east of Shayuchong. On 14 February, the New First Corp, under General Sun Liren, and the 63rd Army Corps launched a full-scale attack on the liberated area in Dapeng Bay, and 1,400 paratroopers from the corps landed in Nantou. The paratroopers teamed up with warships to go on a sweeping operation in the coastal area of Dapeng Bay.

It was obvious that the CCP's priority was to bring about a spell of peace in order to consolidate and regroup their armed forces, pending the outbreak of a full-fledged civil war. Therefore, they were sincere in going through with the ceasefire negotiations. So General Fang Fang, his secretary Chen Hua and interpreter Feng Qiuxi, together with other members of Field Team No. 8, promptly arrived from Shanghai in Guangzhou on 25 January 1946. However, they were met with one obstacle after another. Three days after their arrival, the local garrison headquarters' spokesperson expressed "surprise" to the media and commented that the field team's visit was "uncalled for, as there was no KMT and Communist conflict in Guangdong". What they had were "local bandits who were being eliminated".[8]

To the outside world and, particularly to the media, the garrison commander, General Zhang Fakui, displayed a façade of reason and civility. He extended a warm welcome to the team, and he placed an embargo on the media in contacting Fang Fang and Fang's subordinates. At a press conference on 12 February, he again denied the existence of the East River guerrillas in Guangdong Province. Furthermore, he stated that the Guangdong Garrison Headquarters had "never received any information from the higher authority in Chongqing that there were Communist soldiers in Guangdong and Guangxi". If there were such soldiers, he had "no knowledge of their strength and designations". What he had to deal with "at present were only isolated pockets of local bandits who occasionally robbed various villages, puppet soldiers and Japanese soldiers who were stragglers". He said that the armistice agreement signed in Chongqing "had no relevance to Guangdong. Hence, he was in no position to entertain any request from the Communist representative of Field Team No. 8".

General Fang Fang rebutted him by stating that anti-Japanese guerrillas were present in both the northern and southern banks of the East River, particularly in towns and counties such as Huizhou, Huiyang, Boluo, Dongguan and Bao'an. He said, "besides the East River Column, there are the Pearl River Column, Qiongya Column, Nanlu People's Anti-Japanese Liberation Force and the Hanjiang Column", and added "the very fact that the KMT agreed to sign the Double Ten Armistice Agreement is an acknowledgement that there are Communist-led armed forces in Guangdong and that they were allowed to evacuate from Guangdong". When Colonel Miller was asked by the media for his comment, the American soldier could only say that "he was in no position to release any information about Guangdong". He referred the media to the Military Commission based in Beijing. Except for one or two newspapers that were not totally controlled by the central government, the Communist side was operating at a great disadvantage in this area. The only alternative was to lobby and mobilize some of the non-partisan political parties or those not controlled by the KMT, such as the Democratic Union, headed by He Xiangning. In one of the most brilliant political ploys, the Communists managed to lobby He, who actually cabled the Mediation and Implementation Commission in Beijing and Field Team No. 8 in Guangzhou, first, demanding the implementation of a ceasefire in Guangdong and, second, offering to send representatives of the Democratic Union on an inspection tour with officials of the field team.[9] Another person who was sympathetic to the non-KMT elements in the conflict, Bishop Ronald Hall of the Anglican Church in Hong Kong, also intervened. In a telegram sent to both Chiang Kai-shek and Zhang Fakui, dated 11 February, he stated "In the name of Jesus Christ, would you please order your soldiers to stop your attack against the patriotic Chinese Communist soldiers in the East River region".[10] On 17 February, a spokesperson from the CCP told the media that there were "anti-Japanese forces in Guangdong right at the outset of the Sino-Japanese War". The spokesperson also said, "What we earnestly want is that the Committee of Three in Beijing should direct the Guangdong authority to desist in its attack on the anti-Japanese guerrillas in Guangdong so that a general ceasefire can be implemented throughout the entire country."

The Americans who served in Field Team No. 8 were most concerned about the situation in Guangdong. After being obstructed by Zhang Fakui for over two weeks, the team finally set out from Guangzhou to Huizhou and Danshui on 18 February for an on-site inspection. This move materialized only after the Military Commission in Chongqing acknowledged the existence of the East River Column in Guangdong and its legitimate status. Initially, the team wanted to travel to Hong Kong before they went to the areas of conflict. This request was flatly refused by the Guangdong Garrison Headquarters, as they knew full well that there was still a strong East River Column presence in Hong Kong. Also, the media in the British colony were not entirely pro-KMT. As the team had to depend on garrison headquarters to provide transport and other facilities, it had no alternative but to accept the refusal. Therefore, days before the team's arrival in Danshui, various towns in the area such as Danshui, Huizhou, Aotou and Shayuchong were intensively occupied by soldiers of the 63rd Army. Usual civilian activities, such as regular market days, were not allowed to be observed. Even the villagers' daily firewood gathering from the hills was stopped during the field team's visit.

Eight warships from the central government also barred the entrance to Dapeng and Daya Bays, to prevent the team's discovery of the column's marine unit.[11]

During the inspection of the various areas of conflict, however, the team was prevented from contacting representatives from the column's actual fighting force, because they were hiding in the mountains and the civilians who could have told the truth were kept away from the team. So after the three-day abortive visit, the team returned to Guangzhou. In a press release, the team admitted that the inspection tour had achieved nothing and that "the difficulties encountered are the same as before, i.e. the recognition of the East River Column's status and its existence". What General Fang Fang referred to as Communist guerrillas, Major Huang Weiqin from the KMT insisted were "local bandits"; so they made a report to the commission in Beijing and asked for a directive. The only point both sides agreed on was that the "level of military conflict in the East River area has scaled down".[12] In an interview with the media, however, General Fang Fang said that if the garrison headquarters could guarantee their safety, he was certain that representatives of the column would be willing to meet with the team, but that the garrison had consistently refused this proposal.

Subsequently, on 22 February, Fang Fang gave another interview to the media stating that the press release previously issued by the team did not represent the views of every member of the team, and therefore, he did not agree that the "level of military conflict had scaled down".

In fact, neutral European observers who visited the area estimated that there were as many as 5,000 guerrillas in the Huizhou area alone.[13] Huizhou and Dongguan were the two main bases where the column had been launched in 1938. Both towns were centres of Hakka culture, where most of the rank-and-file guerrillas originally came from, so they were hiding very effectively and blended well with the local people. The end result was that, despite the KMT forces being better equipped in weaponry and strength, they could not find the main body of the East River Column's combat troops.

However, Colonel Miller was most concerned that if General Zhang Fakui were allowed to go on like this, the Communists might see this as a ceasefire violation. They then would be justified in attacking the KMT soldiers in the north-eastern provinces where they were in a strong position. This was a scenario that Miller did not want to happen: it would mean a total breakdown in the ceasefire in many parts of the country. In fact, a spokesperson from the CCP who was based in Chongqing told the media on 15 February: "Unless Zhang Fakui stops attacking the Communist guerrilla forces in Guangdong, our Eighth Route Army will reconsider its stance on the quisling soldiers who surrendered to the central government and take appropriate action against them." This was a real threat that the central government had to take seriously, as many quisling soldiers had been accepted and incorporated into the regular KMT armed forces in those regions where regular government forces were relatively under-strength. The bulk of their better-equipped and better-trained soldiers had been sent to the north-east by American air transport.[14]

One further complication was that the Hong Kong military authorities were teaming up with the KMT military in conducting "anti-pirate drives" in the Bias Bay area. There was no doubt that pirates were in that area, particularly during the volatile period immediately after VJ Day. Both the KMT government and the military administration in Hong Kong had their hands full with other more urgent problems, so dealing with pirates was not a priority. In the meantime, the British consul general in Guangzhou advised Hong Kong's military governor to suspend these activities, as the KMT marine units were not keen to distinguish between the genuine guerrilla marine units and pirates when KMT marines came into actual armed conflict. It was well known that the East River Column's marine unit had eleven vessels in the area. Consul General R. A. Hall's main worry was that this might provoke Communist retaliation in Hong Kong. The Hong Kong authorities accepted the consul general's advice and played a neutral and passive role thereafter throughout the conflict and the ensuing negotiations.

On 9 March, Zhou Enlai instructed General Lin Ping, the political commissar of the column, to fly to Chongqing. Zhou's directive was that Lin should appear as the representative of the South China People's Anti-Japanese Guerrilla Forces and the secretary of the Guangdong Committee of the CCP, to confront the central government. Lin then held a press conference in the city to expose Zhang Fakui's obstacles in preventing Field Team No. 8 from commencing its work in Guangdong. At the conference, Lin disclosed to the media the history of the East River Column, including details of its war record such as the number of rescued Allied pilots, prisoners of war and civilians. Letters of commendation of its work from Lord Louis Mountbatten, General Joseph Stilwell and General Claire Chennault were shown to the media. Zhou Enlai followed by holding another press conference in Chongqing, on 18 March when he appealed to "friends from other political parties and friends from Allied countries" who could monitor the "overall implementation" of the armistice agreement. One of the Communists' trump cards in their propaganda campaign was the number of commendation letters sent to the East River Column's headquarters by US Air Force pilots and other Allied prisoners of war who were rescued by the column during the war. Zhou's appeal received a positive response from the China Democratic Union, represented by people like He Xiangning and General Cai Tingkai from Hong Kong. He also spoke at length at one of the committee of three meetings of General George Marshall, Zhang Zhizhong and Zhou Enlai himself, held on 27 March in Chongqing. Zhou spoke about Zhang Fakui's stalling tactics and the lack of a "detailed and formal order from the central government" enabling him to act. Zhang Fakui actually stayed in Chongqing for two weeks, but he met briefly with Zhou only once. When Zhou requested a second meeting, he refused. Zhou said in conciliatory terms that he was prepared to send another representative of the column to Guangzhou to "improve" the relationship between the column and Zhang Fakui.[15]

In the meantime, Singapore and Malayan Chinese of Huizhou origin, i.e. Hakka descent, raised a strong protest against the central government's stance and the incessant armed conflict in the East River region. As mentioned, most of the Hakka in Southeast Asia originally came from this area. Fundraising campaigns were launched to assist those who had been affected by the armed conflict and had moved south to Hong Kong.[16] A mass meeting of the Huizhou, Dongguan and Bao'an Hong Kong Residents Association was held in Hong Kong on 15 March. It disclosed details of the central government's attack on the civilians and the column's soldiers in the region. Separate telegrams appealing for a ceasefire were sent to Chiang Kai-shek and Zhang Fakui. When a ceasefire was eventually declared, another telegram was sent to Field Team No. 8 to request the team monitor the situation and enforce the ceasefire.

## The Repatriation Agreement

Eventually, the Military Mediation and Implementation Commission in Beijing told General Fang Fang to relay a message to a representative of the column's fighting force to travel to Guangzhou to meet with Field Team No. 8. Subsequently, on 31 March, after repeated negotiations, the commission agreed to send an ad hoc committee of three to Guangzhou to assist Field Team No. 8. The committee was headed by Colonel Trent from the United States Army, and included Colonel Pi Zonggan, representing the KMT, and Liao Chengzhi, representing the CCP. After his escape from Hong Kong in 1942, Liao had arranged for the guerrillas of the East River Column to rescue and escort his mother and his wife to escape from Hong Kong. After both women settled safely in Guilin in early 1942, Liao went to Qujiang in north Guangdong. During the war, many Hong Kong residents who escaped stayed in Qujiang and Guilin. Because of his Hong Kong experience, Liao was directed by the party to stay in Qujiang to mobilize support for the Communist Party. But his efforts were thwarted. On 30 May 1942, he was arrested by the local warlord and incarcerated with other political prisoners. He was kept there until early 1946. After VJ Day, when Chiang Kai-shek wanted to show to the country that he was sincere in coming to a peaceful settlement with the Chinese Communist Party and through appeals by people like Soong Ching-ling and Liao's mother, Liao was finally released with other political prisoners on 22 January 1946. As he had been involved with the East River Column's activities in Hong Kong before the war, and because of his Guangdong background, he was useful to the party in the negotiations. Officially, he was appointed director of the Xinhua News Agency by the Party. This committee was assigned three tasks: to obtain Zhang Fakui's acknowledgement that the guerrillas in Guangdong and Hainan Island were legitimate Communist armed forces, to meet with the commanding officers of both the Communist and KMT forces in Guangdong and Hainan Island and prevent further armed clashes, and to work with the American military to ship the Communist soldiers to Shandong.

When the committee met with Zhang Fakui, he again refused to acknowledge the existence of Communist soldiers in Guangdong. Liao Chengzhi then confronted him by asking, "If there were no Communist armed forces in Guangdong, then why did you issue your earlier order in the 'Pacification Campaign' and the order to eliminate the Communist guerrillas in the two provinces?" Finally, a meeting of the team was held in Guangzhou on 1 April. Miller then arranged for the instructions from "Generalissimo Chiang Kai-shek to the Guangzhou Garrison Headquarters" to be read to members of the team. The instructions were:

1.  Central Government acknowledged the existence of Communist Anti-Japanese soldiers in Guangdong and Hainan Island.
2.  Both sides agreed to arrange the repatriation of 2,400 such personnel to Shandong. The port of embarkation was the fishing village of Shayuchong on the coast of Dapeng Bay. Those who chose not to be repatriated would be given demobilization certificates and the Central Government would guarantee their personal safety;
3.  The timing of the embarkation was set at one month starting from the day of the survey to the day of embarkation with no extension of the limit.[17]

In addition, there were ten more detailed resolutions:

1.  A total of 2,400 military personnel, including 300 women from areas south of East River, north of East River and north Guangdong, were to be shipped by American naval ships from Dapeng Peninsula to Yantai, Shandong.
2.  The foregoing personnel should assemble and concentrate at the point of embarkation one month from the time sub-teams were sent by Field Team No. 8. For those in north Guangdong who might not arrive on time, extension of time was given, subject to the decision of the Committee of Three.
3.  During the time when the Communist armed forces were travelling to the point of embarkation, KMT forces stationed near Dapeng Peninsula should

withdraw to a safe distance to provide a corridor of safety to the Communist forces.

4.  The Guangzhou Garrison Headquarters should guarantee the safety of the Communist soldiers during their movement towards the point of embarkation.

5.  The Guangzhou Garrison Headquarters should assist the Communist soldiers in obtaining food supplies or provide loans to them to obtain such supplies, during their movement.

6.  In implementing the foregoing, Field Team No. 8 should send three sub-teams to monitor and assist Communist armed personnel to move towards the point of embarkation. The three sub-teams should be equipped with telegraph sets to maintain contact with Field Team No. 8.

7.  The Guangzhou Garrison Headquarters should send some military police to work under the three sub-teams. Such military police should work under the control of Field Team No. 8.

8.  General Lin Ping would accompany General Zeng Sheng and appear before Field Team No. 8 to implement the details of the agreement three days after the signing of the agreement.

9.  Detailed implementation of the agreement should be the subject of further meetings between the three sides in Field Team No. 8.

10. Once the three parties had affixed their signatures to the foregoing agreement, the terms should be implemented forthwith.

On the second day of the meeting when these conditions were being drafted, Liao Chengzhi stated categorically that once a ceasefire was observed, the Communists "would discard armed struggle" in the East River area.[18] In addition, Liao Chengzhi requested that the government guarantee the safety and fair treatment of those Communist armed force personnel and their families who had chosen not to be repatriated and decided to be demobilized. They should be issued with demobilization certificates and treated identically to their KMT counterparts. General Huang guaranteed that as long as they "were law abiding, they would not be discriminated against".

Liao then stated, "Now the problem of armed forces in the East River area is solved. But there are other similar problems in the whole of Guangdong, such as those in Hainan Island." The Qiongya Column in Hainan Island, in fact, had been operating as a guerrilla group as early as September 1927, despite the lack of any material support from other Communist guerrillas in the rest of Guangdong. Colonel Trent and Colonel Pi responded that the problem of guerrillas in Hainan Island had been discussed by the Mediation and Implementation Commission in Chongqing, but no solution had been found. Hence, the question of Hainan was outside the remit of Field Team No. 8. As a concession, Liao did not pursue this point further, after Colonel Trent agreed to refer this particular issue to the committee again. There was evidence that the Communists wanted to settle the problem of Hainan, as they were holding four Australian prisoners of war who had escaped from the Japanese camp in Haikou, Hainan Island, and were a physical and political burden to the guerrillas.[19]

Liao then raised a third point about the telegraph set of the Communist representative in Field Team No. 8 being sabotaged. He hoped that the Guangzhou Garrison Headquarters would guarantee that this would not be repeated and that a new set would be provided. General Huang declared that he knew nothing about this. Colonel Miller's comment was: "When the persons worked on the Communist radio, they evidently did a pretty complete job." He surmised that the sabotage "was done while the team was in Huizhou".[20] The agreement was signed on 4 April and the ad hoc Committee of Three returned to Chongqing.

The foregoing three principles and their appended conditions, after having been signed, were handed down to Field Team No. 8 as a directive from Chiang Kai-shek to be implemented by the two sides of the intermittent conflict in Guangdong.

Before the field team could get down to its actual work in the implementation of the agreed-upon points, they had to overcome other obstacles. The key representative on the Communist side, General Zeng Sheng, was still in Hong Kong, while the rest of the team was in Guangzhou. Zeng would only be willing to go to Guangzhou if his "safety was guaranteed by General George Marshall". After Colonel Miller telegraphed General Marshall to this effect, Miller then contacted the British authorities in Hong Kong through the British Consul General R. A. Hall in Guangzhou. Hall's advice to the military government in Hong Kong was that the British side should "avoid any involvement in this domestic dispute in China, as much as possible".[21] Finally, Zeng travelled to Guangzhou by train on 4 April, but it was never clear to the Americans or the Hong Kong authorities where he boarded the train.

After arriving in Guangzhou, he spent the next two days paying courtesy calls on members of Field Team No. 8 and General Zhang Fakui himself. The first session of the implementation of the agreement started on 7 April. Unfortunately, when Zeng attended the first session, it soon became apparent that there were arguments over the question of "face" and "intentional delay" from both sides. It appeared that the Communist side was keen to secure recognition of the East River Column as a legitimate armed force on the Allied side, by insisting that General Zeng sit across the negotiating table on an equal footing with his KMT counterpart. However, General Wang Heng, on the KMT side, flatly refused, as the arrangement would convey the impression that Zeng was recognized as "a Commander of the East River Column". He could only be accepted as a representative of the "Guangdong Communist armed personnel".[22]

A spokesperson from the garrison headquarters actually said there were "Communist armed forces in Guangdong, but there was no Communist army". To some neutral observers, this sounded like an argument over semantics. KMT negotiators were keen to avoid conveying an impression to the outside world that a Communist commander could negotiate on an equal footing with representatives of the legitimate central government. To the KMT negotiators, the name East River Column was totally unacceptable, but to the Communists, the move was one of many in trying to show the world that the column had been part of the Allied forces in the war. Finally, to show the Americans and, for that matter, the world that they were sincere, General Fang Fang agreed to the concession that he and Liao Chengzhi represented Communist armed forces in Guangdong and dropped any mention of the name East River Column.[23] The suspicions between the two sides were so deep and the bad feelings so strong that some of the negotiations were held with Colonel Miller conducting what he described as "go-between discussions". The patient American soldier had to talk to both sides separately, sometimes in separate rooms inside the same building, even about various trivial details such as seating arrangements at the conference table. During some negotiation sessions, discussions from both sides turned into angry shouting matches only ten minutes after they had sat down at the table. All that Colonel Miller could do was adjourn the meeting to another day. The English interpreter for the East River Column delegation was Lin Zhan, the female guerrilla who had helped the American pilot Donald Kerr, when he was shot down near the foothills of Kowloon during the war. Consul General R. A. Hall was impressed by her dedication and that of some of her colleagues, and mentioned in one of his dispatches to the military governor in Hong Kong that these young guerrilla girls "after having lived and worked in the hills, . . . no longer liked the lights of the city" and he was not surprised that "the Communists were able to make a stronger appeal to the student class".[24]

While Field Team No. 8 started its serious work on 1 April, armed skirmishes in the Huizhou and Danshui areas were still going on. It was not until 12 April that General Zhang Fakui issued a ceasefire order to his troops; General Zeng Sheng had issued his two days earlier. Then Chiang Kai-shek, in his capacity as the supreme commander, issued a "Special Directive" to both sides of the negotiations. The directive threatened "serious punishment to both sides for false or exaggerated reports of ceasefire violations".

After the ceasefire order was issued by both sides, another difficult point in the negotiations arose. General Fang requested the central government advance a Chinese national currency loan of 987,600,000 yuan for the purchase of food and warm clothing for the repatriated soldiers. General Fang gave detailed figures showing how this amount had been calculated and included demobilization pay for 1,700 soldiers. The KMT side counter-offered a much lower figure of only 180 million yuan. A final figure of 270 million was agreed upon after Colonel Miller intervened and expressed his opinion that the demobilized soldiers should be paid "the same rate as their demobilized National Government counterparts".[25]

Again the Communist side requested guaranteed safe conduct from General Zhang Fakui and American protection and transport for the guerrillas' evacuation by sea to Shandong.[26] Throughout the negotiations, both sides staged one-upmanship antics. The KMT tried to brand the armed local guerrillas as no more than "bandits", while General Fang tried to show the Americans, through the Communist propaganda machinery, that they were equal to their KMT counterparts. In the meantime, the Communists made strategic moves in deploying some of their experienced soldiers to the neighbouring provinces of Guangxi and Jiangxi, as they knew full well that a full-fledged civil war was imminent. The Communist party's directive to all the guerrilla units throughout the country was "Disperse. Preserve the weapons and preserve the experienced soldiers and experienced cadres".

A few days later, the Communists' new radio/telegraph set was again sabotaged by KMT personnel when Zeng Sheng and his staff were being entertained by the Guangzhou Garrison Headquarters, away from the Communist quarters that were in the same building where negotiations took place. Zeng was worried that he would be cut off entirely from communications with his own fighting forces that were hiding in the mountains near Huizhou. Both Fang and Lin Ping, the political commissar, were worried that, should the KMT forces unleash their entire unit against the column's soldiers in the Pearl River Delta area, the leadership would not adequately be present to lead the fighting force, as Wang Zuorao, the interim leader of the column, and Yang Kanghua, the interim political commissar, were based in the mountainous district in north Guangdong. It was a rare occasion that the top three leaders — Zeng Sheng, Fang Fang and Lin Ping — were actually staying some distance away from the guerrilla soldiers in the field. So Zeng decided that Lin Ping was the only one of the three top leaders in the negotiations who could be spared. Lin was directed to find an excuse to absent himself from the negotiations and make his way back to the fighting force in the East River area. Because their telegraph set was not working, sometimes Zeng Sheng had to rely on Colonel Miller's own set. In some instances, the Communist side resorted to human couriers. From the beginning of April until the third week in May, Field Team No. 8 made little progress. In fact, many of the so-called "formal" and "informal" meetings were bogged down, as both sides filed charges and counter-charges of "ceasefire violations".

On 18 May, Lin Ping finally gave the excuse that he was suffering from "food poisoning". Instead of seeking local medical attention, he chose to go on "sick leave" and travel to Hong Kong. The KMT side of Field Team No. 8 strongly objected, as they did not want the outside world to know the real situation in the so-called negotiations. Finally, Colonel Miller intervened, and Lin was allowed to travel by train. Details of his itinerary were provided to the KMT so that protection and security would be given. Lin was nearly assassinated, however, when the train was deliberately derailed in Zengcheng, twenty miles south of Guangzhou. Fortunately, at the last minute, Lin had decided to travel by boat.

However, what trivial consensus was achieved, such as seating arrangements of KMT and Communist representatives, was the subject of additional negotiations, as the lack of trust between the two sides was so profound that both tried their best to obtain as many concessions as possible. A twenty-four-point preliminary agreement was reached on 8 April after Colonel Miller talked separately to the two sides. The entire agreement was publicized in a press release issued to the media. Details of this agreement were:

1.  The Communists proposed three points of assembly: Yingde in north Guangdong; Longgang and Pingshan in south Guangdong; and Futian in the North River area.

2.  The Guangdong Garrison Headquarters proposed a line of demarcation drawn from Pingshan to Shataukok. KMT forces south of this line would withdraw to facilitate the guerrillas' movements. After the guerrillas assembled in Bias Bay, they would not be allowed to cross this line except for unarmed members who needed to obtain food supply from the market town of Danshui.

3.  The Communists agreed to the routes of assembly proposed by the KMT, but the actual time required for the troop movement might be subject to variations due to weather conditions. Such variations should be subject to the approval of the sub-teams.

4.  The KMT stated that whenever the guerrilla soldiers passed through areas under the garrison headquarters' control, they should observe existing military orders.

5.  The garrison headquarters raised the issue that the guerrillas should not hold any mass meeting or distribute propaganda materials during their movement to the points of concentration.

6.  The Communists agreed not to increase the numbers of soldiers during their movement.

7.  The Communists agreed not to hide and bury their arms and weapons underground before they departed.

8.  The Communists agreed not to accept food supplies and entertainment from civilians during their movement to the points of concentration.

9.  The Communists agreed not to sabotage any of government's transport and telecommunication facilities during their movement.

10. The Communists agreed not to bring along any of the captured Japanese soldiers and Japanese soldiers of Korean and Taiwan descent in their repatriation.

11. The garrison headquarters requested that the guerrillas use their own means of transport and telecommunication during their troop movement.

12. The garrison headquarters requested that the guerrillas should not hold any military exercise during their movement.

13. The garrison headquarters requested that, during the troop movement, the distance between the vanguard and the rear party should not exceed one day's marching distance.

14. The garrison headquarters requested that the guerrillas should not contact individual village leaders during their troop movement. The Communists agreed to contact through the three sub-teams.

15. The garrison headquarters agreed to provide a telegraph set that could be used by the three parties in Field Team No. 8. They also agreed not to cause undue delay in handling the telegrams sent by the guerrillas.

16. The garrison headquarters requested the guerrillas not to engage in any other activities on the beach in Shayuchong while waiting to embark.

17. The garrison headquarters requested that, when their own survey team moved into the areas occupied by the guerrillas, the guerrillas should co-operate.

18. The Communists agreed to provide maps to the garrison headquarters to show details of their troop concentrations so that the garrison headquarters could issue ceasefire orders in such areas.

19. The garrison headquarters agreed not to take action against the guerrillas who were assembling from the sea in Daya Bay.

20. The garrison headquarters agreed to facilitate the guerrillas' movement when they travelled to Guangzhou and Hong Kong to obtain supplies for their sea journey.

21. The garrison headquarters agreed to issue ceasefire orders once the three sub-teams commenced their movement.

22. The garrison headquarters agreed to send thirty soldiers to accompany each sub-team.

23. The garrison headquarters agreed to send unarmed soldiers to ensure no telegraphic wires were tampered with during the concentration movement.

24. The guerrillas requested that their soldiers be provided with inoculation by the three sub-teams, and inoculation certificates be provided by the government; the garrison headquarters agreed.

In the eyes of the Communists, this was an unequal and one-sided agreement that put their armed forces to be evacuated in a dangerous position. However, to show their sincerity in reaching a peaceful solution, they signed the agreement. Fang Fang was so worried that he telegraphed Zhou Enlai and General Ye Jianying in Beijing about some of the "unreasonable terms" such as condition No. 18. As the Communist side was keen to arrive at an early settlement, Fang was instructed to stick to and implement the terms of the agreement. In the meantime, the Communist cadres based in Shanghai and Nanjing, through their representatives in Guangzhou, transmitted funds to the column's soldiers who were hiding in the East River area, to relieve them from their hardship.

Even after the agreement was signed, there were obstacles, some of which were petty and could easily have been resolved if there had been trust on both sides. For example, as late as 29 April, General Huang Weiqin raised a minor issue with the team that "some villagers" objected "to the passing of Communist evacuees through their villages". As for charges of ceasefire violations filed against the Communists, General Fang always refused to deal with the issue at the local level through Field Team No. 8 or through the sub-teams assigned for this purpose. Instead, he continued to propose that the complaints be lodged with the main Mediation and Implementation Committee based in Beijing. Finally, on 21 May, an additional three-point agreement was reached. The details were:

1.  Field Team No. 8 would send three sub-teams to areas north and south of the East River and areas in north Guangdong to assist the East River Column in implementing its evacuation details. Again, the KMT objected to the use of the term "East River Column" in the agreement. It had to be amended to read "Guangdong Chinese Communist Armed Forces".

2.  The Guangzhou Garrison Headquarters would pay 373 million yuan to assist the column's demobilized soldiers, and 100 million would be advanced to them on 22 May, the balance to be paid in full when the evacuation and repatriation party finally arrived at the repatriation point.

3.  Demobilization certificates would be issued to those who were demobilized and the government would guarantee their safety.

Finally, the Communist representatives hosted a cocktail reception in Guangzhou for their government counterparts, Colonel Miller, community leaders and media representatives, on 12 May, when the agreement was signed. At the reception, in response to the Communists' and the media's complaints that the guerrillas were being attacked, General Wang Heng, from the government side, openly declared that "local vendettas and isolated attacks on the guerrillas were beyond the responsibility and the reach of the Central Government".

On 25 May, the three sub-teams then set out from Guangzhou to the three locations: north of the East River, south of the East River and north Guangdong near Qujiang. The representatives from Field Team No. 8 — Major General Wang Heng, from the Guangzhou Garrison Headquarters, General Fang Fang, from the East River Column, and Colonel Paul Miller — then travelled to Hong Kong on 22 June, in anticipation of their travel to Shayuchong to attend a final meeting at the departure site of repatriation.

The authorities in Hong Kong played only a passive role throughout the negotiations but maintained intense interest. The British Consul General in Guangzhou kept the commander-in-chief of the British forces in Hong Kong,

General Francis Festing, informed throughout, and, towards the end of the negotiation, Francis Festing sent his aide, Colonel Stables, to the headquarters of Field Team No. 8 in Guangzhou as an observer.[27] On the day of the actual repatriation, the Royal Navy sent two junior officers to be observers on the beach of Shayuchong [28]

But there were still other obstacles. One of them was the delay in waiting for the arrival of the three sub-teams, each headed by an American officer and assisted by six US soldiers. In the chaotic situation right after the war, assembling American soldiers from Shanghai and other cities in north China to form the three sub-teams, who had to depend on others for the availability of passages on military aircraft, was by no means an easy task. Finally, three sub-teams, headed by Lieutenant P. Bailey (Sub-Teams A and B), Lieutenant Nelson (Sub-Team C) and Lieutenant A. M. Jones (Sub-Team D) arrived in Guangzhou via Hong Kong in late May. Together with the US soldiers and thirty central government military police, the function of these sub-teams was to assist the various guerrilla units, scattered virtually all over Guangdong, to march to various "assembly points" before they embarked at Shayuchong in the Dapeng Peninsula. Another important function was to enforce the terms of the twenty-four-point agreement. Of most importance, the guerrillas, now totally disarmed, had to rely on these American soldiers for their protection. Despite the signing of the agreement and the repeated assurances of their safety given by Zhang Fakui, the guerrillas had been attacked by government soldiers and local militia. On 25 May, the sub-team headed by Lieutenant Bailey and Zeng Sheng from the East River Column arrived in Huizhou from south of the East River, but the local KMT commander imposed an embargo to prevent them from contacting the guerrillas in the area who were trying to go to the assembly point near Dapeng Bay. After a series of heated debates, the guerrillas managed to arrive at the assembly point only on 11 June.

The group of guerrillas who had the most difficulty in meeting the target of arriving in Dapeng Bay within one month were those dispersed in various counties in north Guangdong, like Nanxiong, Lianping and Yingde. The distance was relatively long over difficult terrain, and the means of transport were rudimentary. While they were travelling to Nanxiong on 18 May, they were ambushed by KMT soldiers. During a short battle, the famous and courageous Liu Jinjin (Darkie Liu) and his political commissar, Su Guang, were killed.

Again, on 13 June, the KMT assigned two battalions to ambush the guerrillas in Yingde County who were travelling from north Guangdong. Three assassins were sent ahead of the main forces to kill the commanding officer of the guerrillas. Fortunately for the guerrillas, the three were caught on the spot before they could take any action. The three of them were then handed over to the American officer of the sub-team.

As late as 19 June, two companies of the KMT 7th Battalion Local Militia launched an attack in Huiyang County against the guerrillas who were travelling from east of the East River area. However, the guerrillas were prepared and put up a stiff fight. As a result, about 300 KMT soldiers were killed, and the deputy commander of the company was captured. Again, the commander and the captured weapons were handed over to the American officers of Field Team No. 8.

In keeping with the Hong Kong government's attitude of benevolent neutrality, General Francis Festing, commander of British forces in Hong Kong, met with all the members of the team and provided them with a marine launch to travel to their destination, accompanied by his aide-de-camp, Colonel Stables.[29] On 24 June, a group of 3,174 soldiers and cadres from various towns and counties finally arrived. Originally, the three landing craft from the US Navy that sailed from Shanghai were to arrive in Shayuchong on 25 June, and the entire repatriation party would depart on the following day. A severe tropical storm was imminent, so Colonel Miller announced that the landing craft would be arriving a few days later. The information was regarded by the Guangzhou Garrison Headquarters as a piece of unexpected good news, because it provided a golden opportunity to eliminate the column's entire armed force. Fortunately for the column, three CCP spies had infiltrated the operations department at the garrison headquarters. The elimination plan was immediately passed by a member of the Chinese Democratic Union, Sa Kongliao, to Lin Ping and Fang Fang in Hong Kong. Fang then lodged a complaint with the Mediation Commission in Beijing. At the same time Fang lodged a similar complaint with Colonel Miller of Field Team No. 8. The news was also publicized in the media in Hong Kong. The repatriation party then devised a route of dispersal and retreat should they be attacked in the place of their assembly.

Even as late as 29 June, when the guerrilla soldiers were due to embark on the beach of Shayuchong, General Wei of the KMT (who was based in Huizhou) threw a bombshell at the team by making allegations of "Communist pillaging in the area" and requesting that Zeng Sheng be detained. General Fang remained defiant by walking out of the meeting and declared they should "come and get him".

Despite repeated ceasefire violations committed by both sides after the signing of the twenty-four-point agreement, over 2,400 guerrillas and some female cadres of the East River Column out of the 3,174 actually arrived at the point of embarkation area of Shayuchong and achieved their mission of "victorious repatriation" on 29 June 1946. As the area was full of KMT soldiers, six US officers who worked in the three sub-teams had to collect the widely scattered small guerrilla units at various assembly points and provide an escort to some of the guerrillas who had to go on a ten-day trek to the embarkation point on the beach north of Bias Bay.

Three landing craft (numbers 585, 589 and 1026) from Task Force 78 (Amphibious Group 3), assigned by the commander of the US 7th Fleet, were provided for the journey. To offer additional protection, USS *George* provided convoy protection from the point of embarkation to the final destination in Shandong.[30] The distrust between the two sides was so intense that, up to the actual day of embarkation, the KMT repeatedly placed obstacles in the process of negotiation and regrouping. When the actual negotiations were concluded and members of Field Team No. 8 left Guangzhou for Shayuchong via Hong Kong on 15 June 1946, the KMT garrison was preparing a plan to ambush the guerrillas while they marched from the East River area to Shayuchong. Again, Fang Fang had to lodge a protest in Guangzhou and through the media in Hong Kong. Fang decided that, if the worst happened, the guerrillas would be ordered to march back to their original areas of operation. As a precaution, Zeng Sheng ordered the column's Marine Detachment to mobilize a fleet of about 300 small boats to stand by near Shayuchong. Should the repatriation party be ambushed, the entire group would evacuate south into Hong Kong's territorial waters. In fact, Zeng Sheng had liaised and made such an arrangement with the British military authorities in Hong Kong beforehand.[31]

At the last minute, just half an hour before embarkation, a KMT army officer demanded the full details of all the evacuees' names that were to be checked against a list in his possession. Finally, through Colonel Miller's intervention (who said that this demand was not a requirement detailed under any of the agreements between the two sides), the guerrillas were allowed to embark. Although the US military had been providing equipment and material to the KMT to help them in the impending civil war, Colonel Miller and his colleagues remained fair and neutral in their work in the mediation. They earned the respect and admiration of General Zeng Sheng, who called Miller "an Ambassador of Peace".[32]

Originally, both sides had agreed that only 2,400 persons, including 300 women, were to be evacuated. However, the actual number that embarked on this long sea journey was 2,583. Colonel R. Dixon, who was in charge of the actual transport, agreed that, as long as the three landing craft could accommodate them, he could raise the original figure. Some of the soldiers who initially were unprepared to be demobilized decided to join the repatriation at the last minute. Among this group were eighty-nine soldiers from the Pearl River Brigade, forty-seven from the Hanjiang Brigade, twenty-three from a south Guangdong group and one from Guangxi. To be fully prepared for the worst, an ad hoc committee of the cadres from the top command of the Communist guerrillas in Guangdong was formed to supervise the evacuation and boarding. Zeng Sheng and Liu Tianfu were assigned to supervise boat no. 585, Luo Fanqun and Xie Liquan were responsible for boat no. 589, and Wang Zuorao and Yang Kanghua were to look after boat no. 1026. Before the three landing craft were ordered to set sail, all heavy weapons such as rifles and sub-machine guns were handed over to the US soldiers to store in the ship's hull for safekeeping throughout the sea voyage. As a precaution, some of the fitter soldiers were directed to hide their pistols. They were also ordered to stand by the navigation room daily. Senior cadres told them that once they were ambushed by "the enemy"; their immediate duty was to seize the weapons in the hulls to defend the repatriation party.[33]

## The Guerrillas Who Stayed in Hong Kong

General Zeng Sheng, Wang Zuorao, Lin Jiangyun and Yang Kanghua joined the repatriation party to Shandong. Initially, Fang Fang and Lin Ping were supposed to join the repatriation party, but at the last minute, the Central Committee of the CCP decided that both should stay behind in Hong Kong. Early on the morning of 30 June 1946, some of the East River Column's hardcore soldiers left their area of operation around Huizhou, Dongguan and Shataukok. Those being demobilized were provided with money and demobilization certificates, which enabled them to return to their respective hometowns.[34] It was obvious that the CCP had made a conscious decision to save their most battle-hardened soldiers for future deployment; of the 3,174 soldiers, cadres and women who assembled in Shayuchong, only 2,583 actually joined the repatriation party. Of this number, 859 were political commissars above the company level, from which 537 were cadres at battalion and regiment levels. Experienced cadres who once dealt with propaganda and indoctrination work outside their regular full-time military duties came to 143. Staff with technical knowledge and armament skills came to 215. Most of the 413 women in the party had training in medical duties and intelligence. It was obvious that experienced combatants who were repatriated were in the minority.[35]

The Communists who stayed behind quickly moved into their respective areas of expertise. Qiao Guanhua, Huang Zuomei [36] and Tan Gan, who had extensive Hong Kong experience, set up the Hong Kong Branch of the Xinhua News Agency and Dade College in Tuen Mun, New Territories, in October 1946.[37] The college was located in a rather handsome weekend house, originally built and owned by General Cai Tingkai, the hero of the 19th Route Army who resisted the Japanese in Shanghai in 1932. General Cai came to live in Hong Kong in 1936 and personally supervised the building work. In October 1946, Zhou Enlai, who was involved in the negotiations with the KMT in Nanjing, instructed Lian Guan and Lin Ping, both senior cadres of the South China Bureau of the CCP, that "the Party needed a base in Hong Kong to accommodate some 'democratic personnel' and cultural workers who were to be evacuated to Hong Kong from Nanjing, as the civil war was imminent". Zhou's directive to Lian Guan was that they "should be prepared to go through ten years of bitter struggle in the south. Therefore you should strengthen the underground party's work in the city."[38]

The man who provided the impetus for establishing the college was Professor Chen Qiyuan, former president of National University in Guangzhou before the war. Chen was not a Communist but belonged to the left-wing faction of the KMT. He had been involved in the building of Sun Yat-sen University in Guangzhou in the 1920s and had met a veteran leader of the Communist Party, Dong Biwu, who attended the signing ceremony of the United Nations Charter in San Francisco in 1945. Dong told him that the Communist Party would like to start a school in Hong Kong. When Chen arrived in Hong Kong, he contacted Lin Ping, who confirmed the party's intention. In the meantime, Lin Ping had discovered that left-wing faction members of the KMT also had the intention of launching a school, so it seemed a marriage of convenience. Through the help of General Cai, Li Jishen and He Xiangning, who were not Communist Party members, a college was built. One month prior to the actual opening of the college, it ran an enrolment advertisement in the media and attracted 100 regular students. Students came from three main sources: the KMT-occupied areas (about seventy percent); various Communist guerrilla cadres in Guangdong; and cadres from Communist parties in Southeast Asia. Regular students from Hong Kong looking for genuine post-secondary training were in the minority. As the campus had limited space, the college rented a nearby barn. Here, intensive training in Marxist-Lenin ideology was provided to Guangdong guerrilla cadres before they were sent to join the main body of the East River Column, who were forming the Guangdong and Guangxi Column as the vanguard of the Fourth Field Army in early 1947. During the two and a half years of the college's existence, over 100 such cadres were trained and sent north.[39] Many Communist leaders who were living in Hong Kong gave occasional lectures there, including Guo Moruo, Qiao Guanhua, Mao Dun and the famous novelist Cao Yu. But the Hong Kong government discovered the real nature of the college, a training centre for Communist cadres and sympathizers. So on 23 October 1949, the Hong Kong government cancelled the registration of the college. The governor, Sir Alexander Grantham, declared "there was ample evidence that the College was pursuing political activities that were inconsistent with Hong Kong's security interests". During the short period of its existence, it trained over 800 cadres for different countries.[40]

It was well known that the college was the training ground not only for potential political cadres in the future People's Republic of China but also for those in Communist movements in Southeast Asia.[41] Most of the East River Column cadres who did not join the repatriation to Yantai, Shandong, in June 1946 also enrolled as students, pending the rallying call from General Zeng Sheng. When the Nationalist-Communist civil war broke out in earnest, about 200 such students who were East River Column veterans went north and joined the Guangdong and Guangxi Column.[42] It was estimated by a village representative in Sai Kung, New Territories, that over 200 able-bodied young men from Sai Kung alone answered Zeng's call and went north to join the Guangdong and Guangxi Column in 1947.

Other guerrillas who stayed in Hong Kong launched another project, a newspaper, *Zheng Bao*, in November 1945. It was quite an achievement, considering that it was barely three months after the Japanese surrendered to the Allies. Due to financial constraints, this newspaper could only appear in tabloid form. On 4 January 1946, Rao Zhangfeng, Yang Qi and Lin Ping relaunched *Hua Shang Bao* that had ceased publication during the war years. In this project, Yang and Lin had extensive help and co-operation from members of the China Democratic Union and the Revolutionary Committee of the KMT, who were not Communists but were mostly from the anti-KMT elements.[43] The newspaper was popular with the Chinese population in Hong Kong, as it conveyed the views of not only the Communist Party but also that of the neutral elements. The other Chinese newspapers, which had to rely on information from China supplied by the KMT regime in Chongqing, were heavily censored. Unexpectedly and unwittingly, *Hua Shang Bao* and another Communist newspaper in Hong Kong provided employment for some of the Little Devils of the East River Column. This was due to the fact that typesetters and printing room technicians all belonged to a trade union controlled by the local branch of the KMT. Subsequently, they were all dismissed from their jobs in 1947, when twenty of the Little Devils had learned the skill from some old and experienced technicians who previously worked for *Xinhua Ribao* in Chongqing.[44] *Xinhua Ribao* was a Communist Party newspaper published in Chongqing throughout the war.

About the same time, Rao Zhangfeng was given the job of publishing propaganda materials and organizing United Front activities. In late 1946, the famous novelist Xia Yan moved to Singapore to set up *Huaqiao Ribao* there and to mobilize support from the overseas Chinese. Rao was then sent by the party to visit various cities in peninsular Malaya to do the same kind of work. He stayed on until late 1947, when he returned to Hong Kong to assist Zhang Hanfu in running *Hua Shang Bao*. To maintain a façade of the United Front policy, a non-Communist veteran newspaper publisher, Liu Simu, was appointed chief editor and Liao Mosha deputy editor. Sa Kongliao, a Communist sympathizer, also worked for the newspaper. In February 1948, Liao Mosha was sent to Singapore to set up the Singapore Branch of the Xinhua News Agency. It was through his contacts and United Front work that he got to know many overseas Chinese who had parents or descendants in Guangdong and Fujian.

Fang Fang was appointed to the important post of secretary general of the Hong Kong Sub-Bureau of the Central Committee of the Communist Party. He directed guerrilla activities in Guangdong, Guangxi and Jiangxi from Hong Kong during the civil war until 1949.[45]

During my many hours of interviews with some of the surviving veterans of the column who remained in Hong Kong after repatriation in June 1946, I posed the question of whether the local party cell in Hong Kong had offered help and training to other Communist comrades in Asia, particularly those from the Malaya Communist Party. Without exception, the East River Column veterans all toed the so-called party line that Mao taught them: "revolution could not be exported". Contrary views were expressed by relatively junior party cadres.

A cadre who had done quite a bit of research and writing about the history of the East River Column himself, but for obvious reasons chose to remain anonymous, confirmed that, as early as mid-1946, a political commissar from the East River Column, Xu Shi, moved from Guangxi to northern Vietnam where he became one of Ho Chi Minh's political commissars at regimental level. Xu assisted Ho in running political indoctrination classes for Vietminh soldiers. After the liberation of Guangdong in 1949, Xu held the important post of director of the Xinhua News Agency in Guangdong. Yuan Geng, who played an important part in liaison work with the military authorities in Hong Kong from 1945 to 1946, also travelled to northern Vietnam in late 1946. Yuan was responsible for training many Vietminh soldiers in artillery. In June 1946, after the main body of the East River Column was repatriated, Rao Zhangfeng also sent one of the journalists, Liang Jia, to Hanoi. He had worked for *Qianjin Bao* of the East River Column and, after VJ Day, *Hua Shang Bao* in Hong Kong. Liang adopted the cover of an overseas correspondent for the newspaper, but his duties, as directed by the party, were twofold. Firstly, he was to mobilize the Vietnamese Chinese to support the CCP in the impending civil war, and, secondly, as *Hua Shang Bao* was operating under stringent financial conditions, he was to raise funds from the overseas Chinese. He stayed in Hanoi until September 1947, when he returned through the Vietnamese border to join the Communist guerrillas in Guangxi.

In addition to China's offering personnel and weapons to Vietnam, it is certain that the CCP cell in Hong Kong actually offered ideological support and, in some cases, training to cadres in other Southeast Asian parties. A recently published memoir by Chin Peng, the long-serving secretary general of the Malaya Communist Party, revealed that Chin had actually travelled from Bangkok to Hong Kong in June 1946, staying in Hong Kong for five weeks. He was on a mission to contact his comrades in "Siam, Indo-China and China" to brief them on the betrayal by the former secretary general, Lai Teck. Chin admitted he had extensive meetings with the Chinese Communists at the newspaper *Hua Shang Bao*. Chin's contact even provided the detail that Lai Teck had "submitted a report to the Chinese Communist Party through Hong Kong on his impending travel plans". One senior cadre of the column, who is still around and wants to remain anonymous, admitted that the person whom Chin Peng and Lai Teck contacted and by whom they were briefed was none other than Li Qixin, who was then in charge of the Liaison Unit of the Communist Party Hong Kong Work Committee.

Li had been a seaman who went to Singapore and Malaya in the early 1930s. The Malaya and Indonesia Communist parties originally had been the South

Sea Branch of the CCP which was formed as early as 1925. By 1930, a separate Malayan Communist Party had been formed, and Li was involved mostly in the work of fomenting disputes in the industries and public utilities. Around June 1934, when Li was the secretary general of the Malaya Communist Party, he was arrested by the Singapore colonial government. After being detained for four years, he was deported to China. He re-emerged as one of the founders of the Thailand Communist Party during the war years. There is evidence that it was he who blew the cover of Lai Teck as a turncoat after the war. Li served for about three years as deputy director of the Xinhua News Agency in the 1980s. At the age of almost ninety, he still held the important post of secretary general of the Liaison Department of the Central Committee of the CCP in Beijing.

There is also evidence that representatives of the Malaya Communist Party contacted Fang Fang in Hong Kong in 1947, when he advised the Malaya Communist Party that they could expect no assistance from the CCP and that a united front should be organized. Fang also advised that, while the Labour Party was in power in Britain, the Malaya Communist Party should work for self-government in Malaya by constitutional means, always ensuring that the Chinese members dominated the party. This is highly plausible, as the party in China and Hong Kong had too many pressing issues to deal with on the eve of a full-blown civil war, despite the fact that the Malaya Communist Party was initially an overseas branch of the party in China.[46]

# 7 After the Revolution:
## The Fate of the East River Column

## The "Guangdong Problem": Friction with the Authorities and the Crackdown on "Localism", 1952–53

On 1 October 1949, when the People's Republic of China was established after three years of civil war, Guangzhou had to wait for two more weeks before it was liberated. Shortly after the province's liberation, some unusual difficulties not found in other provinces were encountered. People in Guangdong and, for that matter, Guangxi, spoke a totally different dialect from that of the rest of the country. In Guangdong, after the first and second Opium Wars, quite a few of the big cities had come under foreign influence.

In October 1949, Zeng Sheng and his comrades in the East River Column found themselves back in Guangdong at the head of the triumphant Communist forces. Almost immediately, however, they were in conflict with the central party leadership in Beijing; Guangdong had a strong tradition of local independence going right back to the early twentieth century, which had been strengthened by the guerrilla activities that took place in the province from the late 1920s.

If one looks at the history of China since the 1911 Revolution, one will see that some of the southern provinces such as Guangdong, Guangxi and Fujian were a source of trouble and defiance to the central government in the north. Because of a strong tradition of independent thinking and of not accepting the dictates of rulers from the far north, the people of Guangdong and Fujian, particularly the Hakka, have always had closer links with the outside world than have most of their compatriots in other provinces. On a number of occasions when there was a political turmoil, these three provinces would declare a form of de facto "alliance and independence". For example, when Yuan Shikai declared himself the emperor of China in December 1915, Guangdong, together with a few other provinces, declared independence. Also, when General Zhang Fakui was head of the Military Commission of the Guangzhou National Government in 1931, Zhang teamed up with the warlords in Guangxi and declared de facto independence from the central government, refusing to take any orders from Generalissimo Chiang Kai-shek. Indeed, earlier, during the latter part of the Qing Dynasty, when the Boxer Rebellion broke out in Tianjin and Beijing in 1900, even a minister as senior as Li Hongzhang toyed with the idea of declaring Guangdong and Guangxi independent.

Compared with other liberated areas, Guangdong Province, including Guangzhou, Shantou, and other parts like Hainan Island, had a strong guerrilla presence for a long time before the Second World War. On Hainan Island, the guerrilla movement had been active, without any outside support, from as early as the late 1920s. For guerrillas to be successful, they had to rely on support from the local populace; hence, guerrilla life inevitably would breed "localism". Another important factor was physical distance, as Guangdong is far from Nanjing, the capital during the KMT regime, and even farther from Beijing, the capital since the founding of the People's Republic in October 1949. It is also separated by high mountains. Therefore, localism in Guangdong, which was a force to be reckoned with during KMT rule, did not vanish with the advent of the Communist victory. Local Guangdong cadres were not ready to be submissive to the northerners, and leaders sent down from the capital in the north were equally alert to the sentiments of the Guangdong cadres.

Initially, the battle over Guangdong's localism was not waged with the capital but with the authorities in the Central South Bureau of the CCP based in Wuhan. However, the cadres in this bureau worked under the direct command of the authorities in Beijing.

To begin with, right after the province's liberation, there were four different groups of cadres appointed to various posts in Guangdong. There were the Southbound Work Team and regular People's Liberation Army soldiers from the north, the various guerrilla forces in Guangdong, the underground party and Youth League members from the Guangzhou and Hong Kong areas, and the former KMT officials who remained in their jobs. Within these groups there existed vast differences both in training and in experience during the war years. Most important of all was the cultural gulf, since the Guangdong cadres and the Guangdong guerrillas in particular were far closer to the local people than any of the northerners could possibly be.[1] These differences sowed the seeds of conflict right from the start.

In anticipation of the total liberation of Guangdong, a conference was held on 11–24 September in Ganzhou, Jiangxi. The aim of the conference was to map out ways to administer the cities following the liberation of the province. General Ye Jianying attended with over 200 Guangdong cadres. Since the days of Jinggangshan, Ye had remained loyal to Mao. Therefore he was trusted by Mao with the important mission of liberating Guangdong Province and Hainan Island.

Others who attended were northerners from the Second and Fourth Field Armies and other non-Guangdong cadres from the Central South Bureau of the CCP. Most of the sessions were convened by Ye himself. He emphasized repeatedly the importance of "unity". He said that the Central Committee of the CCP from Beijing ordered that all parties coming into Guangdong "should co-operate and unite in their work". He added, "Now that cadres from all directions are coming together, there are outside cadres and local cadres, new cadres and old cadres, senior cadres and junior cadres, party members and non-party members and cadres from the military and local cadres, we have to pay particular attention to the importance of unity." He then appealed to both the southbound cadres and the local cadres to respect and learn from each other. He said that he particularly trusted Fang Fang, as Fang had been carrying on the "struggle" in Guangdong for a long time. Hence, Fang was given the important task of "formulating" and proposing the administrative and organization structure of the party, the military regional command and the government. Another important duty assigned to Fang was the allocation of equipment and resources to the various government departments.[2]

In two sessions on 21 and 24 September, convened by Ye and held specially for senior cadres, Fang Fang spoke on the "people's armed forces" that had struggled against the enemy for the past three years, the "special" and "different" conditions, and the "customs" in Guangdong and its people. He strongly emphasized that Guangdong people were not "anti-outsiders", by pointing out that there were non-Guangdong people such as General Nie Rongzhen and Li Fuchun, who previously had worked in Guangdong. Nie Rongzhen was one of 1,600 Chinese students who went to France in 1919. He joined the Communist Party in 1923, returned to China in 1925 and took part in the Nanchang Uprising on 1 August 1927. After the failure of the uprising, he worked underground in Guangdong and Hong Kong, before he made his way to join the Chinese Soviet Government in Ruijin, Jiangxi. Like Nie, Li Fuchun went to France in 1919. He was one of the founders of the French branch of the CCP. He returned to China in 1925 and did underground work in Guangdong before he joined the Long March. Additionally Li Bin, commander of the Red Army 46th Regiment, was from Hunan, and Lin Ping was from Jiangxi. Both had led "revolutionary forces in Guangdong before without a problem".

Speaking on the current situation in Guangdong, Fang said most of the villages had been liberated. The total liberated population came to 13.5 million, which was about forty percent of the entire province. Regarding the current strength of guerrilla soldiers, he said that the Guangdong/Jiangxi/Hunan Column had 33,000 soldiers, the Fujian/Guangdong Column had 12,700, the Guangdong/Guangxi Column had over 8,000, the Qiongya Column in Hainan Island had 1,500 to 2000, the Central Guangdong Column had 7,000 and the West River Brigade had 6,000 — a total of about 68,700 soldiers.

He also pointed out that "Guangdong people are by nature brave, adventurous, warm, etc." and "Guangdong people are cleaner, in the sense that they take baths daily, which is different from the northerners' habits". He further mentioned that "As Guangdong was invaded by imperialists earlier than other provinces, there are churches and temples everywhere. Social contact between men and women is more free and liberal."

Regarding armed struggles, Fang said there had been peasant movements and guerrilla groups in the province in such places as Dongjiang, Hanjiang, Nanlu, Hainan Island and Beijiang, as early as 1927. Peasant training schools had also been set up in such places. In the early years of the "revolution", there were local "soviet governments" in places such as Hailufeng and Hainan Island. When the Central Committee of the CCP called a meeting in Ruijin, Jiangxi, in 1934, the East River Column actually had sent representatives to the meeting. "It was no exaggeration to say that armed struggle was never stopped from the late 1920s until Liberation in 1949. Hence overall, the masses have been under the party's education all along." In concluding his speech, Fang made one unusual remark. He said, "Guangdong people in general respect Sun Yat-sen highly." He conceded that in Guangdong's "armed struggle in the past, recruitment for party members was done badly". Hence, in the whole province, there were only 30,000 party members, most of whom had been recruited from the "intelligentsia and peasants with very few from industrial workers". One-third of this total was from Hainan Island.[3]

Ye Jianying followed by speaking on the special conditions of overseas Chinese (*huaqiao*). He said, "Guangdong people have been subjected to oppression by foreigners very early. Hence, poverty has driven many of them to seek better lives overseas, for example in Vietnam, Siam, Burma, Malaya, Australia, Europe and North America." He added, "There are about 11 million overseas Chinese all over the world. Out of this total, between 6 and 7 million of them are of Guangdong origin, i.e. one out of five people in Guangdong has overseas connections." Ye said, "These overseas Chinese had been a source of great help to Sun Yat-sen when he was engaged in his revolutionary activities." He also pointed out that there had been revolutionary bases and revolutionary leaders such as Su Zhaozheng, Deng Fa, Ye Ting and Peng Pai in Guangdong from very early on. "These few revolutionary leaders have led workers in Guangdong in waging anti-imperialist and anti-feudalist struggles in the past. In fact some of them set up the famous Guangzhou Commune." Ye mentioned further "The party in Guangdong has led massive peasant movements before. Land reform is nothing new. The big one was led by Comrade Peng Pai in his famous Hailufeng Soviet." In conclusion, Ye appealed to the southbound cadres and the Guangdong cadres "to learn from one another and respect one another". He emphasized that "the Central Committee of the Party ordered us time and again to pay particular attention to the importance of unity".[4]

It is difficult to know whether the two men were speaking in good faith or were just boasting about the historical revolutionary credentials of the Guangdong people. But with the benefit of hindsight, such remarks must have sounded repulsive and unpleasant to the ears of cadres and soldiers from the north. As Mao's fame and popularity was then at its zenith, the remark about Sun Yat-sen was particularly unwise. The comment about Peng Pai's work with the peasant movement starting as early as January 1923 and preceding that of Mao was also politically insensitive. In parts of Guangdong, Peng Pai was worshipped and respected as a martyr and a great revolutionary leader. The comments about the strength of the guerrilla soldiers almost certainly caused resentment from the southbound cadres, as they maintained that the liberation of the province had been achieved primarily by the "main army", and that the guerrillas had only played a subsidiary role of co-ordination with the main army.[5]

While the Southbound Work Team members came mostly from a better educated background and spoke *Putonghua*, the Guangdong guerrillas, except for a minority of top cadres such as Zeng Sheng, Rao Zhangfeng and Lin Ping, were nearly all relatively uneducated peasants, fishermen, seafarers and workers, with only a few years of schooling. Zeng, Rao and Lin Ping all had better education and were able to speak the Hakka dialect, Cantonese and *Putonghua*. Zeng, who had lived in Australia and worked as a seaman overseas, could mingle with senior cadres as well as the rank-and-file Hakka soldiers, being a Hakka himself. Rao was also a Hakka who had laboured among peasants and workers when he was a journalist in Guangdong before 1949. The overwhelming majority of the leaders and rank and file of the East River Column were members of the tough and independent-minded Hakka community. Veteran guerrillas who fought for years without direction and assistance from the Central Committee of the CCP in Ruijin and subsequently in Yan'an found it difficult to submit themselves to the young and better educated cadres from the north. As some of the Guangdong cadres put it, these northerners had not gone through hard struggles but came to their jobs by merely "riding down on the train". The northerners were told early on by their superiors in Beijing to avoid "commandism" and to co-operate with the local cadres. Initially, many Guangdong officials were appointed to top positions in the province after the liberation of Guangzhou. At the second session of the meeting of the Central People's Government held in Beijing on 19 October 1949, Ye Jianying was appointed chairman of the Guangdong Provincial People's Government and first party secretary. Fang Fang, Gu Dacun and Li Zhangda were vice-chairmen. Fang Fang was the third secretary of the South China Sub-Bureau and held the important post of director of the Land Reform Committee. Rao Zhangfeng, who had been responsible for propaganda work at the East River Column's headquarters during the war years, was appointed publisher of *Nanfang Ribao* of the United Front Department of Guangzhou, secretary general of the Guangdong People's

Congress and vice-chairman of the province's Political Consultative Conference. Deng Wenzhao was appointed deputy director of the Department of Commerce. Obviously, this was done to assure non-Communist members — of these bodies — and the people of Hong Kong and Macao that the party was sincere in its United Front policy (first launched by the CCP in 1924). The United Front meant to "unite all forces that can be united with in order to wage a common struggle against the enemy and to win in revolution and construction". In 1949, the policy was mainly aimed at the national bourgeoisie class. The political policy was to continue in coalition with this class. The economic policy was the implementation of peaceful redemption of assets of the state capitalists. Deng was also appointed deputy provincial governor. Ye and Zhang were sent to Guangdong by the Central Committee of the CCP. While they shared the same linguistic background as the Guangdong guerrillas, they had no direct link with them. Gu had been one of the leaders of the guerrillas at a very early stage, but when he was sent to Guangdong in 1949 at the time of Liberation, he actually was the incumbent director of transport in the north-east, the so-called "old liberated area".

Furthermore, in the eyes of the northerners, overemphasis on local conditions was a hindrance in implementing many of the tasks that had been given by the top leadership in Beijing through the South Bureau of the CCP based in Wuhan.

In little more than a year after Liberation, the simmering conflict between the Guangdong cadres and the non-Guangdong cadres came to a head over the major issue of land reform. The Land Reform Committee was established with the approval of the South China Sub-Bureau of the CCP in October 1950. Fang Fang was appointed director of the committee. The First Guangdong Provincial Conference of representatives from all circles was held in Guangzhou from 5 to 16 October. The conference was attended not only by Communist cadres but also by entrepreneurs who had stayed in the province when the People's Liberation Army moved in and minor KMT officials who had stayed on in their jobs. Fang Fang, as chairman of the conference, spoke at length on this subject. He stated that there should be a plan for "orderly progress" on land reform and the necessity of preserving the economy of the rich peasants. He also paid special attention to the question of dealing with land belonging to overseas Chinese.[6] While Gu Dacun held no formal post on the committee, he took a keen interest in the movement, as he had previous land reform experience in the north-east. He was directed by Ye to help Fang in the land reform work. Initially, he organized a group of 600 cadres to conduct a land reform experiment in Yingde and Taishan. All three senior officials, Ye, Gu and Fang, told their subordinates to pay particular attention to avoid the leftist tendency in their policy and avoid provoking "widespread antagonism". Ye emphasized that the correct policy should "rely on poor peasants, unite the middle peasants and neutralize the rich peasants". Ye also highlighted that "The important point of the movement is to expose the crimes of the landowners' exploitation.

Except for the minority who oppose our policy openly, do not use physical punishment. The aim of the land reform movement is to eliminate landowners as a class and not to eliminate the persons physically." Gu and Fang repeatedly pointed out that they "must not repeat the mistake made by the party in the north-east of physically evicting landowners from their homes and the imposition of hard physical labour".

Ye again emphasized that "there are many overseas Chinese in the province. Trade and commerce are more developed than those in other provinces. Overseas Chinese and national industrial and commercial interests should be protected." Regarding fishermen, Ye said, "Fishermen's interests should be properly reformed and protected and their exploitation by intermediaries should be eliminated." He added, "Small landholding owners who made their living from land rental, professional people, former KMT officials who joined the People's Republic should all be protected." Time and again, Fang Fang considered that there were special conditions in Guangdong, as there were significant numbers of overseas Chinese who owned a few *mu* of land (one-sixth of an acre) to generate income as a means of livelihood. Therefore, such people should not be classified as "landlords" and should not be purged.[7] He set a target of three years, beginning in autumn 1950, to complete the land reform programme. Initially, he launched experiments in the three small counties of Xingning, Longchuan and Jieyang to acquire experience before launching a full-scale programme in the whole province. Rao Zhangfeng, who had ample experience in United Front work among overseas Chinese, took an even softer line: those who had helped the guerrillas in Hong Kong and elsewhere would be protected. He even remarked that "those people who were friends of the Communist Party yesterday should not be treated as enemies today".[8] Fang Fang made the point that there were seven special conditions relevant to the overall land reform situation in Guangdong. They were:

1.  There were large tracts of land held under the name of "clan" and "family" property. Such property was about thirty-three percent of the cultivable land in the province. There were descendants from such clans who actually cultivated the land themselves or relied on the land to generate income to spend on religious activities and on building local schools.
2.  Ten percent of the coastal land was controlled by fragmented and multiple ownership.
3.  Substantial landholdings were owned by overseas Chinese or their descendants, many of whom depended on the income generated by land rental.
4.  The practice of land mortgage was widespread.
5.  The existence of a large number of overseas Chinese and their descendants in the province should be recognized. Most of the poor descendants should be protected.

6. Overall, trade and industry in many cities and towns in the province were well developed. For those landowners who were concurrently owners of industries and businesses in the cities, only their landholdings should be dealt with.

7. There were many "patriotic democratic" people, fishermen and minorities in the province. Also there were plots with special features, such as sandy soil, fish ponds, and orchards. The policy after confiscation of such land is that fragmented plots would be distributed to poor peasants while the larger plots would be jointly cultivated as joint ventures between the government and peasants. Land owned by clans which was used to finance the building of local schools would not be confiscated.

In fact, there had been widespread debate within the party on how to handle land reform in the "later liberated areas" as early as 1949. The *Agrarian Reform Law*, which was promulgated in June 1950, was moderate and reasonable. Article 6 decreed that rich peasants were allowed to retain their property as well as their land. Article 10 decreed that landlords were allowed to retain their land, which they themselves could cultivate. At the second session of the Chinese People's Political Consultative Conference held on 14 June 1950, a major speech was delivered by Liu Shaoqi, who had been a party member since 1921 and had done important work in the KMT-controlled areas in north China in the 1930s. He had become vice-president of the government and vice-chairman of the important Military Commission on the founding of the People's Republic in October 1949. He argued for a milder approach to land reform, stating that during the Chinese Civil War from 1945 to 1949, landlords in the north (or the "old liberated areas") had sided with the enemy and more radical methods had been required to subdue the landlords. In 1950, when most of the country had been liberated, land reform in "later liberated areas" could be achieved with less violence. China required economic development; hence, it was important not to interfere with the contribution of the rich peasants and landlords.[9]

When the broad outlines and guidance had been laid down by the central government, cadres of the South China Sub-Bureau began making plans for land reform in the areas under their jurisdiction. In a keynote speech made at the bureau meeting in September 1950, Li Xuefeng, chairman of the Land Reform Committee, declared that there were disagreements among the cadres on the course that the land reform should take. He stated that, while some of them wanted to take a harsh line and move fast, he and his committee preferred an orderly and non-violent approach. "We must carry on the struggle in accordance with law and reason," he added.

It must be noted that voices demanding a "peaceful land reform" were not restricted to Guangdong alone. Such demands came from cadres in other coastal provinces such as Jiangsu, Zhejiang and Fujian. The main point of their demands was that land reform could be implemented without first staging a class struggle and the liquidation of the landlord class by violent force. Another point was that there was "no feudalism in the south" because the land tenure system in the south was different from that of the north.[10]

Overall, it was the Central-South China Bureau of the CCP, with the approval of the central government, that endorsed this gradual approach. Furthermore, it was the People's Government of Guangdong Province that adopted this policy at its forty-first meeting held on 12 November 1951. Indeed, the decision to complete the land reform was based on a directive issued by the Central Committee of the CCP. Ye actually kept the top leadership in Beijing informed and obtained their approval at every stage of the process.

With the benefit of hindsight, it is easy to understand the reasons for the perceived resistance from the Guangdong cadres. In Guangdong, the fertile areas in the Pearl River Delta were highly commercialized, and land holdings were much smaller than those in the north. Some of the so-called "landlords" usually owned a few *mu* of land, the majority of which was cultivated by the landowners themselves. A significant percentage of such landlords owned their land as a result of inheritance from their ancestors, who had received a share from clan property. The concern of the Guangdong cadres about overseas Chinese was real and justified, as some of the older landowners had bought the land when they returned from overseas and used the property as a "retirement fund".[11] Another important factor was that the various guerrilla columns that once operated in the entire province prior to Liberation had received considerable assistance and support from the local people and, to a large measure, the overseas Chinese. It was unimaginable for leaders such as Fang Fang and Rao Zhangfeng to turn against these people so soon after Liberation.

However, on the outbreak of the Korean War in June 1950, the attention of the top leadership in Beijing began to concentrate on the policy of "Resist US Aggression and Aid Korea". There was tension within and outside the country that caused perceptible changes in the original patient and gradual attitude of the central government towards the land reform movement in newly liberated areas. In fact, there had been simmering disagreements for quite some time between the Central-South Bureau, headed by Lin Biao and Deng Zihui, and the South China Sub-Bureau, headed by Ye Jianying, over the gradual approach. Lin, however, did not dare to bring the disagreement into the open because of Ye's status and prestige.

The gradual build-up of pressure on the Guangdong cadres was so intense that, by spring 1951, Fang Fang said he had realized that "land reform was not simply a division of land but a political struggle" and that Mao "was using land reform as a test to see which cadres had the correct standpoint".[12]

During May and June 1951, when the land reform movement actually commenced in Guangdong, both Ye and Fang repeatedly stopped a number of excessive policies carried out by some cadres. Both of their speeches were carried by *Nanfang Ribao* on 1 July. However, *Changjiang Ribao*, which was the official mouthpiece of the Central South Bureau, published two editorials called "On the Progress of the Guangdong Peasant Movement" and "Study Seriously, Steady Progress: More on the Guangdong Peasant Movement", on 10 and 17 July respectively. Without actually naming Ye and Fang, the two editorials were rebuttals of their policy. The first editorial carried veiled criticisms against Ye by stating, "When the highest leadership in the party issued repeated directives to all cadres to lead the mass movement and to satisfy the masses' demands, there were still people who did not fully realize the importance of peasants in the revolutionary movement in Guangdong. Either their realization and understanding was restricted to a superficial level, or this question was relegated to an unimportant level." The second editorial criticized Ye because he was "not firm enough and in a state of panic in the land reform movement". Ye was so upset on seeing these two editorials that he pulled rank by reminding his critics in the newspaper that he was still the vice-chairman of the Central and Southern Military and Political Committee. He pointed out why "that differences of opinions within the party should be disclosed to the media and that he was not being consulted first".

In late 1951, there was a perceptible change of tone from the Central Committee of the CCP on land reform in the "newly liberated areas". A report stated that the land reform carried out during the civil war was "incomplete". Now that the country was under Communist rule, things were different. The following message was publicized all over the country:

Land reform should be a violent struggle.

A report in *Changjiang Ribao*, dated 4 September 1951, stated that 62,000 party cadres and soldiers had been sent to the countryside in Guangdong to mobilize the peasants. The report said, "The peasants had to be disciplined into discontent and revolt against the landlords." However, almost at the same time, a report submitted to the Central South Bureau described the "difficulty" in "arousing the masses", as many peasants were reluctant to act; in some instances they sympathized with "the persecuted landlords".

Another article in *Changjiang Ribao* on 9 December 1951, stated "Land reform was a violent activity." The article further said, "Land reform is a struggle. It is not a peaceful reform. The land reform must be combined with the campaign for the suppression of counter-revolutionaries and with the nation's support of the Korean War, the 'Resist US Aggression and Aid Korea' policy."

By mid-November 1950, Mao was already showing signs of impatience with the rate of progress and personally intervened. By then, Tao Zhu had caught Mao's attention, particularly because of his harsh and ruthless ways.

Tao, like Mao, was Hunanese. Driven by poverty, he became an apprentice in a timber factory and, in 1926, he enrolled successfully at the Huangpu Military Academy in Guangzhou and took part in the Northern Expedition in 1926. In the same year, he became a member of the CCP. In the eyes of the "Old Revolutionaries", he had impeccable credentials, as he took part in the Nanchang Uprising on 1 August 1927. Subsequently, he worked in the underground party cell in Fujian, where he organized peasant uprisings against landlords. In 1950, he was appointed party secretary of Guangxi Province. Mao personally assigned him to handle "bandit suppression" work. Well known for his harsh and ruthless policy, he reported to Mao that, from November 1950 to mid-January 1951, over 100,000 "bandits" and "counter-revolutionaries" had been executed.[13]

In November 1950, Tao was transferred to Guangdong with the job titles of fourth secretary of the South China Sub-Bureau and second political commissar of the South China Command of the People's Liberation Army. He took the young Zhao Ziyang with him. Zhao was born in a peasant family in Henan, went to primary school and at the age of thirteen, joined the Youth Corps of the CCP. He worked as a junior local party secretary in the Shandong area during the war years. On 1 October 1949, he became the party secretary of Nanyang County, Henan Province. When he was summoned to assist Tao Zhu in Guangdong, he was barely thirty-two years of age. The party in Beijing wanted Tao to replace Fang Fang in running the land reform work. In fact, an enlarged cadre meeting was held in Guangdong from 19 to 25 April 1951. The theme of the meeting was "rely on the main army", i.e. the local organization could be subordinate to those soldiers who came from the north. At the meeting, Fang Fang went through a session of self-criticism and apologized for the errors of many Guangdong cadres who had difficulty overcoming their "guerrilla" attitude. He then appealed to his Guangdong comrades from the guerrilla forces to make a serious effort to rely on the main army.[14]

In order to implement this policy and to push self-criticism down to the basic level, regional meetings in the North River, East River, Pearl River and central Guangdong areas were held with thousands of cadres in attendance. However, the policy was evidently resented and resisted — at least passively. For example, at a North River district meeting, some Guangdong cadres said, "We were told only to rely on the poor peasants. What is this about having to rely on the main army?" They also said, "We are under the leadership of the party. Why must we also have the leadership of the army?" Some cadres at the county level were even reading novels during small group meetings.[15]

An editorial published by *Nanfang Ribao* on 11 May 1951, carried the message that local cadres "should rely on their big brothers from the north". The main criticism from Li Xuefeng, director of the Land Reform Committee of the Central-South China Bureau who penned the editorial, was "Some comrades did not analyze the problems of class. They only emphasized the special conditions of Guangdong, such as the access to the coast, the development of trade and industry and the existence of overseas Chinese." The editorial further stated, "In some of the counties where land reform was carried out, some cadres did not side with the peasants firmly and did not engage in the struggle for the elimination of feudal elements." The main criticism from the Central-South Bureau against the Guangdong cadres was that they were "ideologically impure" as party members. Most of them had numerous overseas connections and had "no previous experience in land reform". Li even compared the Guangdong comrades with some of the Menshevik leaders in the Provisional Government period of March to November 1917 in Russia.

When Gu Dacun arrived in Guangdong soon after its liberation, he was appointed one of the deputy provincial governors, specifically in charge of the day-to-day administration. At the same time, he held the posts of party secretary in the provincial government and the director of civil affairs. The latter post included the duties of politics, urban renewal, social welfare and human resource management. Except for Ye, who was a member of the Central Committee of the CCP, Gu was the only alternate member in Guangdong. He kept with great care copies of various directives from the Central Committee, dating from 1947, that gave all members or alternate members the authority to address the party chairman or any member of the Central Committee on any issue. Therefore, he was quite forthright and outspoken.

Although he was not assigned to deal with land reform, he went to small and poor counties such as Taishan and Yingde where the land reform movement was first launched, to study the real situation. He was alarmed by the leftist tendency of some cadres, and he supported Ye and Fang Fang in the gradual policy in land reform. In direct reference to the harsh policy of the northern cadres, he said, "The Guangdong situation is different. We should not adopt the policy of other provinces. We should restrict the number of executions to the minimum. Even landlords can be reformed. After being reformed, they are a useful labour force." He added, "We are sitting on top of a volcano. Who can tell when it is going to explode if we continue with the present policy?" He was so confident of his position as an alternate member of the Central Committee of the CCP that he openly disagreed with Li Xuefeng's two editorials, despite their reflecting views of the Central-South Bureau and, for that matter, Tao Zhu's personal views. Gu maintained that Ye and Fang's policy of gradually carrying out land reform in three counties first was quite a normal and regular measure.

In April 1952, the South China Sub-Bureau called a larger meeting to discuss the state of land reform work in the province. It was decided that land reform should be given priority over all other duties. Guangdong cadres were told to "depend more on the cadres from the Southbound Work Team". Family backgrounds of all Guangdong cadres who had been doing land reform work were checked. By

May, 6,515 such cadres had been "dealt with". Ultimately, 317 were dismissed from their jobs, while another 405 were detained for further investigations. Fang Fang objected to such accusations, particularly the point about the "impurity" of the Guangdong comrades and their "right-wing" tendency. He maintained that the Guangdong land reform team was moving in the right direction. In fact, one of Fang Fang's main areas of responsibility in the South China Sub-Bureau was the management of human resources, which included the appointment and deployment of cadres. In appointments, he followed Ye's directive that was issued during the Guangzhou conference, before Guangzhou's liberation. Ye's directive was to follow the principle of *wuhu sihai*, i.e. to spread out the appointments among candidates of widely different backgrounds. Appointments to posts above the county level always came after discussions held within the South China Sub-Bureau. There were northern cadres appointed to posts at the provincial level.

In June 1952, Mao finally lost patience and intervened personally by convening a meeting in Beijing to deal exclusively with "the problem in Guangdong". Others who attended the meeting were Zhou Enlai, Bo Yibo, Luo Ruiqing, Deng Zihui, Ye Jianying, Fang Fang and Tao Zhu. Without mincing words, Mao directly condemned Fang and accused him of committing two serious errors: "One is the right-wing tendency in the land reform work. The other is that the Guangdong cadres adopt 'localism' in their attitude." Mao also said, "The entire land reform movement in Guangdong has lost its direction. I want a piece of fast-beat music. But Fang plays a slow-beat piece. There are three slow-moving turtles in the whole country, i.e. Guangdong, Guangxi and Fujian. Now when Guangxi and Fujian have made progress in their work, Guangdong is still crawling slowly." Mao continued, "Out of ten jobs done by you, nine of them are well done. But the one on land reform was not done well. Therefore, you are demoted by one rank."[16] Tao was told to immediately replace Fang in land reform duties and to be in charge of party work in the South China Sub-Bureau. Ye was also criticized for overemphasizing the so-called "special conditions" in the land reform situation of Guangdong. Fang Fang was not allowed to explain or to offer any comment on the accusations levelled against him. In conclusion, Mao also issued a stern warning to Fang Fang, Zeng Sheng and Lin Ping that they "must follow the central government line closely. Otherwise you will not be allowed to stay in Guangdong." Following that meeting, Fang was seen repeatedly asking himself "What have I done wrong?"

But because of Ye's reputation and credentials, even Mao had to tone down his criticism. At a meeting he convened in Zhongnanhai on the "problems in Guangdong" in June 1952, Mao said there was no doubt that there had been localism errors committed by Guangdong cadres, but "Comrade Yc Jianying's work in Guangdong showed actual results and achievements". Mao added, "He is not the leader of the localism gang. We should understand his difficulties and all comrades should learn a lesson from this whole issue so that such mistakes will not be repeated." Mao further said, "Despite this, Comrade Ye went through a session of self-criticism and took full responsibility himself. It showed that he is a magnanimous man and takes his responsibilities seriously."[17]

With a full mandate from the highest authority in Beijing, Tao Zhu pushed through the land reform with full vigour. After this meeting, he reportedly deployed fifty percent of all the cadres in Guangdong to the work of land reform.[18] Land reform was immediately extended from three to eleven counties. Tao then called a meeting of the South China Sub-Bureau in June 1952, with the sole purpose of criticizing the Guangdong cadres for their errors in the land reform work. The meeting lasted from 29 June to 6 July, during which Tao Zhu made serious accusations against Fang Fang. There were three main criticisms. First, he "refused to learn from the land reform experience of the north", hence he "rejected the experience of the old liberated areas and rejected cadres from outside". Second, he was "harbouring an attitude of defiance when facing his superiors". Third, he was covering and protecting "bad and criminal elements". In order to protect his subordinates, Ye underwent two long sessions of self-criticism. He admitted that he had committed serious mistakes on peasant movement work and on localism attitudes. As he was the leader of the South China Sub-Bureau and Fang Fang's superior, he stated that he was solely responsible. He admitted that for the past two years, "the South China Sub-Bureau's work on the problem of agriculture has lost its direction. Fortunately, with Tao Zhu and Zhao Ziyang's leadership, and particularly that from the southbound comrades who worked at the district level, we have achieved significant results. Land reform that involved 5 million people has been successfully completed."

Fang Fang, in his self-criticism session, admitted that serious errors had been committed by Guangdong cadres in the land reform work in thirteen counties in 1950. He said it was obvious that he was "incompetent in handling the land reform work in the entire province". The meeting was then thrown open for all the cadres to comment on the two speeches. Zhao Ziyang, obviously aware of Ye's reputation and prestige, was mild and restrained in his comments, stating that Ye "was not sensitive enough on the question of class struggle". The comments on Fang were harsher, as he was accused of committing an "extremely serious error of localism".[19] Tao Zhu then submitted a report from the South China Sub-Bureau to Mao and the Central Committee of the CCP that incorporated the full self-criticism reports by both Ye and Fang. It gave details of the "serious harm" caused by the "localism" attitude of Guangdong cadres. Tao even exaggerated the criticism by saying that the "localism" attitude was equivalent to the "contradiction" between the enemy class and the people.

Before Tao could get the senior cadres out of the way, he targeted the relatively junior ones. The first victim was Zuo Hongtao, who was head of the United Front Department of the South China Sub-Bureau and assistant secretary general of the Guangdong provincial government. During the war years, he had worked as a journalist in the East River Column, and before Guangzhou's liberation had worked closely with Fang Fang in Hong Kong in the South China Sub-Bureau. The second victim was Yang Qi. Like Zuo, Yang had worked at the East River Column headquarters during the war years and, in fact, had managed single-handedly their only newspaper, *Qianjin Bao*, during the war. In one incident in 1951, when Yang Qi could not find the money to import the necessary newsprint for *Nanfang Ribao*, it was Deng Wenzhao's brother and Yang's brother, Yang Huanzhi in Hawaii, who provided the funds to import the newsprint from Hong Kong. Both Yang Qi and Zuo Hongtao were dismissed and expelled from the party in April 1952. When the anti-localism movement was launched, contacting people associated with Hong Kong and Macao was considered a serious crime.

In a public trial on 18 April 1952, Yang was accused of "corruption" and of being a political ally of Rao Zhangfeng, who was one of the prime targets of the anti-localism movement. Eventually, when he was dismissed from his post as the assistant director of *Nanfang Ribao*, the very newspaper that he served carried the news of his expulsion from the party, in an article on the front page. He was then demoted to a junior job inside the printing room of the newspaper. His membership in the party was restored only in June 1958.[20] Deng Wenzhao, who had given up his entire personal fortune to help the country, was also relieved of his two posts on the direction of Tao Zhu, who gave the excuse, "Deng is physically unwell. Hence he should not be re-elected for the next term."[21] Fang Fang, in particular, is thought to have been targeted by the anti-localism movement because of his great popularity in the southern provinces. It had even been suggested that his experience and prestige in the peasant movement overshadowed that of Mao.

In August 1952, Ye was moved by the Central Committee of the party in Beijing out of Guangdong to Beijing. In 1953, he requested Mao to transfer him back to Guangdong. However, the request was rejected. Instead, he was appointed to the relatively unimportant post of director of Inspection and Audit of the People's Liberation Army in Beijing, in November 1953. When some of his Guangdong subordinates went to Beijing to see him, Ye was bitter, lamenting he was aware that "there are people who made secret reports behind my back". He further said, "This man Tao Zhu kicked out Zhang Yunyi from Guangxi. When he arrived in Guangdong, he kicked me out from Guangdong." Ye also told Gu that being assigned to be the ultimate authority on land reform in Guangdong was a "thankless task". Gu commented that Fang Fang, in taking on the land reform duty, "thought he had firm local support, [but] was in fact asking for trouble".[22]

By October 1952, Fang Fang was further demoted to the rank of fifth secretary of the South China Sub-Bureau. When the "Three Anti's" Movement — anti-corruption, anti-waste and anti-bureaucracy — was launched within the party and the government in late 1951–52, again Fang became a target. Tao Zhu attacked Fang for having committed "serious *guanliao zhuyi*" (bureaucratism) in some of his earlier work, for example the closure of the salt mines and the rectification work on primary school teachers. Fang had closed some of the salt mines in April 1952 and was accused of having done so without consideration for the mine workers. In fact, what Fang did was implement a policy directive issued by the central government in Beijing to close and rationalize "small and inefficient mines". As a result of the closure, 30,000 workers were put out of work, which indirectly affected the livelihood of 130,000 people by not providing the workers with other employment. Part of the accusation was that, due to such closures, twenty-six workers had died. After an extensive investigation, however, a report revealed that three of the twenty-six had committed suicide, and of these suiciders, only one was attributed to the closure. Two workers committed suicide because of marital problems. The remaining twenty-three had died of natural causes.

Regarding the rectification work on primary school teachers, again Fang was acting strictly in accordance with a directive from the South China Sub-Bureau to rationalize and close some of the inefficient primary schools. Shortly after the policy was implemented, however, the South China Sub-Bureau realized that the policy was more complicated than expected, as the closure of schools had resulted in the unemployment of some teachers. Although the deadline of the closure was extended by the bureau several times, Fang continued to face pressure from the Provincial Department of Finance, as it was experiencing a shortage of funds. Fang was in a serious dilemma. Tao's accusations were that Fang did not respect the leaders of the South China Sub-Bureau and such errors were the "further development of his 'localism' attitude".

The end result was that Fang was dismissed from all his posts and had to go to self-criticism sessions in the poor rural areas in north Guangdong for two years. He was then sent to Beijing to fill the post of deputy director of the Overseas Chinese Commission in 1955. He was given an honourable exit from Guangdong, with the help of some of his Chaozhou clanspeople who held senior positions in the commission. After Fang was out of the way, eighty percent of the Guangdong cadres who held county-level positions or above lost their jobs. The minority of junior Guangdong cadres who managed to cling to their positions had to prove themselves and to protect their chances of survival by testifying about Fang's mistakes. They also had to go through self-criticism sessions on their own "localism" errors.

One of the senior leaders in the party, Bo Yibo, recalled his experience many years after the event in an article in *People's Daily*, dated 8 April 1997. He said that there was a need to "to say a few words of fairness for the Guangdong cadres". Bo related that it was Tao Zhu who made secret reports to Mao, first accusing Ye and Fang of "adopting a localism policy in Guangdong". Bo Yibo was the party secretary of the North China Bureau when he was directed by Mao to carry out an inspection tour of Guangdong in early 1952. He met with Ye and discovered that he had some "unspeakable grievances". When Bo returned to Beijing, he reported to Mao that "it was quite normal and usual for Ye and Fang to appoint some cadres who were familiar with local conditions to some of the posts in Guangdong". Such a practice should not be branded localism. In 1975, over twenty years after the event, and when both Tao Zhu and Lin Biao were out of the way, Ye bitterly recalled that "our land reform measures in Guangdong were carried out according to the orders and directives from the Central Committee of the party and those of the Central-South Bureau". He added, "Comrade Deng Zihui told me that the launching of the anti-localism movement was prompted by someone telling stories behind my back." No doubt he was referring to Tao Zhu, who made unsubstantiated reports to Mao.[23]

Deng Zihui was a leader of the peasant movement in Fujian and Jiangxi in the late 1920s and early 1930s. During the civil war in 1945–49, he was the political commissar of the Fourth Front Army Corps of the People's Liberation Army. In September 1949, when the government of the People's Republic of China was formed in Beijing, he was one of the 198 "candidates" elected from among members of the Chinese People's Political Consultative Conference, together with senior figures like Mao Zedong and Zhou Enlai. When the central government was formed, he was appointed to the post of Minister of Village Works in 1950.

By May 1953, when Ye Jianying was out of the way, Tao became the first secretary of the party in Guangdong. Zhao Ziyang was appointed deputy secretary, although he was only in his early thirties. Tao was so ruthless in carrying out the land reform activities that physical torture was inflicted on landowners. Some former KMT officials who had switched allegiances before the province's liberation were executed. The pressure on the landowners and the cadres who were involved in land reform work was so great that, in spring 1953, in west Guangdong alone, 1,165 cadres committed suicide. In February, 805 landowners were driven to suicide, and approximately 20,000 Guangdong cadres were affected. Some were imprisoned, some were executed and many of the more junior ones were dismissed and sent home. It was estimated that by 1953, when the first anti-localism campaign was launched, as many as 7,000 senior Guangdong cadres had been punished.

By 1953, Tao realized that his harsh policy in implementing the land reform movement might have been excessive. In two reports he filed in the name of the South China Sub-Bureau to the Central Committee of the CCP on 24 February and 7 April, he admitted there had been "serious errors in the land reform movement, as we have not been able to unite the masses". Also, he said, "There were too many deaths." He admitted the errors were in the way that he had dealt with the property of overseas Chinese, in that seventy-five percent of them were dealt with either wrongly or too severely. One further admission was that he had confiscated up to ninety percent of the estates and property owned by overseas Chinese. But

Tao put most of the blame on the Overseas Chinese Commission headed by He Xiangning.

Tao's harsh way of dealing with the overseas Chinese and their descendants drew strong criticism inside and outside the country. He Xiangning personally intervened by writing to Fang Fang and demanded that Guangdong should follow the party's policy in dealing with overseas Chinese. Situ Meitang, a prominent overseas Chinese leader from North America who had supported Sun Yat-sen in the 1911 Revolution and the Communist Party as far back as the 1930s, heard about some of the complaints lodged by Guangdong cadres from his hometown and the execution of some of them. He visited Jiangmen in 1953 to find out for himself the actual situation. Some junior local cadres actually threatened to chase the old man out of the city, but they were stopped by Ye Jianying himself.[24] It is not certain whether this threat to Situ was simply excessive behaviour on the part of the junior cadres at the district level, or was made because Situ was an overseas Chinese. Situ and Tan Kah Kee had been the only two overseas Chinese invited by the CCP to attend the founding ceremony of the People's Republic of China held on 1 October 1949. Both had been elected to the sixty-three-member Preparatory Committee to form the government, and both were members of the Standing Committee of the Chinese People's Political Consultative Conference.[26]

By 1958, when a second campaign was launched, up to ninety senior Guangdong cadres at the provincial level had been dismissed or punished.[27] In the Qiongya Column, nearly 10,000 soldiers and cadres were dismissed without being awarded their demobilization certificates or given any monetary compensation. Of this total, 2,000 female soldiers ended up homeless and jobless. Some were driven to begging in the streets, and some were driven to suicide.[26] A report issued by the South China Sub-Bureau on 25 March 1958 admitted that the "serious problem of such a high suicide rate was the direct result of the wrongful adoption of policy by junior cadres". One of Fang's cousins recalled many years later that some cadres had told Fang Fang that Tao "wanted bloodshed in every village". It is not certain whether this was a policy directive from Tao himself or the demand of some of the overzealous cadres under him.[28]

When Ye and Fang were out of the way in Guangdong, the central government in Beijing abolished the South China Sub-Bureau on 1 July 1955.

A Guangdong provincial committee was set up in its place. Tao was appointed provincial governor and secretary of the party in the province. Gu Dacun was appointed deputy provincial governor and deputy secretary of the committee. Zhao Ziyang, at the age of thirty-four, was appointed deputy secretary of the party at the provincial level. On the surface, Gu was second in command to Tao at the provincial level, but he remained bitter because Tao had persecuted many of his old friends and subordinates who had helped the various guerrilla groups, purely because these people were Guangdong natives. He was also alarmed by the large number of deaths from execution or suicide. The ongoing bickering between the two was so serious that Zhao Ziyang appealed to Gu to be a little more conciliatory towards Tao, for the sake of "maintaining unity among comrades". Gu, having a long history and impeccable credentials that went back to his days in Yan'an in the 1930s, disdainfully dismissed Zhao as "young and inexperienced".

Rao Zhangfeng, who had done a great deal of United Front work among overseas Chinese and Hong Kong Chinese who had supported the guerrillas during the war years, suffered the most. He was accused of being "infirm in his political stance and harbouring right-wing elements", was severely criticized twice, in 1952 and again in 1957, and was demoted to the junior rank of party secretary in the small town of Lianping.[29]

A further comment by Tao Zhu was, "Fortunately the party apparatus has not been completely controlled by the localist elements. But the party is already in a dangerous state." Tao added, "If we allow this trend to continue, the party in Hainan will be derailed from its proper leadership, and it will be turned into a localist party." From Hainan, he extended his comments to other parts of Guangdong, "For over a year, the spread of localist activities in other parts of Guangdong has been dangerous and pervasive . . ."

The accusation against Lin Ping was the most unjustified. As early as 1929 he had participated as a peasant guerrilla in his hometown in Jiangxi and joined the Communist Party in 1931. Between 1937 and 1938, he had been the party secretary in the Guangdong Provincial Military Commission. During the tough negotiations between the Communist Party and the KMT in Beijing, he had been advisor to General Ye Jianying. Subsequently, during the negotiations in Guangzhou, he had been a member of Fang Fang's negotiation team. After the liberation of Guangdong, he was appointed deputy political commissar in the Guangdong Military Headquarters. His concurrent duty as head of the highway construction unit in Guangdong attracted Ye's attention, and he was transferred to Hainan Island to do the same kind of work. During the first wave of attacks against localism among Guangdong cadres, he was forced by Tao Zhu to criticize Gu Dacun and Feng Baiju. He was accused of being a member of the "localist clique". Lin was well known for being outspoken, so he confronted Tao Zhu face-to-face, demanding that Tao produce evidence to substantiate his accusation. It has been suggested that he offended Tao by refusing to toe the correct line. Hence, he was implicated despite his impeccable credentials. Furthermore, he was not even a Guangdong native himself.[30]

As far as being a revolutionary was concerned, Feng Baiju had impeccable credentials. He had been a party representative in the Qiongya Column as far back as 1927. In 1939, he was promoted to the position of commander. During the Chinese Civil War from 1945 to 1949, he held positions as both commander and political commissar of the column. For decades, the column had to struggle under extreme conditions without any help from the top leadership of the party. When Guangdong was liberated in 1949, Feng became one of the deputy provincial governors in charge of industries.

## Personality Cult, 1960s

In the mid-1960s, when Lin Biao launched the personality cult to worship Mao throughout the country, Guangdong, under Tao's command, was not slow in jumping on the bandwagon. In August 1965, the Chinese Communist Party Committee launched a seminar "To Study Chairman Mao's Writings". Over 700 senior cadres attended the conference, at which both Tao and Zhao made long speeches. In October, an exhibition of Mao's works was held in Guangzhou, and in one month over 700,000 people visited. In early 1966, at a meeting of the Central-South Bureau convened by Tao, Guangdong showed it was one of the most active provinces in its zeal in studying Mao's thought. At the meeting, Tao said "Mao's thought is the pinnacle of modern Marx-Leninism . . . to learn and grasp the great Mao thought is a timely requirement of our time. To study Chairman Mao's books and to be his lifelong students are the innate duties of party members and cadres." As a result of such words and activities, Tao's influence and position rose rapidly. In early 1965 Zhou Enlai nominated Tao Zhu, together with fifteen others, to the rank of vice-premier, subject to the endorsement of the National People's Congress. In June 1966 Tao went to Beijing to assume the post of vice-premier and minister of propaganda, but he maintained an intense interest in Guangdong, to the extent that Zhao Ziyang was instructed to send him regular up-to-date reports on the situation there.

## The Column Veterans in Later Years

During the Cultural Revolution, which started in 1966, individuals like Fang, Rao and Zeng Sheng were, in the eyes of the Red Guards, people with "foreign connections". They were arrested and imprisoned very early. In December 1966 Fang Fang was arrested, imprisoned and tortured for five years, until he died in September 1971. In 1960 Rao was partially rehabilitated when he was transferred to the newly founded Foreign Languages Institute.[31] However, he was arrested in 1969 and then sent to a hard labour farm in Lechang in north Guangdong; he was brutally murdered in September 1970. Huang Guanfang, who led the Hong Kong and Kowloon Independent Brigade towards the end of the Second World War, was also imprisoned without trial. As he had occupied only a relatively junior post in Foshan during the land reform period, he was released after seven months, without suffering physical torture. Huang was rehabilitated fully after 1972 and occupied the post of director of the United Front Department in Foshan until early 1980.

One leader initially not caught up in the purge was Zeng Sheng, commander of the Guangdong and Guangxi Column when Guangdong was taken by the Communists in October 1949. He was appointed first deputy chief of staff of the South China Military Region. In October 1960, when the anti-localism movement subsided for a while and the whole country was facing the serious economic crisis resulting from the failure of the Great Leap Forward movement, Zeng Sheng was appointed deputy provincial governor and mayor of Guangzhou.[31]

Despite the extreme economic difficulties, both in the province and in the city, Zeng completed a number of substantial projects during his seven-year tenure. These included redirecting the Pearl River; re-housing some of the fishermen who were living in boats that were not seaworthy moored on land in the city slums; and increasing the number of hotel rooms and other tourism-related facilities. This last project was particularly important, not only for the city but for the entire country. The China Import and Export Fair (Canton Fair) was held twice annually in April and October and, from 1956, was the only way for foreigners to visit China. It was also an important source of foreign exchange earnings for the entire country. However, no new hotels of any sort had been built since the 1930s, and the airport was inadequate. To cater to the very few foreign airlines that flew directly into China, Zeng Sheng supervised the extension of the Baiyun Airport. The whole project was completed in a record time of less than two years.

When the Cultural Revolution was launched in Beijing in 1966, Zeng had just returned from leading a Sino-Japanese friendship delegation to Japan. By this time, he had a premonition that he would be targeted sooner or later, as he felt that he had been discriminated against by Lin Biao and Huang Yongsheng as early as the 1950s. On the eve of the Lunar New Year in 1967, while Zeng was convening a meeting of the Municipal Committee of the CCP in Guangzhou, Huang sent one of his junior officers in the Security Department of the Guangzhou garrison to see Zeng. Zeng was told that Zhou Enlai would like to see him immediately. The moment Zeng stepped out of the meeting venue, he was forcefully arrested and taken to Beijing under duress. He was beaten on the head by Red Guards, which probably caused him to suffer from recurring serious headaches until the day he died. Being the most senior among all the former guerrillas and holding the rank of lieutenant general of the People's Liberation Army, he was treated somewhat better than his comrades. Initially he was kept in the Qincheng Prison in Beijing together with a Korean War hero, Lü Zhengcao, but for most of the time during his seven-year incarceration, he was kept in solitary confinement.

Zeng was interrogated 96 times during the first year, 128 times in 1969 and over 80 times in 1970 by a special committee under the direction of Lin Biao. In a case of extreme irony, he and his East River Column soldiers were accused of being "bandits" — the same accusation used against him and his soldiers by the KMT authorities in Guangdong right after the war. The old chestnut of working with the

KMT warlord Luo Fengxiang, in 1938, was also raised. The fact that the column had dealings with the Americans and the British during the war years was used as evidence that he was a secret agent of the "imperialists". The most ridiculous accusation was the charge that he had had an illicit affair with a Japanese geisha during his official visit to Japan.

As a result of all the physical torture and ill treatment, Zeng had difficulty in communicating with other people when he was allowed visitors for the first time six years after his initial arrest. He continued to suffer from extremely bad health and in July 1974 was finally released, to his family who provided him with medical treatment. Zeng was appointed vice-minister of communications in October 1975, and from October 1977 to February 1979 he served as first deputy minister. In this new post he readily admitted that he knew very little about the subjects in his portfolio (land and sea navigation matters and transport), but he put in long hours to learn from the professionals who were his subordinates. He was appointed minister in February 1979. He and his old comrade Yuan Geng saw the potential of the seaside village of Shekou and developed it into a prosperous industrial town next to Shenzhen Special Economic Zone. Yuan Geng was another East River Column veteran who had escaped the anti-localism purge, by spending a long time in Guangxi and Vietnam training the Vietnam Communist cadres.

Zeng retired from active duty in 1983, while retaining the nominal post of member of the Central Advisory Committee of the Central Committee of the Communist Party. On the fortieth anniversary of the founding of the East River Column, a series of celebrations were held in Dongguan, Huizhou and Shenzhen, from November to December 1983. While making a welcoming speech at the ceremony on 3 December 1983, Zeng wept openly when he recalled how his comrades suffered during the anti-localism activities and during the Cultural Revolution. He lamented sadly how they were let down by "the country and the party" and vowed that this should not be allowed to happen again. In ending his speech, he called for *pingfan*, i.e. the rehabilitation of all his comrades accused of localism. Those who attended echoed his comments in a loud chorus.

In 1984, Zeng toured Hawaii and North America, and revisited many old battlegrounds in south China and Hong Kong, where he gave his blessing to the building of a second monument to commemorate his old comrades who had died in active service. He died in Guangzhou in November 1995.[32]

After the downfall of the Gang of Four in 1976, the Central Committee of the CCP examined many cases of persecution and imprisonment of various cadres since 1949. The work was conducted personally by Hu Yaobang, who had made his name by spending a long period as head of the Youth Corps as early as the late 1950s. Because of his close relationship with Deng Xiaoping, he became general secretary of the party in the early 1980s. Hu was well known for his pragmatic and liberal views and was responsible for rehabilitating many people wrongly purged in the 1950s and 1960s. Directive No. 8, dated 19 February 1983, was issued to party members and emphasized that cadres such as Gu Dacun, Rao Zhangfeng and their subordinates had been wrongly accused of committing the "serious errors" of localism in the 1950s and 1960s. They were totally exonerated. However, when the book *Modern China* was being researched by the Central Committee of the CCP in 1988, the author consulted twenty-eight cadres who had served under Tao Zhu and Zhao Ziyang in Guangdong in the 1950s. Some of these cadres and the Guangdong cadres who had been victimized during these years seriously disagreed about the history of the province in the period 1950–70. The Guangdong cadres insisted that the part on localist errors of the Guangdong cadres be totally deleted; the twenty-eight old cadres strongly resisted. The old cadres stated that, while Gu Dacun, Fang Fang and others had suffered unjust punishment during the relevant period, the localist errors made by the senior cadres in the provincial government of that time must be retained in the text. They believed that, although Tao Zhu might have been a little too harsh towards a few of the cadres, his policy in general was correct. To leave out this part of his work would mean discrediting his entire policy and achievements while he was governing Guangdong. At this time, Zhao Ziyang, who had assisted Tao so energetically during the purging period, was now premier of the country, and the twenty-eight cadres were on the point of lobbying Zhao for support. There was no doubt that they wanted Zhao to lend his name and influence to side with them. At this juncture, however, Ye Jianying intervened. He told Zhao, "I have never clarified my position on the Guangdong problem and neither have you". It was a veiled warning that Zhao had better steer clear of the controversy.

Finally, Fang Fang's widow, Su Hui, had to petition the Central Committee of the CCP to "re-examine" Fang Fang's case in December 1992. Gu Dacun's widow, Zeng Shiwen, and her son, Gu Wanxian, also went to appeal personally to Jiang Zemin. Xi Zhongxun, who earlier had been a vice-premier and currently was second party secretary of Guangdong, was sympathetic to those Guangdong cadres who had suffered. A stumbling block, however, was Tao Zhu's widow, Zeng Zhi, who had been appointed a deputy director of the Organization Department of the CCP by Hu Yaobang in 1977. The post carried a deputy ministerial rank. As Mao had known her personally during the Yan'an days, she was still influential. When Tao Zhu arrived in Guangdong in the early 1950s, Zeng Zhi had also worked as the party secretary of the Department of Electricity in Guangzhou. She claimed that she knew the situation in Guangdong then, and it was wrong to totally discredit the anti-localist policy that Tao carried out so energetically. So Xi Zhongxun had to be extremely careful and tactful.

When Xi Zhongxun was transferred from Guangdong to the central government in Beijing in November 1980, he recommended Liu Tianfu to succeed him, and appointed him the provincial governor. Liu was a native of Sichuan but had worked in Guangdong since 1939. During the war, he had worked for a while as the political commissar of the Guangdong People's Anti-Japanese Guerrillas. Upon his new appointment, he spoke up on behalf of the Guangdong cadres who had suffered during the anti-localism movement. He recalled that, for over fifty years, since the founding of the Communist Party in 1921, there had been more than ten non-Guangdong natives who had worked as party secretaries in various cities and counties in Guangdong. The majority of these cadres had worked harmoniously with their Guangdong colleagues. He himself had also worked for nearly fifty years in Guangdong. Hence, it was "unscientific and untrue" to accuse the Guangdong cadres of having harboured localist and anti-outsider sentiments. He also said that the two anti-localism movements launched in 1952 and 1957 were seriously wrong. And both of them were due to the wrong policy and sectarian tendencies of some "senior cadres". This point was no doubt a veiled criticism of Tao Zhu.[33]

As a result of the insistence of people such as Zeng Shiwen and Su Hui, and earlier personal intervention from Hu Yaobang and Liu Tianfu, a special committee set up by the Central Committee of the Communist Party, acting on the recommendation of a special disciplinary committee set up by the Guangdong Provincial Committee of the CCP, finally concluded, in April 1994, that the accusations and punishment inflicted on Fang Fang had been wrong and that there had been no justification for branding any Guangdong cadres as localists. The Central Committee also acceded to the Guangdong cadres' request to delete all reference to their errors when the anti-localist policy prevailed in Guangdong. At a meeting held in Guangzhou when the decision from the Central Committee of the CCP was handed down, Liu Tianfu, the provincial governor, spoke on behalf of the old comrades who had suffered during the period. He thanked the Central Committee for "doing a good deed" and said that the "unjust accusations" against the old comrades had finally been eliminated, albeit forty years after the event. Many old comrades were in tears and lamented, "The decision was not only an exoneration of Comrade Fang Fang alone, but also an exoneration of all the Guangdong comrades who were victimized." The old comrades further said, "For decades, we suffered under the dual stigma of having pursued rightist tendencies in the land reform and a localist policy. We could not even breathe freely and the price we paid was excessive." They also said, "If the central government had allowed Ye and Fang to manage Guangdong according to their ideas then Guangdong's economic development would be even better today. Unfortunately the price we paid was too great."[34]

## Hong Kong and the Legacy of the East River Column

Veterans who did not join the repatriation to Yantai, Shandong in June 1946 followed different paths. Some of them stayed in Hong Kong and worked at the

Xinhua News Agency. Some stayed in other parts of China, most of them in various small towns in Guangdong, such as Foshan and Nanhai. A few of them worked in places far from Guangdong, such as Kunming, Yunnan.

Tan Gan, who had a good command of English and was a close colleague of Huang Zuomei, worked in the Liaison Department of the Xinhua News Agency until his retirement in the early 1990s.

Chen Daming held the post of political commissar in an air force school in Beijing after Liberation. When the Sino-British negotiations commenced in late 1982, his Hong Kong and Guangdong background was considered useful. He was transferred and promoted to the post of deputy director of the Xinhua News Agency in Hong Kong, an organization which functioned as a de facto consulate.

Yang Qi, one of the first East River Column veterans purged in the 1950s, was subjected to accusations during the Cultural Revolution of having "foreign connections". Probably due to his low profile and mild manner, he did not suffer any physical torture. In September 1968, *Yangcheng Wanbao* (Yangcheng Evening News) in Guangzhou, where Yang Qi worked, was banned, and Yang was sent to work as a manual labourer at a cattle farm in a mountainous region in north Guangdong. He worked there until 1974, when he was transferred back to Guangzhou to head a publishing company. After the downfall of the Gang of Four, Yang was posted to the Xinhua News Agency in Hong Kong, where he headed the regular news section.

In 1982, Yang was promoted to the important post of secretary general of Xinhua. After the signing of the Sino-British Joint Declaration in December 1984, the social and economic conditions in Hong Kong returned to an even keel. Then Yang made a horizontal move to head the newspaper *Ta Kung Pao* when he was already in his mid-sixties. He stepped down as the publisher and retired in 1992.

Some of the rank-and-file members who had strong Hong Kong roots re-emerged in different jobs. Chan Wahing, who had been a young fisherman in Ting Kok, Tai Po, New Territories, when the war broke out in 1941, compelled by his sense of patriotism, had followed others in his clan from the area and walked across the mountains to Sai Kung, where he met Cai Guoliang. He joined the East River Column in mid-1942. Because he was no more than a teenager, he was never assigned actual combat duties and spent most of the war years as a guard whenever enemy soldiers or collaborators were captured. He witnessed, therefore, the execution of some of them in Ho Chung, Sai Kung.

On VJ Day, he was with his detachment in Shataukok, but instead of joining the repatriation to Yantai, he returned to his village and resumed his role as a fisherman. Because he had had a few years of schooling and some training in the column during the war, he was better educated than most other fishermen and was therefore recruited by the officer-in-charge of the Fish Marketing Organization Station in Tai Po in 1947. He worked there until the mid-1980s. Dignified, honest and intensely proud of his wartime experience, he never joined the Communist Party. To echo the words of Ken Barnett, he said the reason he joined the column was that he felt the need "to defend his hometown against the Fascists".

Wong Lapkwong was not yet ten when the Japanese invaded Hong Kong in 1941. Compelled by patriotism, he joined the column in Yuen Chau Tsai, Tai Po, in late 1942. Owning to his youth he was employed as a Little Devil, whose duty was to carry messages between various locations where the column's soldiers were stationed. In addition he was assigned duties in the transport section as a casual labourer, but because of his age he could only manage to carry light items such as sweet potatoes and firewood.

After the war he resumed his schooling in Kwun Hang, north Sai Kung. After a few years he dropped out, as he could not cope with the schoolwork. His father in San Francisco sent him the fare to sail to England on the SS *Canton* in 1952. In England he re-enrolled in a secondary school in Norwich but after three years, dropped out, returned to Hong Kong and started a grocery store in Tai Po Market. After a few years, he made enough money to sail for England again in 1960. By then, he had enough experience and confidence in life in England to start a Chinese restaurant in East Anglia. Up to the late 1990s, his restaurant business brought a steady and comfortable income. His children all went to good schools in Britain, so Wong now shuttles back and forth between Hong Kong and the United Kingdom.

Cai Songying is one of the few female veterans who has led an active working life up to the present. She was born in Hong Kong and was studying in a primary school in 1938. Through the influence of her teachers she joined in the Anti-Japan and Save the Nation student activities even then. She also joined a children's choral group called The Ants, who followed their secondary counterparts in staging anti-Japanese cultural events in Hong Kong. In early 1940 she went to evening school while working part-time in a metal factory as a child labourer. When the Japanese began their occupation of Hong Kong, she secretly left home and went to Wu Kau Tang, Tai Po, to join the East River Column. As she was relatively young but better educated, she was not assigned any active combat duties. Throughout the war years, her main duties were propaganda, indoctrination and, occasionally, intelligence work.

As most of the soldiers in the column were illiterate, she spent long hours in literacy classes, particularly for the female members. For propaganda work, she was involved in staging song and dance activities with patriotic and anti-Japanese themes. Her main areas of activities covered Shataukok, north Sai Kung and the surrounding villages near Sai Kung Town. She met her husband, who was a schoolteacher, in the East River Column and they were married during the war.

After VJ Day, she did not join the repatriation but ran a private primary school together with her husband in Sai Kung, New Territories. She worked at the school until her husband died in the late 1960s. Then she worked for a small trade union.

Despite the fact that people of the East River Column were treated as members of the Allied forces after VJ Day and the British government and the People's Republic of China had established diplomatic relations in 1950, the Hong Kong government's policy was to discriminate against those who had any Communist connection or sympathy. Sometimes this took the form of suppressing institutions, for example closing Dade College in the late 1940s.

Except for those who have held posts in the Xinhua News Agency, members of the column who have stayed in Hong Kong for the past decades have all lived in the lower stratum of the community. However, their influence in various parts of the New Territories had been significant. Every year on the anniversary of VJ Day, there are invariably references in the media to their heroism. Schoolchildren are directed to the long silk banner on permanent display at the Sai Kung Rural Committee, given by General Sir Neil Ritchie.

At a reunion held on 3 February 2002, on the sixtieth anniversary of the founding of the Hong Kong and Kowloon Independent Brigade in Guangzhou, over 300 surviving veterans turned up. It was estimated by the organizers of the event that there are still about 600 such veterans who live all over China and overseas. Many live in poverty, but all live with dignity and pride for contributing towards the overall Allied victory over Japan in the Second World War.

# Notes

## Chapter 2

1.  The term Hakka, which literally means "guest people", was probably coined by local residents who had settled in the south before the Hakka arrived. The term was derived from the fact that these people came in waves from north and central China to southern provinces like Guangdong, Guangxi and Fujian. The first wave came around the Eastern Jin Dynasty, A.D. 317–419. The last wave came around the end of the Taiping Rebellion in 1864. Hakka are found in at least seventeen provinces and over 230 towns and cities. In Guangdong alone, they are found in over seventy-one cities and market towns. It was estimated by a well-known Hakka academic, Professor Lo Hsianglin, that there are at least 80 million of them within China and some 20 million outside China, the majority in South and Southeast Asia. For at least the last three centuries, they have produced well-known revolutionary leaders like Hong Xiuquan and Yang Xiuqing, both Taiping Rebellion leaders. Of the later anti-Qing rebel leaders, most of the seventy-two martyrs of the Huanghuagang Uprising in Guangzhou were Hakka. Other notable Hakka were Sun Yat-sen, Soong Ching-ling, Zhu De, Ye Jianying, Liao Chengzhi, Aw Boon Haw, Han Suyin and Guo Moruo. The famous KMT soldiers Zhang Fakui, Xue Yue and Chen Jitang were Hakka. (For details, see William Skinner, Regional Systems in Late Imperial China, paper presented at the 2nd Annual General Meeting of the Social Science History Association, Ann Arbor, Michigan, 1977; and Luo Xianglin, *Kejia Yanjiu Daolun*, Xingning, Guangdong: Shi-shan Library, 1933.)

2.  Israel Epstein, *Woman in World History: Life and Times of Soong Ching Ling* (Beijing: New World Press, 1993), p. 323. In order to garner widespread support, Soong managed to rally not only political leaders from the KMT and the CCP but also some international personages to join the league, e.g. T. V. Soong, Foreign Minister of China; Sun Ke, Dr. Sun Yat-sen's son, who was president of the Legislative Yuan in the KMT government; General Feng Yuxiang, the famous "Christian General" who did not agree with Chiang Kai-shek's policy of appeasement of the Japanese aggressors; J. Nehru; Paul Robeson, the famous African American singer; Pearl Buck; Clare Boothe Luce; Thomas Mann; and Bishop Ronald Hall, Anglican Bishop of Hong Kong. The Hong Kong members who were office bearers were: Norman France, a professor of history at the University of Hong Kong; Israel Epstein, an assistant editor of *South China Morning Post*; and Hilda Selwyn-Clarke, the wife of Sir Selwyn Selwyn-Clarke, Director of Medical and Health Services in the Hong Kong government.

Chan Kwanpo was the Chinese secretary of the league. Chan was a lecturer in Chinese at the University of Hong Kong. He was well known for his patriotism and was well connected with many literary figures, such as Lu Xun and Xu Dishan in China. Liao Mengxing was Liao Chengzhi's younger sister. She married Li Shaoshi, who was an aide to Zhou Enlai when Zhou was staying in Chongqing during the Second World War. Deng Wenzhao (or Tang Manchiu to his friends in Hong Kong) was the deputy Chinese manager of the Belgian Bank in Hong Kong. He returned to China after Liberation in 1949. He married Liao's second cousin and hence came under his influence. In the 1930s he studied in Cambridge. He admitted he had acquired his socialist outlook because he came under Harold Laski's influence. For a while he was the deputy director of the Commerce Department in Guangzhou and vice provincial governor of Guangdong just before the onset of the Cultural Revolution in 1966.

3.    Chen Daming, *Xianggang Kangri Youjidui* (Hong Kong: Huanqiu Chubanshe Youxian Gongsi, 2000), pp. 15–7.

4.    Wang Zuorao, *Dong Zong Yi Ye* (Guangzhou: Guangdong Renmin Chubanshe, 1983), p. 87.

5.    Zeng Sheng, Jiangjun Zhuan, unpublished article by the editor of *Zhongguo Qingnian Bao*, 1986.

6.    Wang Man, *Jiangjun de Fengcai* (Guangzhou: Huacheng Chubanshe, 1987), pp. 1–20.

7.    Zeng Sheng, *Zeng Sheng Huiyilu* (Beijing: Jiefangjun Chubanshe, 1991), pp. 141–66.

8.    Interview with Zeng Sheng, 20 October 1984.

9.    Interview with Zeng Sheng, 20 October 1984.

10.   War Office Papers 208/254.

11.   *Xianzhe Bu Xiu: Lian Guan Tongzhi Jinian Wenji* (Beijing: Zhongguo Huaqiao Chubanshe, 1995), pp. 163–5.

12.   Colin Smith, *Singapore Burning: Heroism and Surrender in World War II* (London: Viking, 2005), p. 67.

13.   Colin Smith, p. 100.

14.   Xia Yan, *Liao Chengzhi Zai Xianggang* (Guangzhou: Guangdong Renmin Chubanshe, 1987), p. 88.

15.   Xu Shihui, Two Negotiations between the Hong Kong British and the Chinese Communists in the 1940s, paper presented at the International Conference on Hong Kong and Modern China, organized by the Centre of Asian Studies, the University of Hong Kong, 3–5 December 1997; and Chen Daming, *Xianggang Kangri Youjidui* (Hong Kong: Huanqiu Chubanshe Youxian Gongsi, 2000), p. 11.

## Chapter 3

1.    Anthony Haydon, *Sir Matthew Nathan, British Colonial Governor and Civil Servant* (St. Lucia, Queensland: The University of Queensland Press, 1976), pp. 118–26.

2.    *Hong Kong News*, 12 January 1942.

3.    *Hong Kong News*, 28 January 1942.

4.    Lin Huaxin, *Liu Heizai Chuanqi* (Guangzhou: Huacheng Chubanshe, 2000), pp. 12–21.

5.    H.C.K. Woddis, Hong Kong and the East River Company, *Eastern World*, August 1949.

6.    David Faure, Sai Kung, 1940–1950 (oral history project, Centre of East Asian Studies, Chinese University of Hong Kong, 1980), p. 52.

7.  *Gangjiu Duli Dadui Shi* (Guangzhou: Guangdong Renmin Chubanshe, February 1989), pp. 192–3.

8.  Lin Huaxin, p. 187.

9.  *Gangjiu Duli Dadui Shi*, p. 31.

10. Sally Blyth and Ian Waterspoon, *Hong Kong Remembers* (Hong Kong: Oxford University Press, 1986), pp. 17–8.

11. David Faure, p. 49; and my interview with Zhang Xing on 19 December 1984.

12. Mao Dun, *Tuoxian Zaji* (Hong Kong: Shidai Tushu, 1979), pp. 194–5; and interview with D. Scriven in Hong Kong on 13 December 1983. Scriven served with the Indian Army during the war and earned a Military Cross and a decoration of D.S.O. For a long period after the war he was the only practising psychiatrist in Hong Kong. During my interview with him, while he was full of praise for the rescue work of the East River guerrillas, as a professional soldier himself, he was not very complimentary about the guerrillas' practice of operating mostly at night and their avoidance of open warfare.

13. Sally Blyth and Ian Waterspoon, *Hong Kong Remembers* (Hong Kong: Oxford University Press, 1986), pp. 18–23; and interview with Liu on 9 February 1985.

14. David Bosanquet, *Escape Through China* (London: Robert Hale, 1983), pp. 111–3.

15. *Gangjiu Duli Dadui Shi*, p. 25.

16. Lindsay Ride, Spheres of Military Influence in Kwangtung, unpublished Lindsay Ride papers, dated probably in mid-1942.

17. Lindsay Ride, Series 2, No. 9.

18. Lindsay Ride, Series 11, No. 9; and War Office Papers 208/451.

19. War Office Papers 208/451.

20. Interview with Lin Zhan and Cai Songying, 16 July 2000.

21. Edwin Ride, *BAAG, Hong Kong Resistance, 1942–1945* (Hong Kong: Oxford University Press, 1981), pp. 217–8.

22. *Dongjiang Zongdui Shiliao* (Guangzhou: Guangdong Renmin Chubanshe, 1984), pp. 584–5.

# Chapter 4

1.  Chan Kingtong, Hai Shang Jiaolong — Wang Jin, paper presented at the Second International Symposium on Maritime Defence of China, 6–8 June 2002.

2.  Chen Daming, *Xianggang Kangri Youjidui* (Hong Kong: Huanqiu Chubanshe, 2000), p. 29.

3.  *Gangjiu Duli Dadui Shi*, p. 88.

4.  David Faure, Sai Kung, 1940–1950 (oral history project, Centre of East Asian Studies, Chinese University of Hong Kong, 1980), p 34.

5.  David Faure, p. 52.

6.  Lin Huaxin, *Liu Heizai Chuanqi* (Guangzhou: Huacheng Chubanshe, 2000), p. 44.

7.  War Office Papers 208/451.

8.  Interview with Lee Hokming, 2 November 1982, and War Office Papers 235/1112.

9.  *Guangjiu Duli Dadui Shi*, pp. 174–7.

10. Lindsay Ride, letter to Military Attaché, H.B.M. Embassy Chongqing, 1 August 1943.

11. Guerrilla War in Kwangtung, *Eastern Horizon* (London, 1979).

12. *Dongjiang Zongdui Shi*, a magazine published on the East River Column's 40th Anniversary in December 1983 (Guangzhou: Guangdong Renmin Chubanshe, 1984).

13. Lu Quan, *Dongjiang Zongdui Shiliao* (Guangzhou: Guangdong Renmin Chubanshe, 1984), pp. 665–94.

14. *Gangjiu Dadui Ge Zhongdui Shi* (Shenzhen: Zhonggong Shenzhen Shiwei Dangshi Bangongshi, December 1985), p. 90.

15. War Office Papers 235/1112.

16. War Office Papers 208/318.

17. Chen Daming, *Xianggang Kangri Youjidui* (Hong Kong: Huanqiu Chubanshe Youxian Gongsi, 2000), pp. 153–9.

## Chapter 5

1. Interview with Zeng Fa, 17 March 2001, in Shenzhen. Zeng did not join the repatriation on 30 June 1946. He stayed behind and worked for a while in the Fish Marketing Organization, Tai Po, Hong Kong. He fought as a guerrilla soldier during the civil war and held the rank of captain when Shenzhen was liberated in October 1949. He retired from the post of mayor of Jiangmen, Guangdong, in 1985.

2. *Gangjiu Duli Dadui Shi* (Guangzhou: Guangdong Renmin Chunbanshe, February 1989), pp. 18–26; Zeng Sheng, *Zeng Sheng Huiyilu* (Beijing: Jiefangjun Chubanshe, 1991), pp. 426–9.

3. War Office Papers 208/750.

4. War Office Papers 235/993.

5. Tse Wing-kwong, *Zhanshi Rijun zai Xianggang baoxing* (Hong Kong: Ming Pao Publishing House, 1991), pp. 218–20. In the war crimes trials staged by the British military authorities in 1946, Kishi, Matsumoto and Uchida were sentenced to death by hanging. Sergeant Kamiyo was sentenced to ten years' imprisonment. Sergeant Yoshimura was given a jail sentence of eight years, and Kodama was jailed for five years.

6. Interview with Kwong Pingyau, chairman of Cheung Chau Rural Committee, on 13 April 1986.

7. Eddie Gosano, *Hong Kong Farewell* (London: Greg England, 1997), pp. 36–7.

8. Stephen Harper, *Miracle of Deliverance* (London: Guild Publishing, 1968); Colonial Office Papers 129/591/16.

9. Tse Wing-kwong (ed.), *The Chan Kwan Po Diary* (Hong Kong: Hong Kong Commercial Press, 1999), p. 834.

10. Colonial Office Papers 129/594/6.

11. Colonial Office Papers 129/594/6.

12. Interview with K.M.A. Barnett, 4 February 1987.

13. Colonial Office Papers 537/60/67.

14. Foreign Office Papers 371/537/41.

15. Foreign Office Papers 371/537/41.

16. *Gangjiu Duli Dadui Shi*, pp. 184–5.

17. Chen Daming, p. 164.

18. Foreign Office Papers 327/538.

19. The Third Supplement to the *London Gazette*, 27 June 1947, carried the following citation on the award of the decoration of M.B.E. "Raymond Wong, student, Kowloon. In recognition of his contribution to the British military activities in South East Asia

before 2 September 1945." Huang Zuomei used his English name Raymond Wong in his dealings with English-speaking friends. The reason his occupation was described as "student" is unknown. Note: Previously referred to as Raymond Huang.

20. *Kung Sheung Daily*, Hong Kong, 16 February 1947.
21. Arthur Clegg, *Aid China 1937–1949: A Memoir of a Forgotten Campaign* (Beijing: New World Press, 1989), p. 167.


**Chapter 6**

1. Zhou Yi, *Xianggang Zuopai Douzheng Shi* (Hong Kong: Liwen Chubanshe, 2002), p. 16.
2. *Sannian Jiefang Zhanzheng* (Shenzhen: Zhonggong Shenzhen Shiwei Dangshi Bangongshi, 1986), pp. 40–5.
3. Colonial Office Papers 129/592/6.
4. *Hua Shang Bao*, Hong Kong, 18 January 1946.
5. Interview with Lin Zhan, 1 August 2000. Lin was one of Fang Fang's English interpreters during the negotiations.
6. *Hua Shang Bao*, Hong Kong, 18 January 1946.
7. *Hua Shang Bao*, Hong Kong, 17 January 1945.
8. *Hua Shang Bao*, Hong Kong, 29 January 1946.
9. *Hua Shang Bao*, Hong Kong, 31 January 1946.
10. *Hua Shang Bao*, Hong Kong, 15 February 1946.
11. *Hua Shang Bao*, Hong Kong, 19 February 1946.
12. *Hua Shang Bao*, Hong Kong, 25 February 1946.
13. Public Records Office Papers 371/537/41.
14. *Dongjiang Zongdui Shi* (Beijing: Jiefangjun Chubanshe, 2003), p. 470.
15. Zhonggong Nanjing Shi Weiyuanhui, *Zhou Enlai 1946 nian Tanpan Wenxuan* (Beijing: Zhongyang Wenxian Chubanshe, 1996), p. 175.
16. *Hua Shang Bao*, Hong Kong, 23 March 1946.
17. *Hua Shang Bao*, Hong Kong, 8 March 8 1946.
18. *History of Field Team No. 8*. Second Quarter Report. Washington, DC: Assistant Chief of Staff, Intelligence. US Army Publication, June 1946.
19. *History of Field Team No. 8*. Second Quarter Report, p. 35.
20. *History of Field Team No. 8*. Second Quarter Report, p. 36.
21. Foreign Office Papers 371/53760.
22. *History of Field Team No. 8*. Second Quarter Report, pp. 1–30.
23. Letter from the British Consul General in Guangzhou to the Commander-in-Chief, Hong Kong, 17 April 1946.
24. *Hua Shang Bao*, Hong Kong, 21 April 1946.
25. *Dongjiang Zongdui Shi*, p. 472.
26. Foreign Office Papers 371/53760.
27. *History of Field Team No. 8*. Second Quarter Report, pp. 1–30.
28. L. S. Houchief, The East River Column Evacuation, June–July 1946, American Naval Involvement in the Chinese Civil War, unpublished PhD thesis, University of London, 1971.
29. L.S. Houchief.
30. *Dongjiang Zongdui Shi*, p. 480.

31. Zeng Sheng, *Zeng Sheng Huiyilu* (Beijing: Jiefangjun Chubanshe, 1992), pp. 450–76.

32. Zeng Sheng, p. 472.

33. Zeng Sheng, p. 478.

34. *Dongjiang Zongdui Shi*, p. 479.

35. Arthur Clegg, *Aid China 1937–1949: A Memoir of a Forgotten Campaign* (Beijing: New World Press, 1989), p. 171. Qiao Guanhua succeeded Huang Zuomei as director of the Xinhua News Agency in Hong Kong when Huang was posted to London to set up the branch office of Xinhua. In London he had the help of Jack Chen and some of his British friends, including Mary Sheridan Jones. The agency was initially based in Fleet Street but moved to Gray's Inn Road in 1948. Huang also tried to run the agency's work in Prague from his base in London.

36. *Liang Guang Zongdui Shi* (Guangzhou: Guangdong Renmin Chubanshe, 1985), pp. 9–10.

37. Zeng Sheng, p. 511.

38. Duan Haiyan, *Xianzhe Bu Xiu* (Beijing: Zhongguo Huaqiao Chubanshe, 1995), p. 200.

39. Lu Weiluan, Dade Shuyuan De Lishi, paper presented at the Hong Kong and Guangzhou Literary Activities Seminar, November 1985.

40. Zhou Yi, p. 16.

41. Duan Haiyan, p. 181.

42. Lu Weiluan.

43. *Ta Kung Pao*, Hong Kong, 22 January 2002.

44. *Ta Kung Pao*, Hong Kong, 22 May 1991.

45. Nanfang Ribao Baoye Jituan, *Huashang Jiaziqing*.

46. Anthony Short, *The Communist Insurrection in Malaya 1948–60* (London: Frederick Muller Ltd., 1975), p. 44. The fact that the Malaya Communist Party was a branch of the party in China was admitted by Chin Peng, secretary-general of the Malaya Communist Party, in an interview conducted in June 1998 with *Yazhou Zhoukan* (Asia Weekly). See *Yazhou Zhoukan*, Hong Kong, 15 June 1998.

**Chapter 7**

1. There were at least ten recognizable guerrilla groups that operated in Guangdong Province (including Hainan Island) during the Second World War: the East River Column, the Qiongya Guerrilla Column, the Zhongshan Zhongdui, the Guangdong People's Anti-Japanese Liberation Army, the Guangdong Nanlu People's Anti-Japanese Liberation Army, the Gaolei People's Anti-Japanese Force, the Xingmei Hanjiang Column, the Chaoshan Hanjiang Column, the Hanjiang Renmin Youjidui and the Guangdong Northwest People's Anti-Japanese United Army.

2. Zhang Leichu, *Huiyi Fang Fang* (Hong Kong: The Joint Publishing Co., 1986), p. 78.

3. Yang Li, *Gu Dacun Chenyuanlu* (Hong Kong: Cosmos Publications Co., 1999), pp. 77–84.

4. Yang Li, pp. 77–80.

5. Zhao Wei, *Zhao Ziyang Zhuan* (Hong Kong: Xianggang Wenhua Jiaoyu Chubanshe, 1988), p. 62.

6. Ezra Vogel, *Canton under Communism: Programs and Politics in a Provincial Capital 1949–1968* (Cambridge, MA: Harvard University Press, 1969), p. 97.

7.  Zhang Leichu, p. 16; and interview with Yang Qi, 12 October 1985.

8.  Zhonggong Guangdong Sheng Dangshi Yanjiu Weiyuanhui, *Huiyi Rao Zhangfeng* (Hong Kong: Joint Publishing (HK), 1989), p 82.

9.  Ezra Vogel, p. 95.

10. "No Feudal Exploitation in South China?" *Xuexi* (Study), Vol. 3, Guangzhou, November 1950.

11. Conversation with Yang Qi, 14 December 1987.

12. Ezra Vogel, p. 111.

13. Zheng Xiaofeng, *Tao Zhu Zhuan* (Beijing: Zhongguo Qingnian Chubanshe, 1992), pp. 219–26.

14. Ezra Vogel, pp. 112–3.

15. *Nanfang Ribao*, 28 May 1951.

16. Zheng Xiaofeng, p. 226.

17. Fan Shuo, *Ye Jianying Zhuan* (Beijing: Dangdai Zhongguo Chunbanshe, 1995), p. 493.

18. Zhonggong Guangdong Sheng Dangshi Yanjiu Weiyuanhui, p. 144.

19. Zhao Wei, *Zhao Ziyang Zhuan* (Hong Kong: Wenhua Jiaoyu Chubanshe, 1988), p. 64.

20. Li Chunxiao, *Ji Yuegang Yidai Baoren Yang Qi* (Guangzhou: Huacheng Chubanshe, 1995), pp. 1–45.

21. Deng Guangyin, *Wo De Fuqin Deng Wenzhao* (Beijing: Zhongguo Wenshi Chubanshe, 1996), p. 91.

22. Yang Li, p. 134.

23. Zhang Leichu, p. 61.

24. *Xin Wanbao*, 26 October 1986.

25. Chen Xiajian, *Shi Lun Guangdong De Tudi Gaige* (Guangzhou: Guangdong Dangshi, July 1994).

26. Zhang Jiangming, *Dangdai Guangdong* (Guangzhou, 1995).

27. Wu Zhi, *Feng Baiju Zhuan* (Guangzhou: Dangdai Zhongguo Chubanshe, 1992), p. 763.

28. Interview with Fang Zhanhua, 14 December 1983.

29. Ezra Vogel, p. 122.

30. Wang Man and Yang Yong, *Tie Gu Ling Shuang: Yin Linping Zhuan* (Guangzhou: Huacheng Chubanshe, 1992), p. 290.

31. Zeng Sheng, *Zeng Sheng Huiyilu* (Beijing: Jiefangjun Chubanshe, 1992), p. 652.

32. Zeng Sheng, p. 745.

33. Yang Li, p. 361.

34. Zhang Jiangming, *Dangdai Guangdong* (Guangzhou, 1995).

# References

Birch, Alan and Martin Cole. *Captive Years: The Occupation of Hong Kong 1941–45*. Hong Kong: Heinemann Asia, 1982.

Blake, Robert and Jardine Matheson. *Traders of the Far East*. London: Weidenfeld and Nicolson, 1999.

Bosanquet, David. *Escape through China: Survival after the Fall of Hong Kong*. London: Robert Hale, 1983.

Carew, Tim. *The Fall of Hong Kong*. London: Blond, 1960.

Chan Lau Kit-ching. *China, Britain and Hong Kong 1895–1945*. Hong Kong: The Chinese University Press, 1990.

——. *From Nothing to Nothing: The Chinese Communist Movement and Hong Kong, 1921–1936*. London: Hurst and Company, 1999.

Cheng Po Hung. *Hong Kong during the Japanese Occupation*. Hong Kong: University Museum and Art Gallery, The University of Hong Kong, 2002.

Chesneaux, Jean. *The Chinese Labor Movement 1919–1927*. Stanford: Stanford University Press, 1968.

Chin Peng. *My Side of History*. Singapore: Media Masters, 2003.

Clegg, Arthur. *Aid China 1937–1949: A Memoir of a Forgotten Campaign*. Beijing: New World Press, 1989.

Cruickshank, Charles. *Special Operations Executive in the Far East*. Oxford: Oxford University Press, 1983.

Endacott, G. B. and Alan Birch. *Hong Kong Eclipse*. Hong Kong: Oxford University Press, 1978.

Epstein, Israel. *Woman in World History: Soong Ching Ling*. Beijing: New World Press, 1993.

Faure, David. Sai Kung, 1940–1950. Unpublished paper, Hong Kong, 1982.

Foot, M. R. D. and J. M. Langley. *MI9: Escape and Evasion 1939–45*. London: Bodley Head, 1979.

Freedman, Maurice. *The Study of Chinese Society*. Taipei: SMC Publishing Inc., 1979.

Goodwin, R. B. *Hong Kong Escape*. London: Barker, 1953.

Harrison, Brian. *The First Fifty Years: A History of the University of Hong Kong*. Hong Kong: Hong Kong University Press, 1964.

Hewitt, Anthony. *Bridge with Three Men: Across China to the Western Heaven in 1942*. London: Jonathan Cape, 1986.

Leong, Sow-Theng. *Migration and Ethnicity in Chinese History: Hakkas, Pengmin and Their Neighbors*. Taipei: SMC Publishing Inc., 1998.

Lindsay, Oliver. *At the Going Down of the Sun: Hong Kong and South East Asia 1941–45*. London: Hamish Hamilton, 1981.

Melson, P. J. *White Ensign-Red Dragon: The History of the Royal Navy in Hong Kong 1841–1997*. London: David Tait, 1997.

Poy, Vivienne. *Building Bridges: The Life and Times of Richard Charles Lee, Hong Kong, 1905–1983*. Toronto: Calyan Publishing Ltd., 1997.

Ride, Edwin. *British Army Aid Group Hong Kong Resistance 1942–1945*. Hong Kong: Oxford University Press, 1981.

Short, Anthony. *The Communist Insurrection in Malaya 1948–60*. London: Frederick Muller Ltd., 1975.

Thompson, Robert. *Defeating Communist Insurgency: Experiences from Malaya and Vietnam*. London: Chatto & Windus, 1974.

Thorne, Christopher. *The Far Eastern War: States and Societies 1941–45*. London: Unwin Paperbacks, 1986.

Toyojiro Maruya. *Guangdong: "Open Door" Economic Development Strategy*. Hong Kong: Centre of Asian Studies, The University of Hong Kong, 1992.

Tsang, Steve. *Democracy Shelved: Great Britain, China and Attempts at Constitutional Reform in Hong Kong, 1945–1952*. New York: Oxford University Press, 1988.

——. *Hong Kong: An Appointment with China*. London: I. B. Tauris, 1997.

Tsui, Paul Ka-cheung. Unpublished Memoir.

Vogel, Ezra. *Canton under Communism: Programs and Politics in a Provincial Capital, 1949–1968*. Cambridge MA: Harvard University Press, 1968.

——. *One Step Ahead in China: Guangdong under Reform*. Cambridge MA: Harvard University Press, 1989.

Ward, Robert S. Hong Kong Under Japanese Occupation. Unpublished report by the American Consul, 1943.

Watson, James L. *Village Life in Hong Kong*. Hong Kong: The Chinese University Press, 2004.

Welsh, Frank. *A History of Hong Kong*. London: Harper Collins Publishers, 1993.

Wilson, Dick. *When Tigers Fight: The Story of the Sino-Japanese War, 1937–1945*. New York: Penguin Books, 1983.

## Other Sources

Guerrilla War in Kwangtung. *Eastern Horizon*. May to September 1979.

*History of Field Team No. 8*. Peiping Executive Headquarters based at Canton, Kwangtung Province, China. Office of the Assistant Chief of Staff, Intelligence. Records of the Army Staff.

Ride, Lindsay. The Lindsay Ride Papers.

Woddis, H.C.K. Hong Kong and the East River Company. *Eastern World*, London.

Papers from the Public Records Office and the Imperial War Museum, London.
CO—Colonial Office Papers
FO—Foreign Office Papers
WO—War Office Papers

## Sources in Chinese

(*Chinese entries arranged in pinyin order*)

《長江日報》，上海
《南方日報》，廣州
《羊城晚報》，廣州

本書編輯組：《勝利大營救》，解放軍出版社，北京，1986
陳達明：《香港抗日游擊隊》，環球（國際）出版有限公司，香港，2000
《當代廣東》，廣州，2004年7月
鄧廣殷：《我的父親鄧文釗》，中國文史出版社，北京，1996
鄧開頌：《粵港關係史 1840–1984》，麒麟書業有限公司，香港，1991
東江縱隊志編輯委員會：《東江縱隊志》，解放軍出版社，北京，2003
范碩、丁家琪：《葉劍英傳》，當代中國出版社，北京，1995
高華：《紅太陽是怎樣升起的》，中文大學出版社，香港，2000
廣州地區老游擊戰士聯誼會：《懷念周伯明同志》，廣州華南印刷廠，廣州，1998
軍事科學院：《全國解放軍戰爭史》，軍事科學出版社，北京，1998
李春曉：《路漫漫兮求索——記粵港一代報人楊奇》，花城出版社，廣州，1999
連貫同志紀念文集編寫組：《賢者不朽：連貫同志紀念文集》，中國華僑出版社，北京，1995
林華新：《劉黑仔傳奇》，花城出版社，廣州，2000
凌鋒：《中共風雨八十年》，The Epoch Publishing Corp，New Jersey，2001
盧權：《東江縱隊史料》，廣東人民出版社，廣州，1984
羅香林：《客家研究導論》，台北南天書局，台北，1992
南方日報報業集團：《華商甲子情》，聯合出版有限公司，香港，2001
瓊崖武裝鬥爭史辦公室：《瓊崖縱隊史》，廣東人民出版社，廣州，1998

孫其明：《和談、內戰交響典》，上海人民出版社，上海，1994

鐵竹偉：《廖承志傳》，三聯書店，香港，1998

王曼：《將軍的風采——記一級紅星勛章獲得者王作堯》，花城出版社，
　　廣州，2000

王曼、楊永：《鐵骨凌霜——尹林平傳》，花城出版社，廣州，1998

王心鋼：《張發奎傳》，珠海出版社，珠海，2004

王作堯：《東縱一葉》，廣東人民出版社，廣州，1983

香港海員工會：《紀念香港海員大罷工八十週年特刊》，香港海員工會，
　　香港，2002

謝永光：《香港抗日風雲錄》，天地圖書，香港，1994

———：《戰時日軍在香港暴行》，明報出版社，香港，1991

徐月清：《活躍在香港——港九大隊西貢地區抗日實錄》，三聯書店（香
　　港）有限公司，香港，1993

楊立：《古大存沉冤錄》，天地出版社，香港，1999

姚永康：《回憶饒彰風》，三聯書店（香港）有限公司，香港，1989

曾生：《曾生回憶錄》，解放軍出版社，北京，1992

曾志：《我在共產黨內七十年》，香港中華兒女出版社，香港，1999

張樂珠：《回憶方方》，三聯書店（香港）有限公司，香港，1988

趙蔚：《趙紫陽傳》，文化教育出版社，香港，1988

鄭笑頻：《陶鑄傳》，中國青年出版社，北京，1992

中共中央文獻研究室：《周恩來一九四六年談判文選》，中共文獻出版
　　社，北京，1996

周奕：《香港英雄兒女》，利文出版社，香港，2004

## List of Interviewees

K. M. A. Barnett, Alastair Todd, Jack Cater, Roger Lobo, Alfred Prata, Oswald Cheung, Chen Daming, Zeng Sheng, Huang Zuocai, Huang Guanfang, Fang Lan, Cai Songying, Chan Wahhing, Lee Hokming, Chung Pun, Lau Wanhei, Wong Lapkwong, Zhang Xing, Liu Jinwen, Luo Oufeng, Zeng Fa, Lin Zhan, Yang Qi, Li Chong, Tan Gan, Yuan Geng, Daniel Heung, Xu Zhiming, Kwong Pingyau, Feng Keecheung and 25 other veterans of the Hong Kong and Kowloon Independent Brigade of the East River Column who want to remain anonymous.

# Name Index